Garden Conservancy Open Days™

Directory 2024

*Open Days:
Celebrating and sharing America's gardens since 1995*

gardenconservancy.org/opendays

With gratitude to the John W. and Dorothy M. Bohannon Family Trust

Copyright © 2024 The Garden Conservancy, Inc.
All rights reserved. No part of this book may be reproduced or transmitted in any form by any means, electronic or mechanical, including photocopying, recording, or by any information storage and retrieval system, without permission in writing from the publisher.

Printed in Canada.

Publisher's Cataloging-in-Publication
(provided by Quality Books, Inc.)
The Garden Conservancy Open Days Directory
2023 ed., 27th ed.
p. cm.
Includes index.
ISSN: 1087-7738
ISBN: 979-8-218-35320-9
1. Gardens-United States-Directories.
2. Botanical gardens-United States-Directories.
3. Arboretums-United States-Directories.
1. Garden Conservancy
II. Title: Open Days Directory
SB466.U65G37 2020 712'.07473
QB100-836

Published and distributed by
The Garden Conservancy
P.O. Box 608, Garrison, NY 10524

Garden Conservancy Open Days

Directory 2024

Open Days online

Table of Contents 1

About the Garden Conservancy 2

From the Director of Public Programs and Education 3

Which garden is on your cover? 4

How to Use This Directory 8
    Getting the Most of E-Ticketing 12
    Know Before You Go: Plan Your Garden Visits 13
    Once You Get There: Guidelines for Visiting 16

Preserving and Fostering America's Diverse Gardening Traditions
    Garden Futures Grants 20
    Our Preservation Work 26

All About the Nibbled Leaf 32
    Nibbled Leaf Bibliography 33

Illustrated Open Days Map 34

Descriptions by State
    Alabama 38
    California 44
    Colorado 76
    Connecticut 90
    Delaware 128
    Illinois 134
    Maryland 140
    Massachusetts 146
    Michigan 180
    Missouri 184
    New Hampshire 188
    New Jersey 202
    New York 230
    Ohio 304
    Pennsylvania 310
    Rhode Island 320
    South Carolina 326
    Vermont 330
    Virginia 336
    Washington 344
    Wisconsin 362

Get Involved 370
    How to Get Involved 374
    Planned Giving 378
    Membership Matters 379

Index
    Open Days Gardens by Date 382

About the Garden Conservancy

A 501(c)(3) nonprofit organization incorporated in New York State, the Garden Conservancy was founded in 1989 by renowned plantsman Frank Cabot after his visit to Ruth Bancroft's dry garden in Walnut Creek, CA. He recognized the need for an organization that would help preserve such exceptional gardens for future generations.

Today, the Garden Conservancy continues to fulfill his vision through its mission to *preserve, share, and celebrate America's gardens and diverse gardening traditions for the education and inspiration of the public.*

Our Educational Programs provide unprecedented access to otherwise private spaces through our signature **Open Days** program, **Digging Deeper**, and **Garden Masters Series** events, which raise funds for our work in preservation and grant-giving.

facebook.com/The.Garden.Conservancy

instagram.com/thegardenconservancy

🌐 gardenconservancy.org

YOU'RE INVITED

To participate in America's only national garden visiting program. From March through October, more than 350 gardens in 21 states will host tens of thousands of visitors. It's our biggest season in years!

Since 1995 we've been opening gardens out of a conviction that sharing is a fundamental part of the art of gardening. Moreover, participating in Open Days supports the Garden Conservancy's mission to preserve and foster America's diverse gardening traditions. Learn more about our preservation and grant work this past year on pages 20–29.

This year we're delighted to announce the return of Alabama, Maryland, Michigan, and Virginia, as well as Chicago. None of this would be possible without the nearly 500 Garden Hosts and volunteers who make Open Days a reality. Thank you!

Looking forward to seeing you in the garden,

—*H. Horatio Joyce, PhD*
Director of Public Programs and Education

Celebrating and sharing America's gardens since 1995

Which garden is

As for 2023, this year's *Directory* has four different covers representing Open Days from different regions across the country. Read more about why we chose these regions for our cover, and be sure to share which cover you received using the hashtag #GardenConservancy.

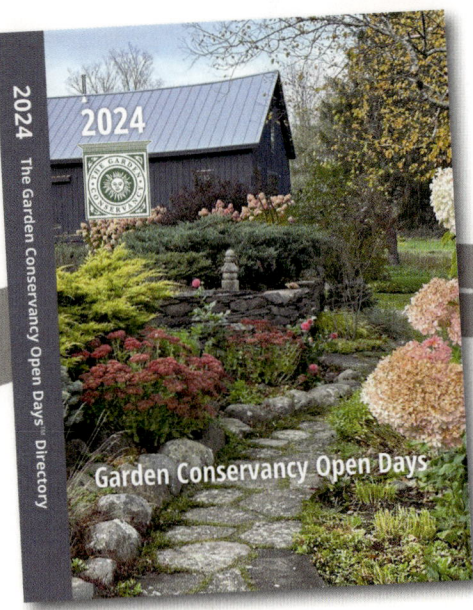

Gunhouse Hill Garden - *Hobart, NY*
Photo: Zone4 Landscapes

While our program has a long tenure in New York, we are pleased to present newer areas for the 2024 season, including Open Days in Delaware and Sullivan Counties, New York.

Road trip anyone? For the full listing of New York gardens, see page 232.

Louise Wrinkle's Southern Woodland Garden - *Birmingham, AL*
Photo: Mick Hales

2024 marks our return to Alabama for the first time since 2009!

We are also celebrating the completion of our documentation of Louise Wrinkle's native garden.

Read more about this garden and project on page 40.

gardenconservancy.org/opendays

Which garden is on your cover? 5

on your cover?

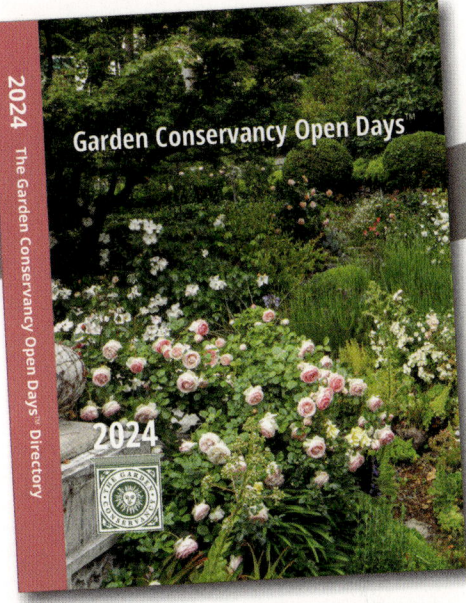

Panayoti Kelaidis
Quince Garden - *Denver, CO*
Photo: Christine Ashburn Photography

2023 saw our return to Colorado for the first time since 2018, and 2024 sees the expansion into Pueblo for its first-ever Open Day.

To see the full line up of Open Days in Colorado, see page 78.

Aging Gracefully - *Berkeley, CA*
Photo: ML Righellis

While California gardens are perennially popular Open Days destinations, we are particularly proud that this season's California Open Days run from March until October and span the entirety of the state.

To see the full season of Open Days in California, see page 46.

Celebrating and sharing America's gardens since 1995

GARDEN CLUB
OF VIRGINIA

Historic Garden Week
TOURS STATEWIDE

April 20-27, 2024

Proceeds fund the restoration of Virginia's historic public gardens and a research fellowship program.

Hydrangea macrophylla 'Nikko Blue'

For a complete listing of tours and to purchase tickets, please visit **VaGardenWeek.org**

Project SAGE proudly presents

Trade Secrets®

a beautiful gathering for a great cause

MAY 18TH & 19TH, 2024

Saturday, May 18th
Extraordinary garden tours & community events

Sunday, May 19th
Rare Plants & Garden Antiques Sale Event
Lime Rock Park - Lakeville, CT

Tickets & Information:
TradeSecretsCT.com
(860) 364-1080

Rain or shine
No pets on either day

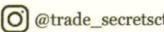 @trade_secretsct
 facebook.com/TradesecretsCT

How to Use This Directory

Be sure to subscribe!
The *2024 Open Days Directory* provides an excellent starting point for the upcoming season, but it is by no means the final schedule.

For the latest news and announcements, be sure to visit our website and subscribe to our e-newsletter. Additional gardens, and even entire Open Days, will be added to the schedule after the Directory is published, so make sure to stay tuned.

The Directory
States are sequenced alphabetically. Within each state, Open Days are listed chronologically by date. Gardens participating in each Open Day are organized alphabetically by county, then town, then garden name.

Each year, we ask all Garden Hosts to submit a description of their garden in their own words to capture the garden's personality and unique voice. Further information about the gardener and their horticultural interests can be found in the Trowel Talk section immediately following the garden's description.

Gardens by Date
To find out which gardens are opening on specific dates, see the "Gardens by Date" index, starting on page 382.

Gardens by State
To find out which gardens are open by county, town, and date, see the list at the beginning of each state's section.

Use these icons for more information about the gardens:

NEW—Gardens opening for the first time this season

[5] Gardens or gardeners that have opened for 5 or more Open Days

[10] Gardens or gardeners that have opened for 10 or more Open Days

[20] Gardens or gardeners that have opened for 20 or more Open Days

['95] Gardens or gardeners that opened during our inaugural year of 1995

Gardens who commit to Nibbled Leaf gardening practices. For more information about this initiative, please visit page 32.

Notes on accessibility. The Garden Host notes that portions of the garden are accessible by wheelchair. Please visit the website for specific notes, when available.

Photography NOT permitted

💬 TROWEL TALK

Learn more about what motivates gardeners, in their own words.

Duck Soup - Harrisville, NH
Photo: Brian Jones

gardenconservancy.org/opendays

How to Use This Directory 9

NONPROFIT PARTNERS

Open Days are presented in partnership with other nonprofit organizations. Learn more about these organizations here.

PUBLIC GARDENS

Public Gardens to complement your Open Day visits.

PRESERVATION PARTNERS

Gardens that the Garden Conservancy has helped to either save or restore.

For more information on Garden Preservation, please see page 26.

DIGGING DEEPER

Dig deeper into a variety of topics with special talks and events.

This schedule will continue to grow; look out for our Spring and Fall Educational Programs Catalogs!

Michael and Betsy Gordon - Peterborough, NH
Photo: Brian Jones

Celebrating and sharing America's gardens since 1995

Wethersfield thanks the Garden Conservancy for the most valuable gift it could have received, the inaugural Jean and John Greene Prize for Excellence in American Gardening. This seminal gift enabled us to document our history with a sweeping cultural landscape study, as we work to plan a sustainable and vibrant future intended to keep green and open space available for all to enjoy.

Photo: Ngoc Minh Ngo

We invite you to experience one of the most important Italian Renaissance Gardens in America, replete with Bosco. Enjoy British Arts & Crafts gardens that surround the Main House, unsurpassed vistas, more than 20 miles of trails amid 1,000 acres of protected land of incomparable beauty in Dutchess County, New York.

Wethersfield
estate & garden
www.wethersfield.org

Getting the Most Out of E-Ticketing

Tickets are released on a rolling basis throughout the season and will be listed on our website when available. Tickets will be released approximately two months in advance of an Open Day, around the first of the month.

Open Days 2024	Tickets Release Date
March	Tuesday, January 2
April	Thursday, February 1
May	Friday, March 1
June	Monday, April 1
July	Wednesday, May 1
August	Monday, June 3
September	Monday, July 1
October	Thursday, August 1

All registrations must be processed online through the Garden Conservancy's website. Once registered, you will receive an electronic ticket that includes all the information you need to visit your selected gardens, including the garden's address, its location, parking instructions, and other information to help plan your visit.

Please note that Garden Hosts do not have the ability to collect admissions or tickets, verify memberships, or make changes onsite—all registrations must go through the Garden Conservancy's website: gardenconservancy.org.

Your ticket will be emailed to you at the email address provided. Be sure to inspect your ticket once it arrives in your inbox. Tickets purchased in advance of the Friday before the Open Day do not need to be printed or presented for entry. Garden Hosts are provided a guest list the Friday before their Open Day.

Tickets purchased after our guest lists have been sent, or on the day of the Open Day will read *Please Present Ticket for Admission*. These tickets must be presented to the Garden Host as either paper tickets or on your mobile device.

You can still be spontaneous!

While advance registration is preferred by us and our Garden Hosts, registration for gardens will remain live until the end of the Open Day or until all tickets have sold out.

You can purchase tickets the morning of an Open Day, or even in between gardens! Be sure to bring your mobile device or printed copies of your ticket if you are purchasing at the last minute.

gardenconservancy.org/opendays

Know Before You Go: Plan Your Garden Visits

Get the most out of your Open Days season with the following reminders:

Whenever possible, we have scheduled gardens to be within a reasonable driving distance from one another. Occasionally, we find a garden that simply must be included, despite its being off the beaten path.

We do our best to make sure the garden directions provided on tickets are accurate. Always check directions before you head out or bring a map or GPS system along with you during your garden visiting adventures.

We send Registration Reminders to all registered participants the Thursday before an Open Day. Be sure to check these emails for any last-minute changes in parking or directions.

Admissions
All registrations are now collected through our e-ticketing system which can be found on our website: gardenconservancy.org/opendays

Admission to Open Days gardens is $5 per person for members of the Garden Conservancy, and $10 per person for non-members. Admission is charged per person, per garden. Children aged 12 and under are always free when accompanied by a registered adult.

For assistance with registration, please call us at 1.888.842.2442, Monday–Friday, 9:00 a.m.–5:00 p.m. ET, or email us at opendays@gardenconservancy.org.

Membership
Membership is not required to attend Open Days gardens, but being a member of the Garden Conservancy offers exceptional value. In addition to receiving 50% off Open Days tickets, members also qualify for discounts to other Conservancy programs.

To learn more about membership please see page 379.

Changes and Cancellations
Occasionally, Open Days and other educational programs must be canceled or changed due to unforeseen circumstances. In the event of a cancellation, we will announce the cancellation on the website and notify everyone who has already purchased tickets.

Inclement Weather
Open Days are considered rain or shine events and will take place in all weather conditions unless the Garden Host deems conditions to be unsafe and cancels the Open Day. We will notify all registered participants of a cancellation as soon as we are made aware that the Garden Host must cancel. Once canceled, we do not reschedule Open Days.

Refunds, Credits, and Exchanges
We do not offer refunds or exchanges in the event you are unable to attend a program that you have registered for.

Children are Welcome at Open Days!
We encourage you to bring your kids and grandkids to your Open Days visits and to share your love of gardening with the next generation of gardeners. Children 12 and under are always free at Open Days.

Celebrating and sharing America's gardens since 1995

TEATOWN
PLANTFEST
Save the date!

FRIDAY, MAY 10
3pm – 7pm
"First Pick"
Admission $25 online,
$30 at the gate
Music • Food • Drinks

SATURDAY, MAY 11
9am – 2pm
Free Admission
Hudson Valley Food Trucks

A SPRING CELEBRATION

Native Plants • Perennials • Annuals
Organic Herbs & Vegetables
Specialty Vendors

1600 Spring Valley Road, Ossining NY 10562 • www.teatown.org/plantfest

WILDFLOWER ISLAND

at TEATOWN LAKE RESERVATION

Curator Chats: 10am – 11am
M: $5 / NM: $10*

Open Gate Days: 11am – 1pm
Free to attend

Sunday, May 26
Sunday, July 14
Sunday, September 8

Learn more at: teatown.org/wildflower
*Member and non-member pricing

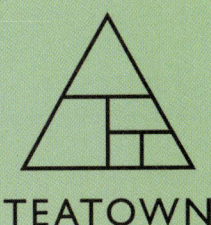

TEATOWN

Once You Get There: Guidelines for Visiting

Open Days are special invitations to visit private gardens. Please reward the generosity of our Garden Hosts by following these simple guidelines:

Check in—On arrival, please be sure to check in with the Garden Host or Greeter, designated by their green and yellow buttons. If your ticket says *Please Present Ticket for Admission,* please print or have it ready to show on your mobile device.

Restrooms—As private residences, restrooms are not available at Open Days gardens. Keep this in mind before you arrive and if needed, ask at the admissions table for the nearest public facility.

Hands Off—Plants and their parts must remain in the garden. Please, no picking, pinching, proplifting, or removing plant pieces of any kind.

Keep it Clean—Do not litter. If you carry something in, carry it back out. Garden Hosts are not responsible for trash disposal.

Smoke-Free—Smoking and e-cigarettes are prohibited.

Follow Signs—Follow any posted signs and directions. Do not enter Garden Host's homes or private buildings.

Pets Not Allowed—Pets and therapy animals are not permitted in Open Days gardens.

Children—All ages are very welcome at Open Days, but please supervise children during your visit.

Parking—Park your car in designated areas. Park so others can enter and exit easily.

Photography and Video—Check if photography or video of the garden is permitted by the Host by asking upon arrival. Tripods are not permitted.

Respect Privacy—Please respect Garden Hosts' privacy and only visit gardens during posted dates and times. Please do not contact Garden Hosts outside of their Open Day.

Give Thanks—Many Garden Hosts will be onsite during their Open Day. Garden Hosts can be identified by their "Garden Host" badge. Please say hello and let them know how much you enjoyed your visit. Or, share words of admiration with Open Days staff at opendays@gardenconservancy.org and we will share your message with the hosts.

Urban Wildlife Habitat - Los Angeles, CA
Photo: Matt Harbicht

Share Your Garden

Become a Garden Host or a Regional Ambassador

See page 374 or contact us at **opendays@gardenconservancy.org** to learn more.

Celebrating and sharing America's gardens since 1995

Visit private Scottish gardens and hidden gems on your next trip to the UK.

scotlandsgardens.org

SC049866

 chanticleer

Chanticleer Gardeners Share Workshop Series

Extend your plant knowledge, learn about dynamic planting design, and discover ways to incorporate craftsmanship into your garden.

April 22–23, June 10–11, October 21–22, 2024

chanticleergarden.org/workshops

ANNOUNCING
HOLLISTER HOUSE
Garden Study Weekend
Symposium

September 7, 2024
at the Heritage Hotel, Southbury, CT

Featuring talks by:

FERGUS GARRETT
Head Gardener and CEO, Great Dixter Garden
Great Dixter Past, Present and Future

Fergus will discuss the history of Great Dixter and the way forward for a sensitive historic garden and estate. He will share his memories of Christopher Lloyd, the way they worked together to develop Dixter, and how they challenged and experimented with garden design.

KATHERINE TRACEY
Horticulturalist and Designer: Avant Gardens
Exuberant Planters

Almost everyone has room for a smashing container planting. Katherine will discuss unexpected plant combinations that exude energy and effortlessness. Using plants that are suited to the garden situation, she will offer innovative ensembles that have that wow factor right up until frost.

PETER DEL TREDICI
Horticulturalist and Botanist
The History of Lawns: From Pasture to Plastic

Peter will present a brief history of the lawn and the techniques used to create and maintain it. He will discuss the social and ecological issues surrounding their use and ways to manage lawns to increase their ecological functionality and decrease their negative impacts.

MATT MATTUS
Plantsman and Author
This Curious Life as a Plantsman

Matt grows most everything in his greenhouse and garden and admits trying grow and collect most plants at least once. He will share his experiments growing plants with trialing classic techniques against the newest horticultural methods to find which has merit and which may mislead.

Following the symposium participants are invited to a special garden party at Hollister House Garden.
Presented by Hollister House Garden and the Garden Conservancy

For more information and to register for the Saturday program, visit
www.hollisterhousegarden.org or call **860.868.2200**

Preserving and Fostering America's Diverse Gardening Traditions

*Your garden visits help support our **Garden Futures Grants** program and our **Preservation** work, documenting and monitoring historic gardens around the country.*

Open Days supports the Garden Conservancy's **Garden Futures**™ Grants!

In 2021, the Garden Conservancy launched a new initiative—since named the *Garden Futures Grants Program*—to award grants between $5,000 and $10,000 to nonprofits nationwide that are making significant contributions to their communities through garden-based programming or the study and preservation of garden history.

The grant program began in response to the many inquiries for aid we received

Garden Futures™ Grants Recipients

Boise Vertical Farm
Boise, ID
Boise Vertical Farm creates a safe community that provides hope, community service, and employment for individuals in substance abuse recovery by growing local produce.

Working with individuals in recovery, we positively affect vulnerable members of society and create a "ripple effect," which influences their families, friends, neighborhoods, and communities.

The participants in our program gain experience working within our greenhouse, learn the history of vertical farming, and learn new trade skills that create employment opportunities and economic security.

Brooklyn Queens Land Trust
Brooklyn, NY
To ensure the conservation and preservation of open space through stewardship and establish a community of gardeners to educate and support community members while promoting interest in green spaces.

gardenconservancy.org/opendays

from small public gardens facing financial hardship brought on by the pandemic.

Committed to turning this grant initiative into a permanent program, in 2022, the Garden Conservancy created a National Advisory Committee to bring diverse perspectives and experiences to the review process.

In reviewing grant applications, the committee considered factors like community impact, diversity of populations served, geographic region, and sustainable gardening practices.

The Garden Conservancy's grant program is unique in that it awards grants for general operating support, with as few "strings attached" as possible for grantees.

In 2023, we were able to award $102,000 to fifteen organizations across the country, and we want to share them with you so you can learn about the great work they do and how you directly support them by participating in Open Days.

Thank you!

Bullington Gardens
Hendersonville, NC
To connect children and adults with the natural world through science-based horticultural education; to demonstrate the beauty and value of native and ornamental plants through themed public gardens; and to enhance life skills for children and adults with physical or mental challenges through horticultural therapy.

Chicago Community Gardeners Association
Chicago, IL
The mission of CCGA is to support community gardens as a vehicle for building sustainable communities and enriching the natural ecosystem in Chicago and beyond. We are committed to creating a space where each voice and perspective is appreciated and heard. We support and encourage the participation of every individual. When a problem or issue is identified, the next natural step is outreach.

Celebrating and sharing America's gardens since 1995

Coggeshall Farm Museum
Bristol, RI

Our mission is to preserve Coggeshall Farm, a 1790s Rhode Island salt-marsh farm. We serve the local community and beyond as a living museum and vital educational resource through demonstration of daily farm activity and honest interpretation that reflects its historical, multicultural influence.

Cultivating Inclusion
Murrieta, CA

Cultivating Inclusion is a nonprofit organization dedicated to providing a job site location for special needs adults in its Adult Transition Program.

The garden/farm provides job training opportunities for special needs adults to learn about gardening and farming as well as providing a therapeutic environment to support their social interactions.

All produce grown is donated to the local food banks to provide fresh healthy food for needy families.

Community Outreach Group for Landscape Design
North Falmouth, MA

Community Outreach Group for Landscape Design (COGdesign) has been an active nonprofit for more than 25 years. Our mission is to provide accessible landscape design to community groups in Greater Boston with a strong focus on historically disinvested neighborhoods. We connect landscape architects, designers, and interested volunteers with grassroots groups to co-create beautiful, resilient, open spaces that meet the needs of local communities.

gardenconservancy.org/opendays

Garden Futures™
Grants Recipients

Gaining Ground
Concord, MA
Our mission is to provide free fresh produce for people who are experiencing food insecurity. We do this work with the helping hands of a diverse community of volunteers who work and learn with us on the farm.

Friends of Robinson Gardens
Beverly Hills, CA
Friends of Robinson Gardens (FRG) develops programs and initiatives that ensure all residents of Los Angeles benefit from the beauty and diversity of Virginia Robinson Gardens.

FRG particularly focuses on programs that benefit BIPOC and underserved children, and on preserving, exhibiting, and disseminating Mrs. Robinson's private archive of historic papers and artifacts. Current programs for underserved children include the Children's Science Fair, Children's Onsite Program, and FRoG.

FRG also provides gardening, art, literature, and landscaping education, and docent-led tours of the gardens for all ages.

Heronswood Garden
Kingston, WA
The Port Gamble S'Klallam Foundation is dedicated to improving the quality of life for Port Gamble S'Klallam tribal members while increasing the understanding of the Tribe's rich cultural heritage with people who reside in the Puget Sound area and visitors from far and wide.

The Foundation works to advance an appreciation and understanding of S'Klallam art, history, and culture. The Foundation also seeks to promote education and wellness and to increase awareness and action to protect the environment. Another primary component of the Foundation's mission is the management of Heronswood Garden.

Celebrating and sharing America's gardens since 1995

Preserving and Fostering America's Diverse Gardening Traditions

Hortus Arboretum
Stone Ridge, NY
The Hortus Arboretum & Botanical Gardens (the Arboretum) is a small family-operated not-for-profit open to the public, whose mission is to experiment and sustain the native, unusual, and historic plant life of the Catskill Mountains–Hudson Valley region.

We serve as a vital educational and recreational resource, focusing on saving rare and endangered plants from around the world with the goal of ensuring that species diversity is preserved, as we present our plantings to a diverse, generally underserved population in this rural area.

Garden Futures™
Grants Recipients

Hunger and Health Coalition
Boone, NC
The Hunger and Health Coalition alleviates poverty through access to healthy foods, prescription medications, and wrap-around services.

gardenconservancy.org/opendays

Preserving and Fostering America's Diverse Gardening Traditions   25

Longue Vue House and Gardens
New Orleans, LA
Inspired by our humanitarian and artistic legacy, Longue Vue's mission is to be a leader in the advancement of innovative thought, creative expression, and lifelong learning, and to engage our resources and exceptional setting to stimulate discussion and action on issues of social justice and community responsibility.

Mezzacello Columbus
Columbus, OH
To model technology, robotics, ecology, and problem-solving in the urban ag space to teach youth to grow, maintain, sustain, and explain the role of food, sustainability, and ecologies.

Neighborhood Gardens Trust
Philadelphia, PA
Our mission is to acquire and preserve community-managed green spaces and gardens to enhance the quality of life in Philadelphia's neighborhoods.

Celebrating and sharing America's gardens since 1995

Our Preservation in Action

Since 1989, the Garden Conservancy has worked with more than 100 gardens in 26 states and two Canadian provinces to advance the Conservancy's mission to "preserve, share, and celebrate American gardens and diverse gardening traditions for the education and inspiration of the public."

The Garden Conservancy's Preservation staff assists garden leaders and community organizations from coast to coast to preserve their garden heritage as community assets, weaving together the practical and the intangible.

Our strategic, multidisciplinary approach supports an array of preservation work—from historic rehabilitation and organizational development to collections management and documentation—while addressing issues like climate change and sustainability, engaging diverse communities, and incorporating new technologies.

Here is how we put our preservation philosophy into practice:

Rehabilitation and Restoration

In 2023, we helped Bard College in Annandale-on-Hudson plan for the restoration of Blithewood Garden. We held a panel discussion with experts on the Gilded Age and a Digging Deeper event to engage more people in the history of this Hudson Valley gem. The Conservancy awarded Bard College a $93,000 grant for the completion of construction drawings which are essential to rehabilitate Blithewood's iconic hardscaping that is more than 120 years old.

In 2024, we celebrate the twentieth anniversary of our partnership with the National Park Service and the Golden Gate National Parks Conservancy to restore the Gardens of Alcatraz. The Garden Conservancy led a comprehensive restoration that involved research and documentation, advising on treatment options, hiring staff, fundraising, volunteer recruitment and training, and increasing national publicity and awareness of this important cultural landscape. Alcatraz showcases the transformative power of gardens in a setting most associated with isolation and hardship. Today, the gardens see hundreds of thousands of visitors!

gardenconservancy.org/opendays

Education as a Tool for Preservation

Building on our existing online preservation education, in 2023 we launched virtual Lunch and Learn opportunities that provide focused learning and resource-sharing for garden leaders, staff, and board members.

We also held in-person Garden Conservancy Northwest Network (GCNN) workshops and garden tours at Albers Marcovina Vista Gardens in Bremerton, WA, and Lake Wilderness Arboretum in Maple Valley, WA. Topics included creating mission-focused and community-centered programming and Board Development with Succession Planning.

Please visit the GCNN members and Preservation Partners listed here in the Directory. Look for gardens highlighted with gray and blue boxes to learn more.

Conservation Easements: Preserving Gardens for Future Generations

During 2023, the Conservancy conducted monitoring visits to sites including The Ruth Bancroft Garden in Walnut Creek, CA, the John Fairey Garden in Hempstead, TX, the Elizabeth Lawrence Garden in Charlotte, NC, and the Gardens at Palmdale in Fremont, CA, and other sites throughout the country.

A conservation easement is a legal contract that identifies historic, cultural, and horticultural significance and promotes practices that preserve them while restricting or prohibiting activities that threaten them. We visit and monitor gardens annually where we hold conservation easements, to ensure the easement terms are upheld and to provide guidance and resources that best protect the garden's conservation and preservation values over time.

At the John Fairey Garden in Hempstead, TX a conservation easement protects a historic collection of rare, endangered, and drought-tolerant plants native to the southern United States and their Mexican and Asian counterparts in perpetuity. Our preservation support helps the John Fairey Garden preserve its significance while managing and mitigating the effects of climate change.

gardenconservancy.org/opendays

Documentary Film: Preserving the Ephemeral

During the spring and summer of 2023, we traveled to Birmingham, Alabama to interview Louise Wrinkle and document her remarkable garden on film. Premiering in Spring 2024, this garden documentary will highlight the nexus of historic preservation and environmental conservation. Interviews were conducted with *Flower* magazine, *Veranda* magazine, and *Southern Living* magazine among others.

Wrinkle was a founding board member of The Garden Conservancy and elevated the importance of native plantings on a national stage through her distinguished career with the Garden Club of America. She is also opening her garden as a part of the Birmingham Open Day on May 4, 2024!

2023 marked the post-production phase for our documentary film of the Anne Spencer House & Garden Museum in Lynchburg, VA. This documentation of the historic home and garden of Harlem Renaissance poet and Civil Rights advocate Anne Spencer chronicles its evolution from a private home and intimate gathering space to a significant cultural landscape.

To see a film short featuring Shaun Spencer-Hester, granddaughter of Anne Spencer, please visit the Documentation section of our website at gardenconservancy.org/preservation/documentation

Advocating for Gardens

Preserving gardens is crucial because of their role as essential community assets, and preservation is stronger and more successful with community support. The Garden Conservancy advocates for at-risk gardens, taking a public stand by writing letters, drafting testimony, and raising awareness to encourage action at the community, regional, and national levels. In 2023, we advocated for the preservation of Oakwell Estate in Villanova, PA, and the Spalding Garden in Milton, MA by writing letters in support of their preservation.

Your Open Days admissions help support this work, thank you!

Celebrating and sharing America's gardens since 1995

MORVEN

MUSEUM & GARDEN

Visit and explore over 200 years of New Jersey and American History!

Wednesday - Sunday, 10 a.m. - 4 p.m.
Guided Tours & Special Exhibitions

55 Stockton Street • Princeton, NJ
609.924.8144 • www.morven.org

PECONIC LAND TRUST

Bridge Gardens

A five-acre gem in the heart of Bridgehampton, Bridge Gardens is a unique public and demonstration garden with a wide variety of native and non-native plants. Come explore it's expansive demonstration vegetable garden, large rose garden, orchard, and four-quadrant herb garden, as well as a story walk through the woodland trail!

Come Visit Us!

Open year-round with free admission, daily 10 am–4 pm.

Scan to learn more about what the garden has to offer!

36 Mitchell Lane | Bridgehampton | New York
www.PeconicLandTrust.org/BridgeGardens | 631.283.3195

What is Nibbled Leaf?

Nibbled Leaf is about showcasing the beauty of nature-friendly gardens.

Created in partnership with the Perfect Earth Project, the Nibbled Leaf program is the native plant and organic gardening initiative within Open Days. Well over half of Open Days Garden Hosts signed up for the Nibbled Leaf icon in their Open Days listing this year.

The only requirement is a commitment to creating gardens that share their bounty with as many lifeforms as possible.

The Nibbled Leaf Booklet, created by Perfect Earth project in 2022, presents a handbook for turning this commitment into practice so that gardens can become havens for all living things.

This year, every Garden Host will receive a copy of *The Nibbled Leaf Booklet* (pictured below) in their Host Kit. Copies are also available for sale by contacting events@gardenconservancy.org or calling 845.424.6500.

gardenconservancy.org/opendays

Nibbled Leaf Bibliography

1. **Douglas W. Tallamy's** *Nature's Best Hope: A New Approach to Conservation That Starts in Your Yard* **(2020)**
This book will change the way you think about yards. Tallamy convincingly explains and trumpets the ecological benefits of planting native trees, shrubs, and perennials.

2. **Aldo Leopold's** *Sand County Almanac: And Sketches Here and There* **(originally published 1949)**
An all-time classic, one of the first of its kind, and still a great read.

3. **Robin Wall Kimmerer's** *Braiding Sweetgrass: Indigenous Wisdom, Scientific Knowledge and the Teachings of Plants* **(2013)**
The new classic. Irresistible stories filled with both ancient and new wisdom.

4. **William Cullina's** *Native Trees, Shrubs, and Vines: A Guide to Using, Growing, and Propagating North American Woody Plants* **(2012)**

5. ***The New England Wild Flower Society Guide to Growing and Propagating Wildflowers of the United States and Canada*** **(2000)**
Excellent go-to books describing native plants and how to grow them. Beautifully written.

6. **Darrel Morrison's** *Beauty of the Wild: A Life Designing Landscapes Inspired by Nature* **(2021)**
A disarming autobiography of one of our great American landscape designers and his passion for our native landscapes across America.

7. **Tom Wessels'** *Forest Forensics: A Field Guide to Reading the Forested Landscape* **(2010)**
Another game changer. Wessels teaches us how to recognize the history of our woods.

8. **perfectearthproject.org/resources/publicationsresearchlinks**
The basics of Nature-Based Land care, in English and Spanish.

9. **Wild Seed Project Publications (wildseedproject.net/)**
Great little guides to the best native plants for landscapes.

10. **Two Thirds for the Birds (234birds.org/access-to-tools/)**
Ask yourself each time you consider planting a new tree or perennial. Am I planting two-thirds for the birds?

Celebrating and sharing America's gardens since 1995

2024 Open Days

Map Illustrator Gregory Nemec:

I grew up with a puzzle of the US with fanciful illustrations throughout. We played with that map so much that the rectangular western states all had rounded corners...

My goal was to depict the ideal version of each flower. The flowers are drawn with ink on board and colored digitally. They are arranged digitally as well, so I can fit them together and overlap them harmoniously, like a bouquet.

gregorynemec.art

gardenconservancy.org/opendays

Illustrated Open Days Map 35

This map celebrates the 21 states with Open Days this year, represented by their state flower.

Celebrating and sharing America's gardens since 1995

Monadnock Vistas - Peterborough, NH
Photo: Brian Jones

Louise Wrinkle's Southern Woodland Garden - Birmingham, AL
Photo: Mick Hales

40 Alabama

Camellia
Camellia japonica

Open Days dates and times by County, Town, and Garden

JEFFERSON
Birmingham
Louise Wrinkle's Southern Woodland Garden
   Saturday, May 4, 10–4
Rooms with Views
   Saturday, May 4, 10–4
The Butrus Garden
   Saturday, May 4, 10–4
The Dancer
   Saturday, May 4, 10–4

Join us for the exclusive Garden Conservancy documentary film premiere and panel discussion this spring in Birmingham, Alabama.

Step into the lush world of Louise Wrinkle's Southern Woodland Garden, an enchanting portrayal of her journey listening to the land.

The premiere will be followed by a thought-provoking panel discussion, illuminating the intricacies of woodland gardening, working with native plants, and the legacy embodied by Louise Wrinkle's creation. Engage with esteemed horticulturists, preservationists, and experts as they discuss the nexus of conservation and preservation and the enduring charm of Southern gardens.

Please be on the lookout for more details and ticket information!

ALABAMA

Jefferson County
Saturday, May 4

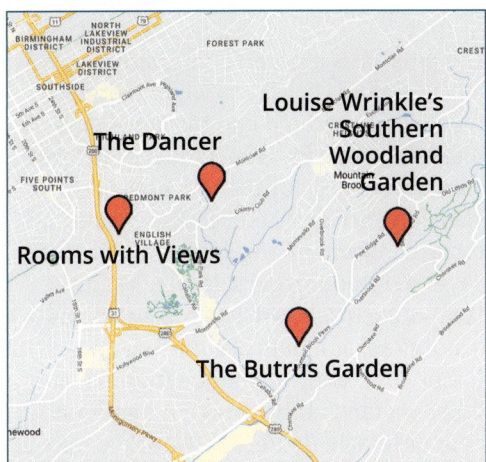

BIRMINGHAM
LOUISE WRINKLE'S SOUTHERN WOODLAND GARDEN

   10–4

Approximately 35 years ago Louise and John Wrinkle moved into the Beechwood Road house built by her parents in 1938 and where she grew up.

To make this 2+ acres of mixed woodland her own, Louise worked with landscape designer Norman Kent Johnson to create accessibility to all areas by a network of paths and added small stone walls where necessary. Her horticultural interests began with natives, but a realization of Asian counterparts has enriched the plantings, which include family collections of hollies, azaleas, and ranunculus.

Through the years the trees have grown to enormous size and new projects have unfolded, the latest of which are a pond in the lower corner and a pit greenhouse at the rear of the cutting garden. A variety of garden areas await the visitor: a sunken boxwood parterre, a Belgian fence of native crabapple, a cutting garden, and a natural brook which flows year-round.

This garden's estimated size is 2¼ acres.

ROOMS WITH VIEWS
NEW   10–4

Set within a framework of original walls and terraces, this garden has been totally replanted during the current owners' tenure of two decades. The results, however, seem timeless.

Designed in the 1920s by notable Birmingham architects Miller & Martin, the house sits at the foot of a sloping lawn, framed with hedges, shrubs, and specimen trees. This graceful, naturalistic landscape presents an almost-Arcadian setting for the house. It also lends dramatic contrast to the walled and terraced gardens behind and below. A tile-paved "balcony" off the formal and family living rooms is furnished for both seating and dining. Container plantings offer seasonal accents of fragrance and bloom.

But the most important feature is the view! A sweeping panorama, the vista extends for miles across Shades Valley to the ridge beyond. One full story down, a bowed parterre of boxwood, cornered by antique terra-cotta urns, provides a

NEW   5   10   20   '95 Year    No Photography    Accessibility   Nibbled Leaf Garden

suitably restrained foreground for the dramatic view. Turf, and a border of lenten roses, Japanese maples, irises, and lamb's ears complete the composition. Below this garden lies a crescent space devoted to fruits: tree, bramble, and bush.

The space beyond is a "wilderness" of ornamental trees and grasses, all enclosed by towering hollies and magnolias. An intermediate-level terrace provides transition between the balcony and lower gardens. Centered on an open lawn, this area is framed with stone-laid walks, box hedges, and a small allée of potted trees. At the far end of the space, a dining table and chairs provide occasion for al fresco entertaining. And over the top of the gardens' far wall, the hint of another view. Tucked away below this level is a walled and hedged enclosure devoted to bocce. Court-side chairs and benches, a games table, and potted flowering shrubs create a casual air of welcome to this almost-secret space.

The plants throughout the property were chosen with seasonal interest in mind. Deciduous flowering trees and shrubs, perennials, bulbs, and annuals lend their interest through the year. And even the garden's evergreens, which give it structure and privacy, were chosen with foliage, flower, and fruit in mind.

This garden's estimated size is 1 acre.

THE BUTRUS GARDEN

 10–4

A 4-acre mature woodland in old Mountain Brook surrounds the grand house built in 1931 of soft gray limestone. Several years ago, visionary new owners revived it and created a new Italianate garden that has settled comfortably around the home.

The emphasis is on greenery, stone, and water. Color is limited to white blooming plants incorporated into the landscape plan and into a few substantial pots filled with seasonal color. Visitors approach via a long driveway and cross a stone terrace in front, then glimpse the first of several outdoor rooms. In the first, the lawn is encircled with low boxwood, tall arborvitae, and pots of colorful annuals. In the next garden, an antique fountain and its pool stand at the center. An antique copper female figure, subtly tucked into one side, overlooks this space, which terminates in a stone pavilion, repeating the architecture of the side porch on the main house.

Stepping down from the gardens, we move along stone paths featuring flowering spring perennials and annuals to a lower grass level surrounded by a woodland garden with large stone statuary focal points. There are many private nooks, including a lower terrace off the side of the house. A greenhouse, the stone base of which matches the house, is surrounded by a new woodland garden designed by noted Birmingham landscape architect Norman Kent Johnson. A sense of complete privacy and peace permeates the place.

This garden's estimated size is 2 acres.

THE DANCER
NEW 10–4

Tucked on the down slope of Red Mountain in Birmingham, Alabama, this 1930s Tudor style home went through a major interior renovation and addition, providing these clients the opportunity to create the garden they dreamed of off the back of their house.

The dream was not specific but in it was water, a ballerina, and roses. The space is about 2,100 square feet (35' × 60') and framed by the garage court and garage, existing magnolia hedge, the new kitchen addition, and a neighbor that needed screening. By using the house geometry and centerlines to pull the architecture into the garden, two garden rooms were created. The Fountain Garden is centered on the new kitchen steel-framed glass doors.

Adjacent to the Fountain Garden is The Rose/Sculpture Garden, centered on the living room. A display terrace for the 8 foot tall bronze ballerina sculpture is surrounded by four Winter King Hawthorns as she overlooks the rose garden beyond.

This garden's estimated size is 2,100 sq. ft.

💬 TROWEL TALK

As the designer, not the 'gardener' for this garden, I can only speak to that. After more technologically advanced methods of 3D models and renderings produced some sterile options, it was a hand-drawn fountain sketch that finally unlocked this garden design and was often referred to throughout construction to verify the vision was still in place.

—*GLA*

Keeyla Meadows Garden and Art - Albany, CA
Photo: Keeyla Meadows

California

46   California

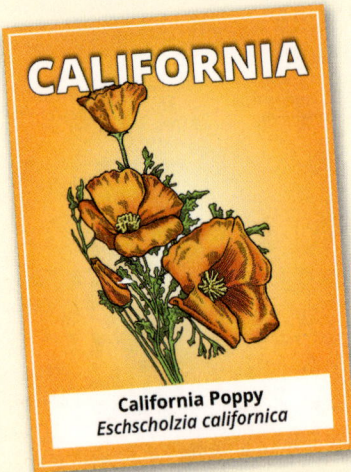

California Poppy
Eschscholzia californica

Open Days dates and times by County, Town, and Garden

ALAMEDA
Albany
Keeyla Meadows Gardens and Art
  Saturday, May 11, 10–4
Berkeley
Aging Gracefully
  Saturday, May 11, 10–4
Berkeley Pollinator Playground
  Saturday, October 19, 10–12, 12–2, 2–4
Berkeley Urban Oasis
  Saturday, October 19, 10–12, 12–2, 2–4
Catalina Sculptural Pollinator Paradise
  Saturday, May 11, 10–4
Marcia's Garden
  Saturday, Sunday 19, 10–4
Oakland
Ann Nichols' Garden
  Saturday, May 11, 10–4
Meadow's Edge
  Saturday, October 19, 10–1, 1–4
Oakland Cramscape
  Saturday, October 19, 10–4
Zumba Gardens
  Saturday, October 19, 10–4

Piedmont
A Garden for Birds
  Saturday, May 11, 10–4
Piedmont Oasis
  Saturday, May 11, 10–4

LOS ANGELES
Altadena
The Abascal Family Garden
  Sunday, April 21, 10–4
Pasadena
Bennett-DeBeixedon Garden
  Sunday, April 21, 10–4
The Schumacher Garden Retreat
  Sunday, April 21, 10–4
Sherman Oaks
Longridge
  Sunday, April 28, 10–4
Studio City
Sustainable Storybook Garden
  Sunday, April 28, 10–4
Wrightwood Estates Hillside Garden
  Sunday, April 28, 10–4

MARIN
Bolinas
Visions of Paradise - Sally Robertson Garden and Studio
  Saturday, May 4, 10–4
Ross
Old Oak Hill
  Saturday, May 4, 10–4
Stinson Beach
The Panoramic Garden
  Saturday, May 4, 10–4

RIVERSIDE
Palm Springs
Casa de las Ardillas
Saturday, March 2, 10–4
Casa Madrina - Godmothers Cottage
Saturday, March 2, 10–4
Casa Mazamitla
Saturday, March 2, 10–4
Dry Falls Garden
Saturday, March 1, 10–4
Monte Vista Garden
Saturday, March 2, 10–4

SAN FRANCISCO
San Francisco
English Tudor Residential Garden
Sunday, June 9, 10–4
Geary Street Gardens
Saturday, May 18, 10–4
New England in San Francisco
Sunday, June 9, 10–4
San Francisco Native Garden
Sunday, June 9, 10–4
The Cottage Garden
Saturday, May 18, 10–12, 12–2, 2–4
The Gaddam Residence
Sunday, June 9, 10–4
Twin Palms
Saturday, May 18, 10–4

SAN JOAQUIN
Tracy
Hutton
Saturday, June 8, 10–4

SAN MATEO
Pacifica
Pacifica Collector's Garden
Saturday, May 18, 10–4

CALIFORNIA

Riverside County
Saturday, March 2

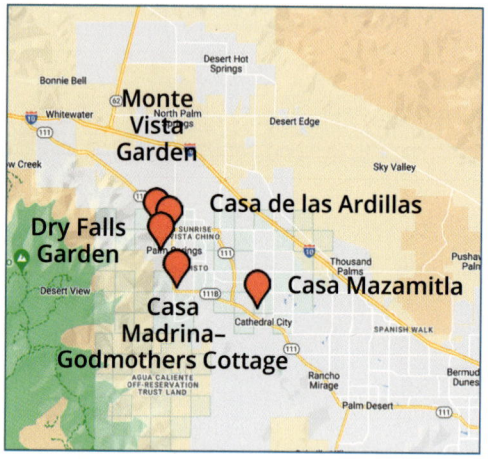

PALM SPRINGS

CASA DE LAS ARDILLAS
NEW   10–4

To enter Casa de las Ardillas, guests pass through a metal portal inserted into the existing hedge and emerge on the other side in a lush oasis facing the San Jacinto mountains.

The garden experience creates a series of outdoor rooms using exuberant planting to frame and delineate each area. Garden views are framed by windows around the house for seamless continuity in every room.

Pink muhly grasses, succulent accents, an olive grove, euphorbia, palo verdes—planting is layered and immersive. At the end of a linear pool, the reflection of a pink neon squirrel shimmers on the surface, blending with the desert sky.

CASA MADRINA–GODMOTHERS COTTAGE
NEW   10–4

We had a chance to acquire this property when it was abandoned and derelict. I envisioned transforming it into a weekend escape—a private lush oasis to enjoy with friends.

Today our 1930s Spanish house is a fiesta of color! with patios of chocolate sandstone to blend with the mountains, earthy red walls, and a violet casita. Plantings include espaliered bougainvillea, fragrant jasmine, native and date palms, citrus trees, and an olive triad that shelters a generous entertaining area. The front yard is my ongoing experiment with desert natives and annual wildflowers.

I designed into the infrastructure all the elements of a sustainable landscape: permeable paving, infiltration zones, laundry-to-landscape greywater system, a smart irrigation timer and drip irrigation, habitat plantings, and good soil-building practices. Because of these elements, native and migratory birds and butterflies are regular visitors.

This garden's estimated size is ¼ acre.

💬 TROWEL TALK

My first garden was a vegetable patch at our summer cottage.

A simple manual fell into my hands as a 12-year-old and my great grandmother offered to buy a load of good loamy soil. I had to spread it and started to plant the seeds. I was so surprised when they started to sprout and diligently watered my garden with a watering can using the rain barrel.

The best memory is harvesting the corn and sharing it for dinner. I guess that got me hooked.

—Laura Morton

CASA MAZAMITLA
NEW ♿ 10–4

This modest condominium garden exudes a sense of calm and order that is enlivened by color, pragmatic in the use of raised vegetable beds, and not so precious as to eschew a whimsical surprise. You are welcomed by artichoke-capped gateposts (a symbol of hope and prosperity) into a discreetly minimalist walled garden with a borrowed viewshed.

Garden designer Joseph Marek has designed a formal series of five small "rooms," defined by hardscape and plant material, that provide a sense of discovery as one progresses through them.

This garden's estimated size is 2,000 sq. ft.

💬 TROWEL TALK

The first thing you should know is that Gardener #1 not only talks to his plants but instructs Gardener #2 to attend to, or water "the children." That also means editing in the garden is done with a "no child left behind" policy; just ask our friends who became adoptive parents of potted plants when we relocated from the moderate microclimate of Silver Lake, Los Angeles to the desert climate of Palm Springs in 2020.

The second thing to know is that Gardener #1 grew up reading Sunset Magazine's "Western Garden Book" cover to cover and inherited his grandparent's green thumbs. Gardener #2 feels that it must have been a combination of domestic vegetable/flower gardens and the descriptions of gardens in 19th century British novels that spurred his gardening ambitions.

Both gardeners enjoy working out of doors and wanted their garden designed for al fresco entertaining. The Silver Lake garden, an evolution of almost thirty years, supported Gardener #1's favorite plants; daylilies, staghorn ferns, and epiphyllum. It also included an extensive collection of cacti and fig trees (the fig being a passion of Gardener #2).

Joseph Marek designed the final iteration of that garden, which made him the natural choice for Casa Mazamitla. His remit was to provide the intimacy and serenity of that first salubrious space in a desert climate where the plant list had to survive triple-digit temperatures for months on end. The Mediterranean-inspired plantings include an espaliered fig. The series of "rooms" he envisioned produce a sense of discovery as guests travel through the garden. Each is defined by hardscape elements or a featured plant - hence a cactus garden that holds some of the specimens from Silver Lake.

The desert location enabled Gardener #1 to pursue his interest in agaves. Another aspect of our oasis is the thoughtful addition of materials, ornaments, and found objects that have accumulated over the past three years. It is axiomatic that all gardens are constantly evolving but this usually refers to plant growth. At Casa Mazamitla, the introduction of new ideas or adornments is often the result of discovery (I love it, where will it go?) like the artichoke finials on the gate posts, or finding a way to repurpose something that might otherwise be discarded—the iron cocktail tabletop, a gate saved from the Silver Lake house, is a perfect example.

Gardener #1 is constantly rearranging and restaging spaces, often to the dismay of Gardener #2. Life in the garden is never dull. Gardens are a grand experiment, and we often fail. We have even killed cacti. Yes, too much water will drown "the children." Our desert garden is yet another experiment that has only just begun.

—*Gardener #1 and Gardener #2*

DRY FALLS GARDEN
NEW   10-4

The inspiration for the garden was the rugged canyons of the adjacent San Jacinto mountains. Our favorite plants are the iconic California fan palms that populate the adjacent canyons from which Palm Springs gets its name. Huge yucca and agaves reinforce this desert aesthetic.

Nestled within a neighborhood of classic Mid-century homes, this garden unfolds as a poetic canvas, embodying the essence of a tranquil oasis. The original design featured amoeba-shaped islands of pristine white gravel, haphazardly within an expanse of verdant lawn. Now, in its rebirth, the garden gracefully draws inspiration from the untamed allure of the San Jacinto mountains, which stand as the focal point of the dwelling.

Nature's rugged elegance is echoed through the meticulous selection of the landscape elements: The colored walls, the agave, yuccas, the California fan palm, mesquite, ironwood, and the graceful palo verde trees are artfully choreographed to pay homage to the majestic mountainous backdrop.

This garden serves as a "desert retreat" carefully sculpted to offer respite from the frantic pace of Los Angeles life creating a landscape that not only soothes the soul but also tells a story of resilience and natural elegance.

💬 TROWEL TALK

In crafting this garden, we drew inspiration from the rugged canyons gracing the adjacent mountains. The clients hold a particular affinity for the iconic California fan palm, a species that

Los Angeles County— Pasadena

Sunday, April 21

flourishes in the nearby canyons and lends its name to the renowned Palm Springs.

The design gracefully incorporates sizable yucca and agave, enhancing the overall desert aesthetic. These botanical elements, carefully chosen and strategically placed, seamlessly weave the narrative of arid beauty throughout the garden. Each plant, a testament to the unique charm of the surrounding landscape, contributes to the creation of an oasis that echoes the untamed allure of the neighboring mountains.

—Steve Martino, FASLA

MONTE VISTA GARDEN
NEW 10–4

The Monte Vista Garden celebrates the geomorphic condition of the neighboring San Jacinto Mountains and Tahquitz Canyon through fractured rock shards. Bringing the language of the rock faces down into the site as if they had fallen from the mountains, the fractured shards are a recurring motif in this Palm Springs garden that unite the architecture and the landscape.

The mirrorlike quality of the pool and spa reflects the surrounding palms, the mountains, the sky as abstractions, reflections, refractions that would otherwise go unnoticed. This desert garden uses low-water native and adapted plant material, carrying the character of an existing smoke bush throughout the garden. Screening plants in shades of grey and silver form a silver cloud that immerses the new architecture.

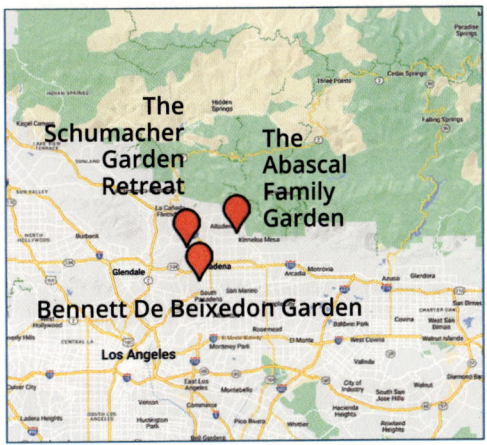

ALTADENA
THE ABASCAL FAMILY GARDEN
NEW ♿ 10–4

Upon entering the Abascal Garden under an allée of white crape myrtles, you feel as though you've been transported someplace else. With the help of the supremely talented landscape architect Sally Farnum, the Abascals created a Mediterranean-inspired garden that is a delight to the senses.

The garden has all the hallmarks of a classic Mediterranean garden such as shady retreats, multiple seating areas, terra-cotta pots, boxwood topiaries, citrus and olive trees, water features, blurred lines between the house and garden, and of course, gravel. The gravel was added over the years not just for aesthetic

52 California

Register online: gardenconservancy.org/opendays

purposes, but for water conservation as well. Much of the water-thirsty lawn and water-impermeable asphalt surfacing was replaced with gravel.

In designing a recent house renovation, careful consideration was given to how the garden would be experienced from inside the house, which is why you have beautiful vistas of the garden and the restful sound of a trickling fountain from nearly every room in the house. An added bonus to the property is a bonsai collection cultivated by Manuel and a gorgeous view of the San Gabriel Mountains!

This garden's estimated size is ½ acre.

💬 **TROWEL TALK**

I seem to have a different favorite plant every year, but there is one basic plant I can't live without. I've been collecting vintage/antique terra-cotta pots for about twenty years and I love to plant them with boxwood topiaries, particularly globes. To me, a simple boxwood in a rustic, patinated pot is perfection.

I find pots at yard sales, antique stores, neighbors, nurseries going out of business, you name it! Some of my favorite pots came from a garden center in Carpinteria, CA. They had a large collection of old pots that were great looking and consigned by a local resident. When I went to purchase them, they asked me to write the check to the consignee, Oprah Winfrey.

—Jane A.

PASADENA
BENNET DE BEIXEDON GARDEN
 partial 10–4

Hidden away at the end of a long gravel drive, our magical garden was created in 2003 on a lot previously abandoned for 50 years. Wrapping around a newly built northern European-style cottage, the site utilizes the sloped and rocky terrain to create a two-level slate patio with river rock walls and steps.

Surrounded by major oak trees and bordered by vines and climbing roses on all four sides, the garden is divided into rooms, including a sunny cottage garden, a shade garden under the oaks, and a culinary garden.

THE SCHUMACHER GARDEN RETREAT
NEW 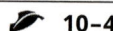 10–4

The fragrance of roses, California native sages, and citrus from the Schumacher Garden Retreat invites those passing by this Linda Vista charmer. As you enter the garden, you'll meet birds, butterflies, and native bees delighting in this Certified Wildlife Habitat.

Begin by walking down the hanging *Epiphyllum* path with *Ficus*-covered privacy walls into the propagation area, where Bea's nursery of seedlings, offshoots, and tiny plantings are tended. The homeowners award-winning cacti are on display in container gardens accenting the four living spaces and two chef workspaces.

The serene sounds of water fill the space, as does dappled light that glitters through the tree canopy on *Dudleya, Haemanthus, Camelia, Ceanothus,* and *Heuchera*. Beneath

NEW 5 10 20 '95 Year

the lush, leafy, low-water beauty, water conservation systems capture and sink stormwater from the roof and permeable hardscapes.

After you stroll through the fire pit, raised herb garden, and spa, reemerge via a gravel path at the front of the home where you'll find a delightfully peaceful sunken meditation garden adjacent to the front entrance. Hidden behind the riot of front yard foliage, this serene space includes built-in seating with a view of yet another fountain.

Exit wandering through the artfully integrated collection of roses, spring-blooming natives; buckwheats, salvias, mallows, and wildflowers.

This garden's estimated size is 8,300 sq. ft.

💬 TROWEL TALK

What is your favorite plant?
The *Haemanthus albiflos* (Elephants Tongue) from South Africa, that has propagated from one single bulb into a carpet of more than 50 blooms.

What was your first garden?
Tom planted a rose garden for his mother in Milwaukee as a teen, and Bea grew up on an acre in Zimbabwe where her mother had rock gardens, jacaranda and cassia trees, as well as chickens, vegetables, fruit trees, and a composting pit.

What is a plant that you have never had any luck with?
We lost our first pincushion, but we think we have learned enough that we are looking forward to having four recent plants blooming this spring.

What is your favorite garden tool?
Toms is his large spongy kneeler that he uses to keep the pink thyme between the pavers neat, and Bea has her favorite needle nose clippers she uses to cut herbs, roses, and miniature Ikebana arrangements.

—*Tom and Bea Schumacher*

Los Angeles County— San Fernando Valley

Sunday, April 28

SHERMAN OAKS
LONGRIDGE
NEW ♿ 10–4

The front garden of this 1940s-built traditional home is dominated by an ancient and rarely-seen-in-Southern California silver maple tree (*Acer saccharinum*). Working with the tree and creating new gardens around and under it was the task presented to landscape architect Joseph Marek in 2020.

The plantings in this white picket–fenced front garden reflect a more East Coast aesthetic while also considering the need for water-wise plantings. Westringias, teucriums, and Little Ollies have been mixed with hydrangeas, pittosporums, and climbing roses. New 'Natchez White' crape myrtles and boxwood spheres line the sides of the path to the front door.

The lawn was reduced in size while still allowing space for the family's young children to play. In time the lawn will be further reduced as the gardens and children grow. The back garden terrace was expanded and now features a roaring fire pit, a grill, and a dining pergola for outdoor entertaining and family events.

There is also a sliver of lawn for play. A play court and a trampoline currently flank the sides of the pool, but there are plans to build a pool house and to expand the pool down the line.

This garden's estimated size is 10,000 sq. ft.

STUDIO CITY
SUSTAINABLE STORYBOOK GARDEN
NEW ♿ 🍃 10–4

It's easy to believe in storybook creatures in this Universal Studios adjacent neighborhood! Homes designed for studio employees evoke wonder. While most wear ho-hum lawns, the Sustainable Storybook Garden offers ample play space for elves, gnomes, and other pollinators.

Watch for those with wings dancing through this Certified Wildlife Habitat. In spring, they alight upon bright blue foothill penstemon and candy-pink western redbud blooms, only to be distracted by wands of white sage and wildflowers.

Travel an original brick and stone walk or gravel paths to meet dragons (aka western fence lizards), who rustle the deer grass cloaking the magic of two bioswales that draw and sink stormwater. Notice the trickle of water and the delightful crunch of gravel on the way to the back garden. There, bold and dynamic container gardens punctuate and define a space that is both drive and extended patio. Valley-indigenous foliage, including forage-worthy coffeeberry, toyon, and Catalina cherry wrap and shade a cozy conversation circle of Adirondack chairs.

Engaging Dustin Gimbel sculptures draw eyes up, while rare native irises offer ankle-height hiding space for Mr. Toad and other creatures...who may just turn to stone if you catch them eavesdropping!

This garden's estimated size is 1,600 sq. ft.

TROWEL TALK

What is your favorite plant?
Big fan of toyon *(Heteromeles arbutifolia).* I love that it grows so readily in the canyons of LA, so it feels relevant and important to have in our home gardens too. Plus, the history behind it is really cool. Early settlers from the East Coast thought it looked like the traditional holly they were accustomed to (red berries), hence Hollywood! Great for birds too—they love eating the berries.

What was your first garden?
I've always done a lot of gardening with containers, which I still love. In our previous home, though, I had a lot of space to do more (big front and backyard). I took that opportunity to do a mix of natives and drought-tolerant friendly plants. Lots of learning there that I've taken with me—the biggest lesson was to go all native! The best decision we could have made in this new garden.

What is a plant that you have never had any luck with?
Have never had any luck with citrus. I have two limes in pots now that seem to be doing ok, but no limes yet. Ask me again next year, haha!

What is your favorite garden tool?
Hard to pick just one, but probably my Felco pruners. They're the best and worth every penny. Second best—my hands! So much better than fussing with gloves or other tools if you can just do it on your own.

—Michael S.

WRIGHTWOOD ESTATES HILLSIDE GARDEN
NEW partial 10–4

The present garden dates from 2007, when it was remodeled by Landscape Designer Jamie Schwentker as part of a major renovation to the Mid-century Modern house, which included the addition of a second story and a new garage.

This is essentially a hillside garden, with the largest portion of the property being a hill that rises up steeply behind the house. This tall slope and the orientation of the house itself create fairly shady conditions for most of the garden areas. There were already many mature trees and shrubs on the property, some of which were rather unusual species, and the designer felt that as many of these as possible should be preserved and integrated into the new design.

The Owners confirmed that they had bought the house from a plant loving "hands on" gardener. Among these mature tree and shrub specimens are a pair of majestic Canary Island Date Palms, a giant Eucalyptus citriodora (lemon-scented gum

tree) a Blue Atlas Cedar tree, *Callistemon citrinus* (Red Bottlebrush tree), some Canary Island Pines and old *Camellia japonica* shrubs. There is also a large specimen variegated English Holly tree in the Rear Garden as well as a nearby *Trevesia palmata*, with its large tropical leaves. Another huge tropical plant in the rear garden is a Split-leaf Philodendron that clambers over an existing retaining wall at the foot of the rear slope. An enormously tall *Agathus robusta* (Queensland Kauri), which is very seldom seen in residential gardens, stands at the very west end of the property along with a couple of mature Aleppo Pine trees.

The Garden Designer thus came to understand this property as a kind of botanical garden boasting a variety of somewhat rare specimen plants, and the theme of the new planting palette would be eclecticism, featuring "unusual" plants that would complement the existing specimens and help create a garden tapestry of foliage textures, shapes, and colors.

The original Front Garden had been mostly lawn, all of which was removed to create an Entry Garden comprised of swaths of various plantings (among them Kangaroo Paw, Red-leafed Azaleas, Fox-tail Agave, Sago Palms, Mexican Weeping Bamboo) through which one walks to reach the front door of the house.

A Cactus and Succulent Garden was created on the far (west) side of the Driveway, which can best be viewed from the sidewalk in the cul-de-sac of the street. A boomerang-shaped lawn was created in the level area just behind the house as an entertainment space and a play area for the Owners' dogs. Shade tolerant flowering plants surround the lawn.

The rear slope above the lawn was already densely planted with an assortment of drought tolerant plantings including agaves, aloes, and a large *Heteromeles arbutifolia* (the native Toyon tree), but mass planting of other flowering shrubs and perennials were inserted into the mix to create a more picturesque design since this steep slope is such a predominant feature of the Rear Garden from both inside and outside the house.

A new Kitchen Garden was established at the far west end of the Rear Garden- beyond the Barbecue area and the stone-paved dining terrace, with its outdoor fireplace, off of the kitchen. Through the years, however, the various fruit trees in this area began to shade out the lower growing vegetables and herbs. Thus, today this area remains only an orchard.

A new raised planter for vegetables and herbs was then constructed at the east end of the Rear Garden, adjacent to the Eucalyptus tree because this spot remained the sunniest in the garden. Alterations such as this one are inevitable in all gardens, and this garden has definitely changed and evolved over time.

A very capable and experienced gardening crew fortunately continues to maintain the Wrightwood Estates Hillside Garden and alter it as various needs arise. Plant varieties have gotten switched out over time. The rear lawn was changed to artificial turf several years ago, when conditions became too shady to support real turf grass, and also facilitated the reduction of water usage in the garden, making it more sustainable.

In recent years, the construction of some landscape tie retaining walls on the rear slope have provided easier human and canine access onto the rear slope as well as level places to sit, rest, and enjoy the beauty.

This garden's estimated size is approximately 12,000 sq. ft., of which about 3,800 sq. ft. is level land.

Marin County
Saturday, May 4

BOLINAS
VISIONS OF PARADISE - SALLY ROBERTSON GARDEN AND STUDIO
 10–4

I like to think of walking through the garden gate as entering an enchanted and magical world. When asked to describe my garden, I refer to the title of one of my favorite garden books, *Visions of Paradise*.

This expression has guided me for nearly four decades. As a painter, I often choose plants as inspiration for a watercolor, but I give much thought to their placement, for the garden itself is a highly orchestrated color palette. As I mature as a gardener, shrubs and trees which give year-round structure become more and more important, and well-shaped shrubs mingle well with exuberant roses.

Succulents have found their place, along with unusual specimens such as the exotic phoenix palm from the Canary Islands, or

NEW 5 10 20 '95 Year    No Photography    Accessibility    Nibbled Leaf Garden

the lovely deciduous dawn redwood from China. The koi pond and water garden offer an idyllic spot to linger and enjoy a reflective moment.

The garden is an ever-changing project, evolving year after year, and I hope that even those who have visited in the past will find new inspiration here. Visitors are also invited to visit the studio, where art and garden meet.

This garden's estimated size is ¾ acre.

💬 TROWEL TALK

For many years I taught a class called Watercolor in the Gardens of France. We visited and painted in many remarkable gardens from Paris to the Côte d'Azur, but it was the gardens of Provence, with their emphasis on shaped shrubs, which probably had the most influence on my own garden, as I love to combine abundant flowering plants and these more formal elements.

Feel free to ask me about the "minor miracle" which saved my expansive koi pond and water garden during the drought.

—*Sally Roberston*

ROSS
OLD OAK HILL
NEW   10–4

A 3-acre garden on a "hogback" surrounds the carefully placed 1905 house designed by Bernard Maybeck. Vintage native oaks frame views of Mount Tamalpais.

Two coast live oaks are particularly grand and are named (by the owner) "General Fremont" and "Mrs. Fremont." They are surrounded by *Chasmanthe* plants and when they are in bloom (red-orange), it is hummingbird heaven. After the Sudden Oak Death pathogen destroyed many oaks in Marin County and notably in this garden, the owner took the opportunity to create new vignettes, always trying not to stress the remaining oaks.

Now winding paths lead to ponds, a waterfall, a golf pitch, climbing roses (including the famous 'Kiftsgate'), a succulent garden, a bee hive, and a micro-farm that generates produce for the owner's daughter, who is also a chef.

STINSON BEACH
THE PANORAMIC GARDEN
  10–4

Huge boulders on a steep hillside provide the framework for this unusual garden perched on the shoulders of Mt. Tamalpais. It was created twenty-plus years ago from a wilderness of brambles, poison oak, and native willows. Now stone walks radiate from a centrally located house to a series of garden rooms defined by their plantings—various fuchsia species, tillandsia, and pendulous epiphyllums grow in the shade of ancient bay trees. On the hillside, protea and dozens of succulent species grow in the sparse soil among the rocks.

In the sunny open areas, azara, *Pseudocydonia psoralea*, and rare shrubs share space with perennials and self-seeding annuals. Water-loving plants such as papyrus and giant gunnera surround the seasonal stream and the koi pond.

The garden contains more than 200 species of plants, including unusual specimens from the Mediterranean, Australia, New Zealand, Chile, South

Register online: gardenconservancy.org/opendays   California   59

East Bay Area
Sunday, May 5

Africa, and Mesoamerican cloud forests. Scattered among the plants are beautiful stone sculptures from Zimbabwe and comfortable weather-worn benches offering diverse views of the garden and the Pacific Ocean below.

This garden's estimated size is 1½ acres.

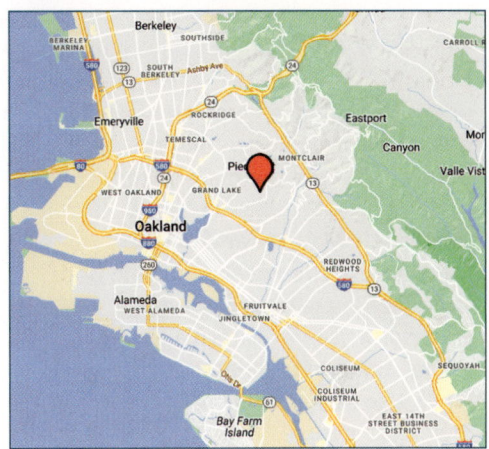

DIGGING DEEPER

Designing a Garden For Pollinators
Valerie Matzger and Keeyla Meadows
Sunday, May 5, 2–4

NEW 5 10 20 '95 Year   No Photography   Accessibility   Nibbled Leaf Garden

60 California

Register online: gardenconservancy.org/opendays

East Bay Area
Saturday, May 11

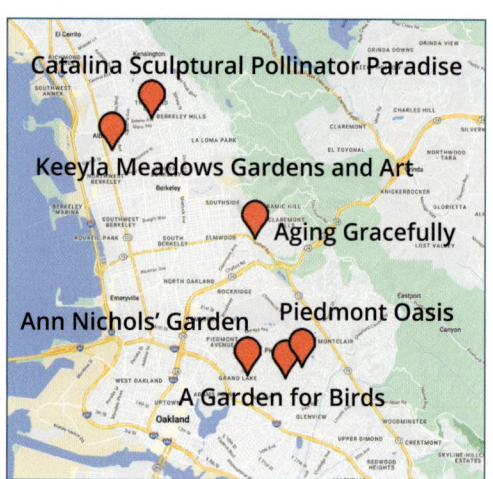

A Garden for Birds
Piedmont, CA
$30 Members | $40 General

Since 1970, bird numbers have plunged along with the insects that they depend upon. Habitat loss, climate change, pesticide use, window collisions, and outdoor cats are the main culprits.

Join Valerie Matzger and Keeyla Meadows, garden designers who both specialize in creating gardens with successful use of California Native plants that put pollinators to the fore while also being visually attractive and inviting to people.

Topics covered will include selection and appropriate placement of Native plants, information on applying color design principles to a habitat garden, fountain construction, irrigation installation, and placement of garden features such as seating areas and water features to enhance pleasures and functionality of habitat gardens. Explore these principles at Valerie's home garden, which has been visited by 47 species of birds, giving the garden peace and animation with their songs and movement.

ALBANY
KEEYLA MEADOWS GARDENS AND ART
 partial 10–4

My whole life, growing up in the wilds of a Native Southern California Canyon, I have been an Avataress of bees, butterflies, and beneficial garden insects. I love the sounds of crickets in the evening garden.

Reading Rachel Carson's *Silent Spring* at 12, I feared for the effects of chemicals on the environment. I grew into a gardener, artist, and landscape designer and learned to write to reach out to others of the joys and "how to do its" of gardening, which led me to authoring two books, *Making Gardens Works of Art* and *Fearless Color Gardening*.

My home garden is a haven to birds, bees, butterflies, dragonflies, crickets, and salamanders. A bounty of year-round colors of foliage and flowers offer bouquets, foraging grounds for birds and

NEW 5 10 20 95 Year    No Photography    Accessibility    Nibbled Leaf Garden

insects. For more than 40 years I've been teaching classes and installing gardens that support pollinators. Come to the garden to be with the bees and butterflies.

💬 TROWEL TALK

A small square canvas presented in art school just did not fit my creative vision. A garden of any size does, Offering an opportunity to create a large scale work of art. My garden invites you to come and visit. Be in the light, pleasures and inspirations that gardens all over our vast country offer.

—Keeyla Meadows

BERKELEY
AGING GRACEFULLY
10–4

When we moved into our old, neglected carriage house and garden in 1987, I did not know a peony from a boxwood. I was busy working and raising children. We were so excited just to have fruit in the yard that we could actually eat and some flowers to put in a vase. Over the years I have read, experimented, divided, planted, replanted, lost, and gained . So much of my knowledge has come from sharing with others.

I have learned much, especially the peace and joy a garden bestows. It is a place to contemplate, feel alive, and delight in the five senses. I am most proud of the way our garden has given back over the years. What started as a clump of clivia is now hundreds, the hedgehog aloe that lived under the European oak has yielded 50+ babies, our agapanthus have graced the pathways of friends and neighbors from Berkeley to Napa, and our ancient acanthus is a spectacle in the spring, spreading its roots in nooks and crannies.

With California's water shortages and raging fires, the garden has evolved into a dryer version of itself. Succulents, grasses, and water-wise plants have edged out hydrangeas and other thirsty perennials The true heroes of the garden have not only persevered but also flourished—regal beech and sculptural oak, the ancient boxwoods and magnolias, the acanthus and elder hellebores—a true testament to the grandeur of nature.

This garden was archived in the Smithsonian Institution's Archives of American Gardens in 2022. Images and more about this documentation project can be found here:

tinyurl.com/hartestate

This garden's estimated size is ⅛ acre.

💬 TROWEL TALK

The Gardener's Passion

I know every inch of you
I close my eyes and see your nuance
Smell you when I'm long away from you
With beauty that permeates my pores
Your needs deplete me
I dream of being with you when I regain my strength
I share my innermost thoughts while basking in your fertility
You are my serenity and safe space
I try to tame you but your beautiful wildness always prevails
With resiliency that knows no bounds
Your adaptability, a lesson for all

I will always need you more than you need me
You will live on long after I'm gone
When I lose my senses the imprint will remain
I'll see your vibrancy
Smell the myriad of fragrances,
Feel your texture,
Hear the others that inhabit your domain,
And taste your fruit
Thank you beloved garden
For gracing me with your beauty,
Your life lessons, and hours of joy and awe—

—*Your grateful Keeper*

CATALINA SCULPTURAL POLLINATOR PARADISE
NEW 10–4

Catalina went from a boring, thirsty, high maintenance lawn to a succulent, pollinator meadow in less than a year's time. The large corner lot in Berkeley's Solano Avenue shopping district attracts butterflies, bees, hummingbirds, and humans. The plant palette is a solid combination of drought- and deer-tolerant species providing year-round color and intrigue.

OAKLAND
ANN NICHOLS' GARDEN
10–4

This is a garden of many levels consisting of a number of outdoor rooms, each with its own plant and color scheme. The front garden, designed around an existing Canary Island date palm, is home to a variety of tropical and subtropical plants. One passes a small orchid garden and meanders along a gentle waterway to enter the upper garden. A shady "entry parlor" welcomes visitors to the back patio, the white garden, and the bright-foliaged, sunny middle garden and finally through the arched entry to the rose garden.

This garden's estimated size is ⅛ acre.

PIEDMONT
A GARDEN FOR BIRDS
NEW 10–4

Although I've designed gardens since 1989, it took the enforced isolation of the COVID epidemic to turn my attention to my own property.

After learning of the catastrophic loss of birds, due partly to habitat loss, I determined to create a garden for birds and the insects that support them. Out went the two sloping lawns in the front and back, and in went curved terraces containing some 100 species of California native plants supported by dry-laid stone walls. Flagstone paths wander through the fragrant sunny garden below the coast live oak and continue through the cool, shady garden anchored by a coastal redwood.

Several seating areas offer places to rest and enjoy the 47 species of birds that visit the little pond/waterfall or the front garden fountain so popular with hummingbirds.

This garden's estimated size is ¼ acre.

NEW 5 10 20 '95 Year   No Photography    Accessibility    Nibbled Leaf Garden

Register online: gardenconservancy.org/opendays   California   63

PIEDMONT OASIS
10–4

Historic 1911 Willis Polk design has been turned into a collector's garden. Formal structures meet controlled chaos. This garden has 100-year-old trees, legacy plantings of traditional species from previous decades, and an eclectic mix of rare and just odd plants. It's a plant nerd's delight.

This garden's estimated size is 1½ acres.

💬 **TROWEL TALK**

My motto seems to be, "there's always room for another plant." The plant usually comes before we've found the spot for it. I'll try any plant once and many twice, or more, before giving up on it. Sometimes it's just a matter of finding the right place for a particular plant.

In the end, the one thing that you can count on is that nature always wins.

—*Jon and Julie*

Nearby Counties

- **SAN FRANCISCO**
- **SAN MATEO**

Saturday, May 18

SAN FRANCISCO COUNTY
SAN FRANCISCO
GEARY STREET GARDENS
   10–4

In the heart of downtown San Francisco lives a secret garden behind twin historic buildings. These structures were erected in the early 1900s in the theater district and are three blocks from Union Square, on the dividing line between upper-class Nob Hill and the notorious Tenderloin districts.

It is extremely urban; however, from the streets and sidewalks you are just a garden gate away from an amazing urban oasis. Sean Stout and James Pettigrew of Organic Mechanics have designed a lush habitat garden for frogs, fish, bees, butterflies,

NEW 5 10 20 '95 Year      ♿ Accessibility

songbirds, hummingbirds, mourning doves, nesting robins, and more.

Even hawks regularly visit, bathing in the mosaic water feature after eating their pigeon in the trees. The garden invites people with its soothing sound of water, many paths, and secret nooks. Recycled materials are used in fresh, creative ways in mosaic paths, unusual planters, and sculpture.

Rare and unusual plants are featured in this can't-miss urban paradise. Organic Mechanics has won numerous awards, including the American Horticultural Society Environment Award and the prestigious Best in Show at the San Francisco Flower and Garden Show. They have appeared in many television programs, newspapers, and magazines. Their design/build firm is founded on organic and sustainable principles.

This garden's estimated size is 4,000 sq. ft.

💬 TROWEL TALK

We are always finding creative ways to juxtapose plant material with found metal objects. The garden is in a very urban setting but sheltered by buildings. This environment allows us to create a large peaceful outdoor room that is in sharp contrast to the hectic street scene.

—*Organic Mechanics*

THE COTTAGE GARDEN
🍃 10–12, 12–2, 2–4

In 2005, the Garden Conservancy acquired an easement on a vacant lot adjacent to the Greenwich Street pedestrian stairway in the Telegraph Hill Historic District. Historically important as open space, the lot was once a garden started in the 1930s by Valetta Heslet, who also planted gardens in an adjacent public right-of-way.

After preparing a landscape plan in consultation with the Garden Conservancy, the owners rebuilt a garden for the public to view and enjoy from the pedestrian stairway. The Garden Lot entrance is off the Greenwich Steps between Sansome and Montgomery streets.

It is a steep lot with seven sets of wooden retaining walls. The entrance is at the lowest elevation and serves as a way to access the gardens. Three brick steps from the Greenwich Steps serve as the entrance to the Garden Lot. A brick path turns east and runs along the eastern edge of the Garden Lot to access two cottages and is separated from the main garden by a simple wooden fence and from the eastern boundary by a wooden balustrade that matches the Garden Lot's stair balustrade.

Entrance to the main garden is through a simple wooden gate. A level lower garden area is planted with trees and shrubs at the edges. Eleven stone steps with a landing and a wooden balustrade connect the lower garden to the terraces. There are two wooden retaining walls between the bottom and the top of the stairs: one located at the stair landing and one at the top of the stairs. At the top of the stairs, five more terraces step up the hill, with five sets of wooden retaining walls.

NEW 5 10 20 '95 Year  No Photography    Accessibility   🍃 Nibbled Leaf Garden

The bottom retaining wall at the top of the stair includes a built-in wooden bench and a narrow wooden garden workbench and storage area. The terraces above this point are extensively planted. A set of three wooden stairs exits this terrace to the west to connect to the deck.

TWIN PALMS
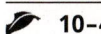 10–4

Perched on a hill with dizzying city skyline and bay views, this urban oasis on a double-plus-sized lot is deeply rooted in the English country garden tradition but with sustainability designed into its heart. Blessed by rich soil and underground natural springs, 80-year-old boxwoods and camellias thrive on their own from the garden's first period, 1939 to 1992.

In 1992 the current owners challenged the landscape architect to incorporate in-situ specimen shrubs to anchor a fresh design that included a new bluestone patio and a freestanding heated all-glass conservatory. The hardscape design now echoes the sweeping curves of the Art Deco architecture of the home.

Over the last 30 years, the landscape has evolved into a bird sanctuary and perennial garden featuring wisteria trained upright. The central recirculating water rock is a year-round magnet that draws in resident hummingbirds, finches, and sometimes even red-tailed hawks for their daily bath.

Native hawthorns, propagated from the original mother, now bloom plentifully throughout the garden in dense stands, as trees, and in bonsai forms. Starting in late June when the hawthorn nuts ripen, they provide a daily feast for a pandemonium of the city's famous wild parrots!

This garden's estimated size is 6,500 sq. ft.

💬 TROWEL TALK

I was the only one of four siblings to share an interest in gardening with both my parents, who taught me much of what I know. I have been an avid gardener for 60+ years, since I was a small child. I have a particular fondness for flowers, and San Francisco is my dream location for a garden because something is always blooming.

—*The Gardener*

SAN MATEO COUNTY
PACIFICA

PACIFICA COLLECTOR'S GARDEN
 10–4

Matt and Annie moved to Pacifica six years ago in order to create a garden for their ever expanding agave, aloe, and succulent collection. In their 5,000 sq. foot lot they've built raised beds with recycled urbanite between winding decomposed granite pathways, and planted a huge variety of drought-tolerant, xeric, rare, and unusual plants like cussonias, dendroseris, and seed-grown *Aloe polyphylla*.

Their sustainable, low-water landscape design business, Xeric Oasis, is run from their home, and as a result the gardens feature an ever-changing cast of new plants and interesting cultivars.

This garden's estimated size is 5,000 sq. ft.

NEW 5 10 20 '95 Year   No Photography    Accessibility    Nibbled Leaf Garden

PUBLIC GARDEN
PENNSYLVANIA STREET GARDENS

251 Pennsylvania Ave
San Francisco, California 94107

In 2008 Annie Shaw and Matt Petty founded volunteer-run Pennsylvania Street Gardens to showcase xeric plants from all over the world and reduce water use in ornamental gardening while inspiring the community to join in.

Their first garden, Pennsylvania Garden, sits on almost an acre of Caltrans-owned land and proves you can have a gorgeous landscape without using much water—if any!

An additional garden, Pennsylvania Railroad Garden, is just down the hill along the 100 block of Pennsylvania Avenue.

Planted in 2012, it has 23 trees, a walking path, and hundreds of the types of plants that performed best at our original garden. Once a derelict expanse of trash and encampments, it has brought peace and beauty to this part of Potrero Hill.

Volunteers are warmly welcomed at our monthly workdays - please visit our website to find out more.

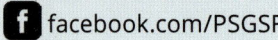 facebook.com/PSGSF

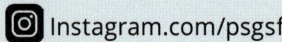 Instagram.com/psgsf

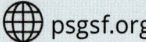 psgsf.org

San Joaquin County

Saturday, June 8

TRACY

HUTTON

NEW 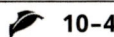 10–4

Thoughtful design is about working with regulating lines, creative problem-solving, and knowing what can contribute to a comfortable, versatile, and beautiful setting. We first edited out 38 trees, including 19 redwoods, and we are in our second spring since the garden installation was completed.

Our home is a resource-conscious mash-up of what I call California Agrarian and Contemporary Tuscan, and it relies on strong lines, order, and consistency in inherited and added materials.

We have introduced 2,000 sq. feet of Italian porcelain pavers, lots of gravel, functional light-etch concrete, and a 30' long by 8' tall brick wall to aid noise abatement. A raised spa is within the garden and alongside a 16' × 38' black-bottom play pool. There are two raised produce beds and easy fruit trees as part of a palette of earthy neutrals, yellows, and warm pinks.

This garden's estimated size is 3/8 acre.

💬 TROWEL TALK

As a gardener and landscape architect, I like to celebrate seasonal interest and varied textures as I play with lines and manipulate order. My mom was a florist and garden enthusiast, and I often think of her as I enjoy arranging and sharing various cuttings. Current favorites include columnar hornbeam, slender veldt grass, and *Heuchera* 'Rosada'.

—Monica Perrone,
Monica Perrone Landscape Architecture

San Francisco— St. John's Wood Neighborhood
Sunday, June 9

SAN FRANCISCO
ENGLISH TUDOR RESIDENTIAL GARDEN
NEW ♿ 10–4

This renovated English Garden surrounds a 1937 English Tudor home in beautiful St. Francis Woods. The landscaping was designed by Arterra Landscape Architects in 2007.

The renovation included assessment of the soil and drainage conditions, and substantial modifications to the hardscape and landscape plans to the front and backyard while complementing the original landscape design with several of the original shrubs left in place in the front and side of the residence.

The backyard now includes an arbor, patio, new fencing, built-in seating wall, flagstone, lighting, and ornamental pots. Over time, some shrubs were replaced, and the garden now consists of a wide variety of trees and shrubs, including *Podocarpus gracilior*, azure, English boxwood, rosemary, azaleas, hydrangeas, loropetalum, anemone, clivia, heuchera, abutilon, camellia, star jasmine, agapanthus, pittosporum, daphnes, 'Biokovo' geraniums, *Coleonema* 'Compact', and more.

💬 TROWEL TALK

I have always enjoyed gardening, but I never knew exactly what I was doing! When I retired from a 30-year career in health care, I became a certified Master Gardener in 2017 and served in the organization for three years.

I now enjoy maintaining my garden with the assistance of my gardener based on solid scientific-based evidence. I am also First Vice-President in my local neighborhood garden club as well as overseeing an HOA landscape committee on a 21-acre second home property. This all keeps me very busy but so rewarding to spend time in my beautiful gardens and neighborhood.

—*Denise S.*

NEW ENGLAND IN SAN FRANCISCO
NEW 🖋 10–4

Our home is one of the few wood-shingled, colonial cape style residences in a historical neighborhood of Mediterranean and Tudor stucco designs. Coming from the East Coast, we were immediately drawn to the house- and tree-lined streets of the neighborhood.

The backyard was a blank slate. We

engaged landscape architect Kate Stickley of Arterra, with two requests: make it feel like we are in New England, and incorporate an ellipse in the design. She accomplished both splendidly. Since it's a small space, most of the area is covered with an elliptical terrace of blue stone, surrounded with trees and shrubs usually found along the Atlantic, rather than the Pacific. River birches allow for privacy during the summer, along with hydrangeas, roses, and geraniums for scent and seasonal colors.

This garden's estimated size is 30 x 30 feet.

SAN FRANCISCO NATIVE GARDEN
NEW   10–4

We replaced our San Francisco gardens 20 years ago, front and back, with virtually all California native plants (the trees being the principal exception). Our goals were to reduce or eliminate irrigation, and invite wildlife in.

Now, our garden has regular bird and insect visitors, and blooms or berries year-round. Everything in the garden is something you'd spot hiking in the Bay Area-we wanted it to match the local native flora as much as possible.

This garden's estimated size is 1,200 sq. ft.

💬 TROWEL TALK

I've become a gardener focused on the ecology of city landscapes: how they interact with and support birds and insects. That's what makes a garden beautiful to me.

I am grateful to see more and more people replacing their lawns, incorporating natives into their landscapes, and replacing their lawns with low-water-consuming plants. It makes for more interesting neighborhoods in our gardens, and the wildlife surely appreciate it!

— *The Gardeners*

THE GADDAM RESIDENCE
NEW 10–4

A captivating urban sanctuary where the timeless elegance of a Georgian home is accentuated by a diverse array of magnolias and cypresses, proudly adorning the front yard. This botanical collection, featuring a spectrum of magnolia species, establishes a stunning living tableau that pays homage to the home's architectural grandeur.

The front yard also features a fountain that incorporates a 1920s bronze vessel that was restored and seamlessly integrated into the walkway. In the secluded serenity of the backyard, the innovation of modern landscape artistry unfolds. Two living walls, conceived by the visionary Davis Dalbok, rise like verdant tapestries, weaving lush textures and vibrant shades of green into the fabric of the space. These vertical gardens stand as a testament to contemporary design, marrying beauty with sustainability.

Complementing this green haven, a bronze water sculpture by the renowned Archie Held stands as the centerpiece, its fluid form and soothing sounds crafting a tranquil urban oasis. Here, the interplay of water and sculpture captures the essence of tranquility, creating an environment that not only dazzles the senses but also provides a soul-soothing retreat from the city's bustling pace.

NEW   5   10   20   '95   Year    No Photography   Accessibility    Nibbled Leaf Garden

East Bay Area
Saturday, October 12

This harmonious blend of historical reverence, botanical beauty, and artistic expression transforms the property into an enclave of peace and beauty, offering an unparalleled urban living experience.

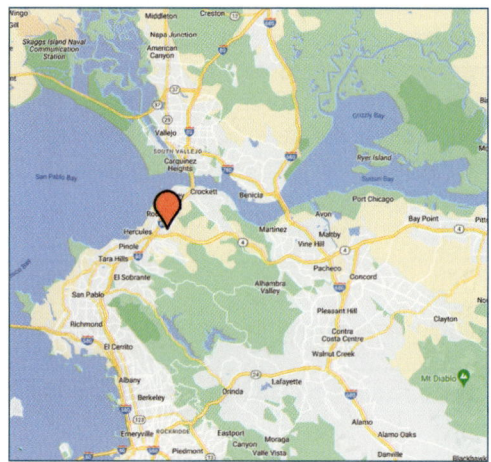

DIGGING DEEPER

Living Works of Art
Mathew McGrath, Artist and Founder at Farallon Gardens
Saturday, October 12, 5–7

Home Garden and Studio of Mathew McGrath
Rodeo, CA
$30 Members | $40 General

As a landscape designer and artist, Mat McGrath's home garden is an ever-evolving, living painting and sculpture garden. The owners collect found objects and salvaged materials to create sculptures set within the garden context. Learn how to incorporate beautiful, unconventional pieces to create works of art and sculpture for your garden.

💬 TROWEL TALK

My favorite plant is agave. My first garden was a small postage stamp San Francisco backyard I filled with cuttings and plants acquired from San Francisco Botanical Garden plant sales.

—Mathew McGrath

East Bay Area
Saturday, October 19

BERKELEY
BERKELEY POLLINATOR PLAYGROUND
NEW   🍃   10–12, 12–2, 2–4

Embark on an enchanting journey at the Berkeley Pollinator Playground, starting with a cobblestone permeable driveway that welcomes you with eco-friendly charm. Follow the pathway lined with colorful flowering perennials and an edible food garden, guiding you through the heart of this captivating landscape.

Discover the vast play area, a lush meadow inviting playful escapades and evoking the whimsy of childhood wonder. Continue to the seed fountain and leaning stone bench area, a tranquil space where the calming sound of trickling water accompanies your observations of birds and pollinators.

Berkeley Pollinator Playground is a symphony of natural delights, inviting you to experience the beauty of the natural world, carefully combined with each

---

NEW   5   10   20   95   Year   📷 No Photography   ♿ Accessibility   🍃 Nibbled Leaf Garden

beautifully crafted element.

💬 TROWEL TALK

Since her early childhood in the 70s, Andrea has been gardening. She grew up in a family of women who were and are very connected to the land. With her mother, on their acre of land in rural Oregon, Andrea would spend Saturday mornings learning how to tend to flower beds, rose trellises, a huge vegetable garden, and multiple fruit trees and berries. This experience led her to starting her own gardening side hustle just out of high school.

At Prescott College, Andrea learned about ecofeminism, and it resonated as it reinforced the lessons of her childhood about developing and maintaining a relationship with the natural world.

—*Andrea Hurd, Founder and General Manager, Mariposa Gardening & Design Cooperative*

DIGGING DEEPER

Find Your Home in Nature
Andrea Hurd, Founder and General Manager, Mariposa Gardening & Design Cooperative
Saturday, October 19, Hours TBD

Berkeley Pollinator Playground
Berkeley, CA
$30 Members | $40 General

At Mariposa, we strive to create gardens that support the lives of birds, butterflies, and bees. We work with rather than against nature, creating life above and below the soil. We design for both beauty and ecological diversity. Our goal is to foster a connection to the natural world for all our clients.

In our gardens, everything works together. Complex associations form from the way plants are placed together. When we work to create complex associations, the garden becomes healthier and more able to resist pests and diseases. The soil teems with life and supports a healthy soil-food web. This creates more resilient plants that are less dependent on water and can resist diseases and pests.

The five fundamental concepts on which we design our gardens are: Be water wise; use no chemical fertilizers or toxic pesticides; enhance biodiversity to build a complex, thriving web of living beings; provide food, water, and shelter for pollinators; and support the larger cycles and systems of nature. We do this by building fertility in the soil, giving plants what they need to thrive, increasing habitat value and adding food for humans too.

If you follow these principles in designing, building, and caring for your garden, you will greatly reduce or even eliminate pest pressure as a result of biological diversity. The production of fruits and vegetables will also increase. Beauty and harmony in the garden for

humans and wildlife will be felt and will contribute to a greater sense of peace and happiness. You will have a place for pollinators to thrive, a defense against decreasing populations, and nutrient-dense, clean food for your table.
This is how we help you find your home in nature.

Photo: Saxon Holt - PhotoBotanic

BERKELEY URBAN OASIS
NEW 10–12, 12–2, 2–4

Welcome to the Berkeley Urban Oasis, where the cityscape seamlessly merges with a haven of tranquility. This unique garden beckons with its defining features—a charming small seating area atop a dry stacked stone patio, ideal for leisurely tea sessions, and a shaded dining space offering a picturesque view of the seed fountain. The modern stone path winds through the shady urban oasis, intentionally landscaped to attract birds.

As you explore, encounter the central lemon tree surrounded by a vibrant mix of flowering perennials, edibles, and a walkable butterfly meadow, creating a harmonious blend of nature and urban living.

MARCIA'S GARDEN
10 10–4

My small urban garden has, over the past 45 years, become mature—that is to say, way over my head. It is an oasis, and a California world of its and our own.

Unusual subtropical plants still intermingle with sculptures in steel, stone, and ceramic that Mark Bulwinkle, Sara Floor, Ted Fullwood, and I have made. Cevan Forristt helped me create a raccoon-proof koi pond. A collection of bantam chickens has the run of the garden by day and sleeps in the Poultry Pagoda (Chicken Kremlin) by night.

I have added a "beach," a faux eroded landfill of pebbles and shards. The ex-driveway is now the Big Beauty Garden, where strong colors and bold foliage embrace a beatific 10-foot-tall ceramic female figure. The "National Collection of Bambusa ceramica" continues to increase in size and varieties. The garden never holds still.

This garden's estimated size is 3,000 sq. ft.

💬 TROWEL TALK

I am still working on my first and only garden. It will never be done, though I joke that I need to plant with a shoehorn. The back garden can only include plants that bantam chickens won't eat, so I favor plants with the texture of plastic. Bromeliads, camellias, and cycads, for example, are perfect for here.

I live in a gentle, subtropical climate and love to take advantage of that. People comment that it looks like Bali here, but it isn't tropical, I just love big marvelously shaped leaves. I enjoy complementing them with sculpture, interesting containers, stones, and other nonliving things.

—Marcia Donahue

NEW  Year   Nibbled Leaf Garden

OAKLAND
MEADOW'S EDGE
NEW 10-1, 1-4

Welcome to Meadow's Edge, a hidden gem boasting a unique redwood understory habitat.

Descend the stadium-style stairway toward an in-ground fire pit set by a stunning dry-stacked stone retaining wall. Discover a secluded lounge area within the redwood understory, creating a tranquil retreat. The landscaping showcases diverse habitats, including the redwood understory, songbird habitat loaded with native shrubs and trees where birds can find food and shelter, and a butterfly habitat meadow resembling a native California hillside.

This garden fosters a thriving community of birds and beneficial wildlife. In October, vibrant blooms from a variety of California native plants add a touch of color to this enchanting oasis.

OAKLAND CRAMSCAPE
NEW 10-4

Our garden started as a barren plot of concrete and hardpan clay in 2017, and our mission has been to create a feeling of oasis in an urban setting. Gardening is our primary tool for self-expression; our palette includes a diverse array of plants, including bromeliads, palms, and succulents.

Vertical elements are a key feature in our very small garden, creating a feeling of enclosure. We have also tried to create intimate seating areas, places we can relax and admire the diverse array of plant forms in our garden. While floral color is minimal and subdued most of the year, foliage color is always a primary concern when selecting and placing plants in the garden. We have emphasized silver and blue in our garden and have used bold paint colors on our home to help create a backdrop for our beloved plants, including a wall inspired by Yves St. Laurent's Villa Oasis.

This garden's estimated size is ⅛ acre.

💬 TROWEL TALK

I've always been the type of person to pull over if I see a good piece of trash on the side of the road. Imagine my excitement when I saw a cleanly stripped mattress spring poking out of a trash bin! No time was wasted dragging it home, I knew exactly what to do with it. Promptly it was hung from the eaves outside our back door. There it became the perfect nursery for my favorite epiphytes: Tillandsia. Completely filled in, it is hard to tell that it is merely a piece of "trash."

Being a gardener has opened my eyes to what potential everyday objects might hold when positioned correctly in the garden.

—*Planty Magoo*

ZUMBA GARDENS
5 10-4

Welcome to my garden. I grew up in the lush, high mountains of Ecuador. For me it was an enchanted, magical forest; it is the inspiration for this garden.

Step into Zumba Gardens and leave the city behind. This is a garden to immerse yourself in and enjoy. As you explore the garden's labyrinth of paths, you will

---

NEW 5 10 20 95 Year    No Photography    Accessibility    Nibbled Leaf Garden

notice typical and exotic plants mixed in unorthodox combinations. Scattered about is traditional and nontraditional art. There are blooms of color interspersed throughout so that it appears natural, random, and playful.

Many of the plants and colors were selected to provide seed and nectar, attracting wildlife that enhances the sense of magic and wonder. As a result, you'll notice an abundance of birds, moths, butterflies, and frogs in the garden. As the sun sets you may notice raccoons, possums, and a red fox. To protect and promote the wildlife, the garden is an organic environment with no pesticides or fertilizers. The mites, larvae, caterpillars, and other "pests" are a necessary component of the garden's well balanced, natural ecosystem.

I hope you will find a visit to Zumba Gardens a feast for the senses and enchantment for your soul.

This garden's estimated size is 1 acre.

Conrad Family Garden - Pueblo, CO
Photo: the Garden Host

Colorado

78 Colorado

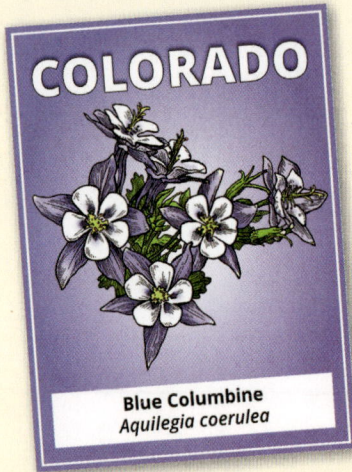
Blue Columbine
Aquilegia coerulea

Open Days dates and times by County, Town, and Garden

DENVER METROPOLITAN AREA
Centennial
Pine Gardens
  Saturday, June 1, 10–4
Denver
Jim and Dorothy's Garden
  Saturday, June 1, 10–4
Panayoti Kelaidis Quince Garden
  Saturday, June 1, 10–4
Prairie Paradise
  Saturday, June 1, 10–4
SummerHome Garden
  Saturday, July 13, 10–4
The Bosler House Gardens
  Saturday, July 13, 10–12, 12–2, 2–4
Virginia Vale Garden
  Saturday, June 1, 10–4
Lakewood
Grummons Desert Garden
  Saturday, July 13, 10–4

PUEBLO
Pueblo
Conrad Family Garden
  Saturday, June 8, 10–4
Midway Xeric Garden
  Saturday, June 8, 10–4
Pollinator Garden
  Saturday, June 8, 10–4

Register online: gardenconservancy.org/opendays — Colorado 79

COLORADO

Denver Metropolitan Area

Saturday, June 1

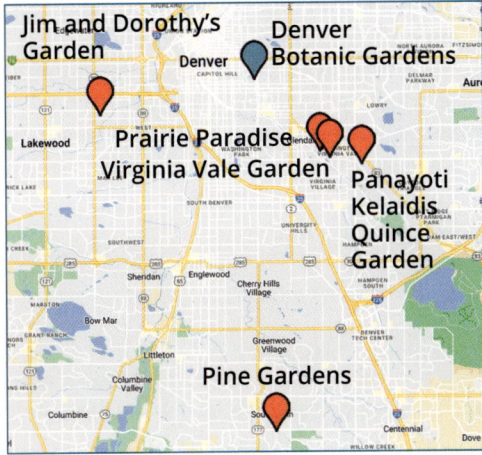

The 2024 Open Days in the Denver Metropolitan area are presented in partnership with Denver Botanic Gardens.

NONPROFIT PARTNER PUBLIC GARDEN

DENVER BOTANIC GARDENS

**1005 York Street
Denver, Colorado 80206**

Denver Botanic Gardens is an urban oasis. Stroll through the world-renowned Rock Alpine Garden or visit the Japanese, Herb, or Water-Smart Gardens, to name a few. The gift shop offers books, gifts, gardening tools, and more. The Helen Fowler Library has an extensive collection of horticultural books and catalogs.

Special events and plant shows are planned throughout the year.

Facebook.com/denverbotanicgardens

Instagram.com/denverbotanic

botanicgardens.org

NEW 5 10 20 '95 Year   No Photography   Accessibility   Nibbled Leaf Garden

CENTENNIAL
PINE GARDENS
partial   10–4

I've spent the last ten years renovating an old, overgrown landscape originally planted in the late 1970s. Most of the lawn has been removed and replanted with variously themed gardens under the large conifers and deciduous shade trees.

Themes include rock/alpine, woodland patio, water feature with disappearing streams, shade gardens, walled cottage garden, raised vegetable beds, tropical back patio, and deck container gardens, and even some espalier fruit trees. The landscape provides four-season interest, and nearly all the seasonal color is provided by perennials, flowering shrubs, vines, and ground covers.

This garden's estimated size is ¼ acre.

💬 TROWEL TALK

You'll notice straight away that I'm a collector of plants with no particular favorites. I tend to focus on perennials, but nothing is really off-limits. If a plant catches my eye, I find a place for it.

—Keith Funk

DENVER
JIM AND DOROTHY'S GARDEN
   10–4

This garden was first planted in 1997 with 10,000 homegrown western native plants. The garden received its only watering during that first summer, at the end of which it suffered a devastating hailstorm that leveled the garden in addition to destroying all neighborhood roofs, cars, and windows.

Though a number of small seedlings managed to survive, replacement continues, now with the aid of a portable drill, tubelings, and no water, even when planting. Visitors from around the world have visited the garden where annuals, perennials, shrubs, and trees exist in harmony with nature.

This garden's estimated size is 5,000 sq. feet

💬 TROWEL TALK

My gardening experience started with a childhood chore of weeding my mother's rock garden in western Pennsylvania when I found an arrowhead. I am still looking for arrowheads.

—The Gardener

NEW 5 10 20 '95 Year   📷 No Photography   ♿ Accessibility   🍃 Nibbled Leaf Garden

PANAYOTI KELAIDIS QUINCE GARDEN
♿ partial   10–4

The garden was begun in 1994, and the current lay of the land would startle the previous owners: almost every square inch has been reworked. The theme is biodiversity: it contains more than 6,000 kinds of plants, from giant trees to tiny alpine cushions, and is home for the widest spectrum one can shoehorn into a half-acre. The garden is never the same from day to day.

This garden on a hill has magnificent views of the Front Range; from Pikes Peak to north of Longs Peak, one can see nearly 200 miles on a clear day! The soil is sand, not sandy loam, and it has been amended by additions of large quantities of humus. The soil of the vegetable garden, the most highly amended, has a pH of 7.9, so acid-loving plants are not too happy here without some serious soil amendment.

The dryland ridges, shrub border, and sub-balcony border (roughly half the total area of the garden) are all designed to be unwatered. Here you will find extensive plantings of steppe plants (East Ridge): tulips, aril iris, acantholimons, and veronicas, while West Ridge is filled with Western American penstemons, buckwheats, cacti, and unusual shrubs.

A small blue gramma prairie boasts a large collection of mariposa lilies, which should be starting to bloom right now. The lawn, vegetable garden, and perennial triangle, most of the rock garden, and the propagation shade frame and growing-on area are all under automatic water. Despite the automatic sprinklers, many spots must be given water by hose in prolonged hot weather. Here you should see lots of peonies, tall bearded iris, and classic perennials in full bloom, as well as early season interest in the large vegetable garden.

The most intensively planted part of the garden, however, is to the east of the house, where one of the largest collections of rock garden plants in America is concentrated around a waterfall and on a series of berms filled with literally thousands of cushions and mat plants with bulbs emerging everywhere in the springtime. The rock is Pikes Peak granite, a rusty orange granite delivered from Colorado Springs where it is used in rip rap. We think this is a more dignified way to use it!

The plantings throughout the garden reflect my love of succulents (such as the hundreds of pots filled with cacti!), African plants, any plant in the mint family, and the rich steppe flora of Central Asia and the American West. This garden is proof positive that a collector can indeed have a garden that is still beautiful.

PRAIRIE PARADISE
NEW ♿ 🌱 10–4

I'm a landscape designer; in my design work, I've always been partial to destination retreats and there are four in the backyard. PV (Puerto Vallarta) is a gazebo-type affair, Paradise has a bistro table and umbrella, Punta de Mita is a small intimate area for two people, and Palmetto (named after a long-gone palm) is the bar and lounge area. There are gardens around all the retreats.

In addition, there is a 30' × 18' redwood-covered patio with a flat-screen TV, recliners, and other amenities one would expect. All the gardens are no to low water except the raised vegetable/flower beds.

We moved in 30 years ago and started the gardens a couple of years later. Initially, the landscape was typical urban blah with overgrown pfitzer junipers, viburnums, and Kentucky bluegrass. Today, I still maintain a huge "throw rug" of turf in the backyard—perhaps 200 square feet, but it offers a nice foil for the gardens to play off.

I am not a maintenance maven; I'd rather enjoy the garden than have it become a millstone. In the last few years, I've strived to change my mindset; instead of thinking of it as a dreaded obligation—then it will be—think of it as an opportunity and it can be, to be a better guardian for my plant communities.

This garden's estimated size is 3,600 sq. ft.

💬 TROWEL TALK

I don't have a favorite plant per se—if it is thriving in my bare-bones environment - I'd have to say I'm partial to it. Although, some of the plants that seem to get the most comments are *Yucca rostrata*, Snow Leopard cactus, and *Sambucus nigra* 'Eva'.

My very first garden was in 1957 when I was in the middle of my tenth year. I was a member of Speedy Seeders, a 4-H group of like-minded youth who enjoyed growing and making themed bouquets for competitions—such as the county fair.

I'm always pushing the zone, or what I call zonal denial, so I've experienced a lot of failures.

Strangely, my favorite tool is probably a very small, yellow-handled screwdriver I use in the greenhouse for so many tasks, such as pricking out seedlings and planting the same.

My inspiration is most likely my next-door neighbor Jake Kelly when I was a kid—he was retired and was always working in the yard. Also Mrs. Scott and her daughter Susan were our 4-H advisors.

—*The Garden Guy*

VIRGINIA VALE GARDEN
NEW ♿ partial 🌱 10–4

Set on a typical suburban lot, this garden is a collection of native, xeric, rock garden perennials, and unusual trees and shrubs. The front yard is largely xeric. The back is a mix of rock gardens, alpines, troughs, natives, various trees, and shrubs chosen for yearlong interest. There is a small propagation area as well.

NEW 5 10 20 '95 Year  No Photography ♿ Accessibility  Nibbled Leaf Garden

Pueblo County
Saturday, June 8

The 2024 Open Days in Pueblo are presented in partnership with Keep Pueblo Beautiful.

NONPROFIT PARTNER
KEEP PUEBLO BEAUTIFUL

Keep Pueblo Beautiful was established in 1969. Its mission is to the preserve the natural beauty of Pueblo. The Board holds monthly meetings and is active in supporting the Hanging Baskets Program, "Wednesday Weeders" volunteer group, Western Landscape Symposium, Fountain Creek Week Clean Up. It holds conservation easements and recognizes people and places that keep Pueblo beautiful. We are grateful for the Pueblo County CSU Extension Service partnership assisting in the Open Days Tours.

facebook.com/Keep-Pueblo-Beautiful

PUEBLO
CONRAD FAMILY GARDEN
NEW 10-4

The garden is situated on 2 acres upon the bluffs of the Arkansas River, overlooking the riparian zone and Pikes Peak. Two continuous springs form a natural wetland which serves as the centerpiece.

Surrounding areas of xeriscape, English garden, and natural prairie make up the rest. Stone pathways with wooden bridges allow access to nearly the entire garden area. Both native and non-native flora provide habitat for a diversity of mostly native fauna.

We enjoy living within and observing a diverse ecosystem. Some of my favorite plants are south African succulents, alpine cushion plants, and carnivorous plants, none of which do exceptionally well. My main tasks are controlling overgrowth and removing those unwanted pesky plants before they go to seed.

This garden's estimated size is 2 acres.

💬 TROWEL TALK

I have always been intrigued with biology and the ways in which plants and animals interact to make up an ecosystem. In my childhood I constructed terrariums, had a freshwater aquarium, and was always

NEW  Year   Nibbled Leaf Garden

adding crayfish, frogs, and minnows to a family fishpond. Then I was on to marine reef aquariums. Size and scale have always increased, and I jumped at the chance to purchase this property.

Now I reside in a complex and diverse ecosystem. I may have been successful in the re-introduction of Northern Leopard Frogs, which seem to be self-sustaining.

—Andrew C.

MIDWAY XERIC GARDEN
NEW 10–4

Nestled in an area known as The Blocks, this urban garden has matured for nearly twenty years. The garden comprises mainly cold-hardy agaves and cacti amid a concrete and natural stone setting. A unique greenhouse provides shelter for plants from warmer zones.

This garden's estimated size is 6,000 sq. ft.

💬 TROWEL TALK

With their understated color, symmetry, and imposing nature, agaves are by far my favorite plants. There are about six varieties present, 'Havardiana' being the most prominent. Maintenance and editing can be quite the challenge. We've had three blossom over the last five years; it's a bittersweet event, seeing the stock grow up to 6 inches per day into a beautiful burst of flowers, only to know the plant will die.

—Bobby Valentine

POLLINATOR GARDEN
NEW 10–4

People are always surprised that we grow primarily flowers and shrubs, and there is not a tomato or zucchini plant to be found in our garden. Our response is that we grow food for insects. This is not a higher calling than growing food for us humans. Just a different calling, but a calling nonetheless.

Our fifteen-year-old garden is watered every two weeks or so throughout summer, and in an effort to push out weeds, is overly crowded with both native and non-native xeric/dryland plants. We have not modified the native soil (shale and clay) in any way. If a plant cannot survive in heat, clay, and on just-enough water—well, it doesn't survive

This garden's estimated size is 3,000 sq. ft.

💬 TROWEL TALK

At 73, I wonder and worry, how much longer can I caretake this garden. It is hard physical work. I find myself saying if I was 37, I would do this or I would do that, or in my next life I will tear out the lawn and redo the backyard.

One of the most satisfying parts of gardening is the anticipation of the future. But, when you are old that future may not be next spring, it may be your next life.

—Warren N.

Register online: gardenconservancy.org/opendays   Colorado 85

Denver Metropolitan Area

Saturday, July 13

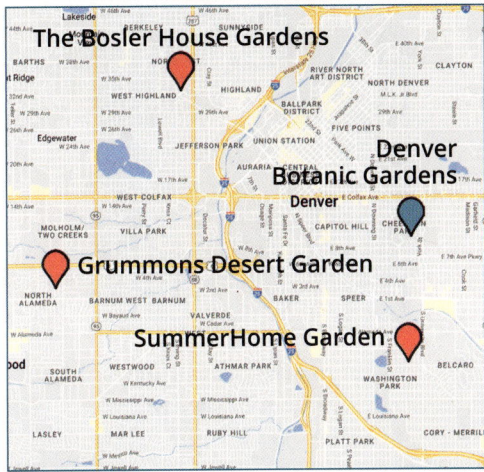

The 2024 Open Days in the Denver Metropolitan area are presented in partnership with Denver Botanic Gardens.

NONPROFIT PARTNER PUBLIC GARDEN

DENVER BOTANIC GARDENS

1005 York Street
Denver, Colorado 80206

Denver Botanic Gardens is an urban oasis. Stroll through the world-renowned Rock Alpine Garden or visit the Japanese, Herb, or Water-Smart Gardens, to name a few. The gift shop offers books, gifts, gardening tools, and more. The Helen Fowler Library has an extensive collection of horticultural books and catalogs.

Special events and plant shows are planned throughout the year.

Facebook.com/denverbotanicgardens

Instagram.com/denverbotanic

botanicgardens.org

SUMMERHOME GARDEN
10–4

SummerHome, an inner-city xeric pocket garden, is built on a residential lot that previously had an uninhabitable house. The intentions of the garden are to instruct and advise gardeners on the use of xeric/endemic plantings, create a community garden and gathering place for all to enjoy, and deter the overdevelopment occurring in the neighborhood.

Plantings center around commercially available species of low-water plants with a rolling bloom from February to October. Pathways, fountains, and art greet visitors as they stroll through the garden. In the back corner, a large crevice garden made of Colorado buff sandstone slabs highlights cold-hardy cactus and succulents from around the

NEW   5 10 20 '95 Year    No Photography    Accessibility    Nibbled Leaf Garden

world. Trees and shrubs, including 'Sucker Punch' chokecherry, red buds, sumacs, chokeberry, and atriplex, present the canvas for the lesser sized agastache, salvias, goldenrod, rabbit brush, Apache plume, and many others.

Thousands of bulbs begin the season in February, including alliums, tulips, fritillaria, anemones, and foxtails. Habitat for pollinators is provided with open areas and solitary bee hotels.

This garden's estimated size is about ⅛ acre.

💬 TROWEL TALK

My fave plants are those that struggle to survive in harsh conditions and then give all their energy to blooming just for me. In my garden, it's all the cactus and succulents.

I began gardening with my Italian grandmother in her rose garden at the age of 7. I can still smell all those roses. But I am not a good rose gardener, just an admirer.

Gardening gives you the full life cycle of a plant in just one year. It's amazing to see what one seed or bulb or cutting can become.

—*Lisa Negri*

DIGGING DEEPER

SummerHome's Path to a Wilder Denver
Lisa Negri and Kevin Williams
Saturday, July 13, 4–6

SummerHome Garden
Denver, CO
$30 Members | $40 General

The creation of SummerHome Garden transformed a dilapidated residential lot in the heart of Denver into an immersive, naturalistic garden championing the use of drought-dynamic, locally suited flora and offering an inspirational community space for all to enjoy.

At the heart of the garden is the spirit of accessibility and defiance. In addition to its aesthetic appeal, SummerHome serves as a vital sanctuary in the midst of the urban jungle and stands as a symbol against the excessive development that looms in the surrounding neighborhood.

Join the founder of SummerHome Garden, Lisa Negri, and garden designer Kevin Philip Williams, of

Denver Botanic Gardens, to discuss the concepts, plants, planting strategies and legal battles that went into creating this cherished and challenging public pocket park.

The presentation and tour will be followed by an opportunity for conversational Q and A with Lisa and Kevin both in SummerHome and in Lisa's private residential garden.

Copies of Kevin's book, *Shrouded in Light: Naturalistic Planting Inspired by Wild Shrublands* (Filbert Press, 2024), will be available for purchase.

THE BOSLER HOUSE GARDENS
NEW   10–12, 12–2, 2–4

The Bosler House in Denver, Colorado was built in 1875 and has been lovingly restored by Jan and Steve Davis, who purchased the house in 2016. It is on the National Register of Historic Places and is a Denver Landmark property.

Privacy and structure have been created in this city garden with hedges behind which is a large flower garden overflowing with traditional garden perennials, Colorado native flowers, and annuals. Outside the kitchen lies a potager garden and a patio for outdoor dining surrounded by potted annuals.

A small orchard of dwarf fruit trees and raised boxes with raspberries and blackberries can be found on the west side of the property. Pollinators are found in abundance in the gardens.

💬 TROWEL TALK

Steve and Jan have been gardening together throughout their 40+ years of marriage. He especially enjoys growing vegetables, and Jan loves her flower garden.

His garden is a collection of vegetable cultivars that has been refined over the years, featuring the most productive and delicious vegetables. The freezer is stocked for the winter with delicious soups preserving the summer bounty.

Jan's garden started with a foundation of perennials, and every winter she searches catalogs and websites for interesting new annuals to keep the garden full of flowers throughout the season.

—*Jan and Steve Davis*

NEW 5 10 20 95 Year   No Photography   Accessibility   Nibbled Leaf Garden

LAKEWOOD
GRUMMONS DESERT GARDEN
partial   10–4

Kelly's garden is a career-long effort to demonstrate the possibilities of the beauty and favorable aesthetic of the low-water garden to other gardeners. His garden features numerous mature specimens of yucca, agave, perennials, grasses, and numerous cactus species.

A great number of the garden's plants are varieties that Kelly developed, tested, and introduced in the Plant Select program over the last twenty-plus years. The extensive gardens are complemented with vegetable and fruit varieties and five greenhouses full of cacti.

The lawn areas feature the super low-water turf grass 'Dog Tuff' that was introduced by Kelly through the Plant Select program.

This garden's estimated size is ¾ acre.

💬 TROWEL TALK

I grew up on a ranch in the Black Hills on the Wyoming/South Dakota border. Occasionally, prickly pear cactus would overrun the pastures, and we would have to eradicate them. When I was six years old, I felt sorry for the baby cacti in the pastures, so I would dig them up and plant them in tin cans. Eventually, my folks helped me to build a small rock garden that looked like a wedding cake: three tiers made with quartz rock from Grandma's collection filled with our local shale for media. In this garden, I planted my baby cacti and then added some local wild strawberries. I thought that this was a great combination!

—*Kelly Grummons*

Adams Family Garden, Los Angeles, CA
Photo: Matt Harbicht

Become a Garden Host or a Regional Ambassador

See page 374 or contact us at **opendays@gardenconservancy.org** to learn more.

Greens Farms Botanical Gardens - Westport, CT
Photo: David S.

Connecticut

92 Connecticut

Mountain Laurel
Kalmia latifolia

Open Days dates and times by County, Town, and Garden

FAIRFIELD

Fairfield
Garden of Kathryn Herman
Saturday, June 22, 10–4
Inwood Cottage Garden
Saturday, June 8, 10–4

Greenwich
Chelmsford
Saturday, June 8, 10–4
Garden of Allison Bourke
Saturday, June 8, 10–4
Sleepy Cat Farm
Saturday, June 22, 10–12, 12–2, 2–4
Saturday, October 5, 10–12, 12–2, 2–4

New Canaan
Ann and Haig's Garden
Saturday, June 8, 10–4
New Canaan Meadow
Saturday, August 24, 10–4

Redding
InSitu
Saturday, August 24, 10–4

Sherman
Cooke-Gribble Garden
Saturday, July 27, 10–4

Southport
The Gould Garden
Saturday, June 8, 10–12, 12–2, 2–4
Saturday, October 5, 10–12, 12–2, 2–4

Weston
Frances Palmer's Garden
Saturday, September 14, 10–4
Wells Hill Farm
Saturday, September 14, 10–4

Westport
Greens Farms Botanical Gardens
Saturday, June 8, 10–4
Prospect Gardens Westport
Saturday, June 8, 10–4
Saturday, September 14, 10–4
Rosebrook Gardens
Saturday, June 8, 10–4

HARTFORD

Burlington
Garden of Robin Lensi
Sunday, July 21, 10–4
The Salsedo Family Garden
Sunday, July 21, 10–4

Canton
Sudden Delight
Sunday, July 21, 10–4
The Marsted's Garden of Whimsy
Sunday, July 21, 10–4

Farmington
Oldgate
Saturday, June 15, 10–4

Glastonbury
The Murray Gardens
Saturday, June 15, 10–4
Sunday, July 21, 10–4
The Stubenrauch Gardens
Saturday, June 15, 10–4

LITCHFIELD

Cornwall Bridge
Garden of Debby and Bart Jones
Sunday, June 23, 10-4

Falls Village
Church House - The Garden of Page Dickey and Bosco Schell
Sunday, June 2, 10-4
Garden of Bunny Williams
Sunday, June 23, 10-1, 1-4

Kent
Sculpturedale
Saturday, July 27, 10-4

Lakeville
Juniper Ledge
Saturday, July 27, 10-4

Norfolk
Fernwood
Saturday, June 27, 10-4

Roxbury
Japanese Gardens at Cedar Hill
Sunday, June 2, 10-4
Lagniappe Garden
Saturday, July 27, 10-4

Salisbury
The Shillingford Garden
Sunday, June 23, 10-1, 1-4

Sharon
Garden of Lee Link
Sunday, June 23, 10-4

Washington
Brush Hill
Sunday, June 23, 10-4
Isabel and Winston Fowlkes
Sunday, June 2, 10-2
The Sumacs
Sunday, June 23, 10-4

West Cornwall
Garden of Jane Garmey
Sunday, June 23, 10-4
Michael's West Cornwall Garden
Sunday, June 23, 10-4
Roxana Robinson - Treetop
Sunday, June 2, 10-4

NEW HAVEN

Cheshire
Goin' to the Dogs
Saturday, July 20, 10-12, 12-2, 2-4

Hamden
Woodland Ridge
Saturday, July 20, 10-4

Oxford
Garden of Susan and Richard Kaminski
Saturday, July 20, 10-4

NEW LONDON

Stonington
Kentford Farm
Saturday, May 25, 10-4
Saturday, October 12, 10-4

WINDHAM

Ashford
My Gardens of Serenity
Saturday, July 13, 10-4
Tranquil Refuge
Sunday, July 13, 10-4

CONNECTICUT

New London County
Saturday, May 25

hillside, and stone walls surround the whole property. For more information, visit kentfordfarm.com

This garden's estimated size is 6 acres.

STONINGTON
KENTFORD FARM

  10–4

This garden is open twice this year: May 25 and October 12.

Kentford Farm is a perennial farm in the making. For 25 years, Paul Coutu and William Turner have been creating grass pathways and planting beds. The farm dates back to 1727, and the previous owner started planting in 1945.

Fifty-foot weeping cherries, a Norway spruce, copper beech, and blue Atlas cedar, to name a few, dot this 6-acre garden. There is a walk-in root cellar built into the

Litchfield County
Sunday, June 2

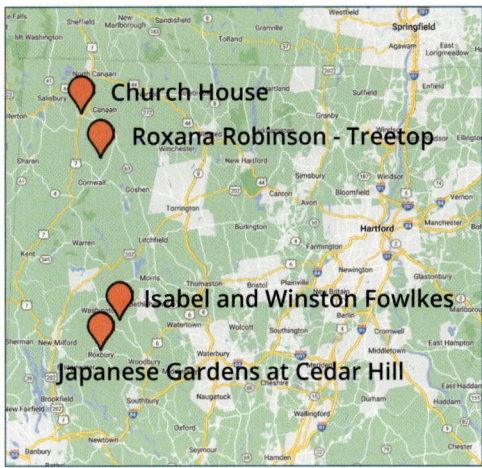

Additional gardens are open nearby :
Dutchess County, NY
  Broccoli Hall—Maxine Paetro, Armenia, NY
  Clove Brook Farm—Christopher Spitzmiller and Anthony Bellomo, Millbrook, NY
  Squirrell Hall, Millbrook, NY
See page 251.

FALLS VILLAGE
CHURCH HOUSE–THE GARDEN OF PAGE DICKEY AND BOSCO SCHELL
   10–4

The garden here is smaller and simpler than the one we had at Duck Hill, but with a few echoes: a patterned cutting garden, a small greenhouse, a young orchard. Mixed borders of flowers run along the front of the house beneath three shadblows. A summer garden of hydrangeas, burnets, and roses surrounds our saltwater pool. Mowed paths strike off through meadows that surround the house, leading to trails in our woods, on the west side high and rocky with limestone outcroppings, on the east side, low, damp, and fern-filled. Best of all, perhaps, is the view beyond the garden, fields, and forest of the Berkshire hills.

This garden's estimated size is 17 acres.

ROXBURY
JAPANESE GARDENS AT CEDAR HILL
 10–4

This Japanese garden is intended to evoke a sense of serenity, as different rooms invite the visitor to pause and reflect. Stones and ledges throughout reside harmoniously with specimen trees and plantings that marry color, texture, and shape.

The water features induce a visual and auditory tranquility, encouraging meditation. From the teahouse, one has a commanding view of much of the garden with its borrowed Litchfield Hills landscape. Proceed through a stone garden to a series of geometrically patterned orchards and connecting footpaths.

This garden's estimated size is 2½ acres.

💬 TROWEL TALK

My garden is the culmination of a lifelong study of Asian culture and philosophy. While representing many elements of the Japanese ethos, it is more accurately a fusion of harmonious concepts of East and West.

NEW  Year No Photography  Accessibility

The careful selection and placement of stones provided the greatest challenge as they formed the underlying structure of the garden. Once they were in place, plants, shrubs, and specimen trees were added to enhance the beauty of the stones.

—Bob Levine

WASHINGTON
ISABEL AND WINSTON FOWLKES
  10-2

This is a mature garden set under large arching red oaks underplanted with spectacular rhododendrons put in nearly 50 years ago. The balance of the garden consists of two perennial borders framed by dramatically clipped boxwood. There are also two richly planted terraces.

WEST CORNWALL
ROXANA ROBINSON - TREETOP
  10-4

Treetop is the garden of the novelist and biographer Roxana Robinson, set on the grounds of a rustic Arts & Crafts house built in 1928 by her grandparents.

It's an idiosyncratic hillside garden incorporating granite ledge, steep ravines, placid greensward, and a wooded slope down to a lake. The gardens are separated into two areas. Closest to the house is the level terrain of "Sissinghurst," with its decorous palette of blues, pinks, silvers, and purples, stone path, and birdbath.

"Margaritaville" is a wild and rocky ravine with a riot of giant ferns, orange tithonia, scarlet crocosmia, red salvias, and orange asclepias. The garden contains a homemade frog pond and a house for the wren.

Around the gardens are deep woods. Here nature plays a larger part than nurture, and natives outnumber the nons. The owner's grandfather was a nature writer, her parents were bird-watchers, and the owner writes about the natural world in her novels and essays.

The gardens are an attempt to make peace between the wild and the domestic, a response to the powerful surrounding landscape of forest and boulder that also reflects the owner's love of roses and clematis.

This garden's estimated size is 15 acres.

💬 **TROWEL TALK**

At the moment, my favorite plants are ferns, which are vigorous, hardy, bug-resistant and look beautiful all season. My first garden was on the grounds of an old farmhouse in Katonah, NY. It was a lovely setting, big sloping lawns, old trees, stone walls and meadows. This one is impossible: steep wooded hillsides, open rock ledge, and broken planes. I love it.

—Roxana Robinson

Register online: gardenconservancy.org/opendays Connecticut 97

Fairfield County
Saturday, June 8

FAIRFIELD

INWOOD COTTAGE GARDEN

partial   10–4

The property is 1¼ acres and offers various soil and light conditions, including sun, dry shade, wetlands, and full shade. Old-growth trees define the garden's perimeter.

We use native plant material, including perennials, evergreens, and deciduous plants, to add seasonal variety and texture. We focus on winter-hardy plant material and use boxwood, yews, azaleas, and rhododendrons for the foundation and perimeter plantings. We have added dogwood, Eastern red cedar, and river birch for the tree midstory.

We have an allée of beauty bush and enjoy the aroma of the harlequin glorybower. We have a significant bulb collection, starting early with snowdrops, crocus, daffodils, and some wetland-loving bulbs. We have a pergola with a wisteria and enjoy climbing hydrangeas on tree trunks and our three-story stone chimney. We refer to that as our "bird hotel."

We love native understory plantings, including fern and mayapple, and have used liriope in mass plantings. Summertime is lush with daylily and hydrangea, and we have a full pollinator garden including Joe Pye weed, butterfly weed, mallow, and sedum.

The season comes to a close with Montauk daisy and aster. We have a natural pond where fish, frogs, and turtles are at home.

This garden's estimated size is 1¼ acres.

NEW 5 10 20 95 Year    No Photography    Accessibility    Nibbled Leaf Garden

GREENWICH

CHELMSFORD
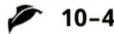 10–4

This 10-acre property was designed variously by Warren Manning and Bryant Fleming (both formerly of the offices of Fredrick Law Olmstead) and Charles Gillette.

The gardens were created in the early 1900s for Blanche Ferry Hooker, daughter of the founder of the Ferry Seed Company, and a competent plantswoman in her own right. The property comprises a swale, ½ mile of shaded walking trails, perennial beds, a root cellar, a knot garden, a 100-foot-long folly of rose-clad stone arches, a dogwood grove, and a riverbank fern garden.

This garden's estimated size is 10 acres.

💬 TROWEL TALK

The perennial beds that were part of the 1943 plan by Charles Gillette were 6 feet deep! We narrowed the width by installing sod (sounds like sacrilege, I know), but the effect is still lovely, and much more manageable.

You don't need to eat the whole box of chocolates, a few will do just fine – a perennial bed does not need many hundreds of plants – a few hundred will do!

—*The Gardener*

GARDEN OF ALLISON BOURKE
  10–4

The owner of this 3½-acre property is a hands-on gardener who designed the garden herself, often using her backhoe in the rocky Connecticut soil to make her ideas a reality.

There is an 80-foot-long mixed border as well as beds of choice and unusual shade-loving varieties, a vegetable/cut flower garden, more than 250 peonies, a greenhouse, a lovingly tended beehive, and more than 30 raised beds used for propagation and experimentation.

Currently underway, we are trialing alliums and camassias.

This garden's estimated size is 3½ acres.

NEW CANAAN

ANN AND HAIG'S GARDEN
NEW 10–4

The heart of our 4-acre garden is our collection of more than 80 varieties of ferns. There are native ferns, ferns from around the world, and ferns that date back to the dinosaurs.

Our property also includes dozens of dogwoods, viburnums, and rhododendron; many Japanese maples; various other specimen trees and shrubs; a wide assortment of hydrangeas; and several stately oaks. The woodland gardens have a variety of ground covers, some carpeting large areas, providing a dramatic contrast to the towering trees. The pool garden has summer blooming plants with of course a few ferns.

A favorite feature of the garden is the 700-

yard woodchip path that meanders around the property. Over the 33 years that we have lived here, several of the ferns have spread into large swaths, including one field of ostrich ferns we affectionately call Jurassic Park.

Our house was built in 1940, part of the modern architecture movement that was popular in New Canaan at the time. It was designed, built, and lived-in by the grandson of H. H. Richardson, one of the leading American architects of the late nineteenth century. The house was built during the Depression by unemployed boat builders from Maine and has nautical features inside and out.

This garden's estimated size is 4 acres.

💬 TROWEL TALK

My favorite gardening tool is a homemade crowbar which I occasionally borrow from a friend. It's about 8 feet long, weighs around 25 pounds, and looks like a harpoon. I use it to move particularly obstinate rocks. It is nicknamed The Persuader.

—Haig

SOUTHPORT
THE GOULD GARDEN
NEW 10–12, 12–2, 2–4

This garden is open twice this year: June 8 and October 5.

I started to think about a garden in 2002, but it took several years to figure out what I wanted to achieve. Since my red brick house was built as a boys' club, it has an assertive presence on a street facing a river, a golf course, and Long Island Sound.

I decided that pastel colors wouldn't be swallowed by the house scheme of orange, purple, chartreuse, and deep red, for the south-facing garden which sits well above the street. This colorful garden has become a destination for monarchs and hummingbirds.

Southport is a unique waterside destination and a great walking town. A brick wall faces the street, and to honor my grandmother, we planted a mix of peach, orange, and dark pink climbing roses and many varieties of clematis on the street level. This location is a perfect microclimate. The May–June bloom has become a "go see" legend in Southport when it is in its full blooming glory.

The backyard is the shade garden, featuring an *Ulmus americana*. This elm is well over 90 years old and has been listed with The Notable Trees Project sponsored by the Connecticut Botanical Society, The Connecticut College Arboretum, and the Connecticut Urban Forest Council.

This garden's estimated size is ½ acre.

💬 TROWEL TALK

My favorite plants are tithonia which

attracts Monarchs, ricinus 'Red Spires' as it looms over the fall garden, and *Trycirtis hirta* that is so delicate and whimsical. *Rosa* 'Climbing Polka' is my favorite rose.

I had my first garden at the age of five. It was a school plot. We grew carrots—I was so proud of my bounty. My grandparents loved to garden, and my grandmother's roses were the best in her neighborhood.

I met Tom when my beloved late husband decided we needed a garden at our new weekend house in Greenwich. My husband and Tom got along so well that when we decided to move to Southport, the one to call was Tom—23 years ago.

My gardens evolved over time to become the colorful fall garden it is today. It has been documented and was accepted into the Smithsonian Archive of American Gardens.

—The Gardener

WESTPORT
GREENS FARMS BOTANICAL GARDENS
 10–4

This nearly 3-acre garden is a combination of three formal perennial rooms that are behind a stone wall and surrounded entirely by 30-foot 'Green Giant' arborvitae. Each room has a unique personality and flows easily to the next, ending in a sculpted hornbeam allée.

There are white perennial gardens throughout the pool area. The highly fragrant roses bloom all summer. A newly added Zen garden features miniature perennial trees and unique plantings.

There are numerous key viewing locations throughout the property. One of the key features of the garden is an apple and pear espalier orchard behind the pool house. The property is tiered and has beautiful perennial flowers and trees on all levels, with more than 70 multicolored and varietal peonies and more than 100 hydrangeas in varying colors and provenance.

This garden's estimated size is 3 acres.

💬 TROWEL TALK

We've always loved gardens, and gardening, and nature in general. What started as a somewhat "small project" became the Beautiful Monster we have today.

It evolved and grew (literally) in directions we never imagined. Every year, we say "This is It; we've maxed out, our hands are full," yet every year there seems to be a new little (or not so little) area. For instance, this year was the Stump Garden, an old 1800s English use for felled trees or stumps, in which they are used as a garden bed, or pot.

We keep bees on the property, which seem to love their home. We believe they, like us, never want to stray too far from home. We are very fortunate to have smart, kind, strong, and creative help, as it seems every year, those pots, plants, and bags seem to get just a little bit heavier.

One of our Dreams/Goals is to plan a Euro Vacation, revolving around the Great Gardens of Italy, France, or the UK!

An old expression we always keep in our hearts is "the earth is very old, yet every spring it's young again"...peace.

—Arlene and David

PROSPECT GARDENS WESTPORT
♿ partial 🍃 10–4

This garden is open twice this year: June 8 and September 14.

Prospect Gardens Westport dates back to the 1812 original Victorian farmhouse and surrounding acres of the Wakeman onion farm.

Through a series of abutting property acquisitions over the last twenty-plus years, the property is now a contiguous arboretum-style garden of almost 9 acres featuring planting collections, gardens, open lawns, and winding pathways leading from one area to the next, allowing the visitor a three-dimensional experience of being "in" the gardens.

Mature deciduous and evergreen trees create a sweeping canvas and provide a sense of scale, shape, and texture reflective of the owners' contemporary style and sense of design.

Some of the property's key features include a Mediterranean graveled entry garden, two orchards, a three stone–tiered vegetable garden, berry houses (blueberry, raspberry), beehives, a sunny perennial garden, a shady perennial woodland walk, a conifer collection, numerous flowering shrub and grass borders, a Japanese-inspired meditation garden and maple collection, red-clay tennis court, two pools, containers featuring citrus and cacti, a glasshouse, an internationally renowned sculpture, and a 1-acre perennial/native wildflower meadow. Most recently added is a four-tiered amphitheater with a stone-medallioned stage.

This garden's estimated size is 8 acres.

DIGGING DEEPER

Erasing the Lines Leads to Good Design
Cindy Shumate
Saturday, June 8, Hours TBD

Prospect Gardens Westport
Westport, CT
$30 Members | $40 General

A well-designed garden of any size has a flow to it, pathways to invite people into it, features that integrate and complement, all while being horticulturally appropriate for the collection of plants.

In this session, we will target some of the major projects on the property where we have created a new feature or collection, or moved mature plant pieces into new places, or started a new area with a vision of what it will be in several years. Our focus areas will include the new grassy amphitheater, a 1-acre perennial meadow, privacy hedging without straight lines, and more.

We will also examine the critical function of pathways, how to make a property into an integrated garden, and how to ensure both functionality and beauty at the same time.

Photo: Cindy Shumate (Cynscape Design)

NEW   Year 🚫 No Photography ♿ Accessibility 🍃 Nibbled Leaf Garden

ROSEBROOK GARDENS

 10–4

Rosebrook Gardens continues to become a coveted garden tour as the energy and soul of this house and property are palpable from the first moment you arrive. Every step closer to the gardens brings visual wonderment in every direction.

You don't want to miss any details of this oasis with glorious design details, a charming Garden Studio, a stunning wisteria-covered pergola, and a classic English Folly. Discover two parterre gardens all surrounded by a profusion of flowers anchored by lush green boxwoods.

This garden tour is packed with layers of ideas and stunning vignettes all designed and curated by a passionate gardener.

This garden's estimated size is ⅛ acre.

💬 TROWEL TALK

What are your favorite plants?
Roses and peonies of course!
Tell us about your first garden.
Playing in the dirt in my grandmother's garden.
What is a plant that you have never had success with?
Boston ivy.
What is your favorite garden tool and why?
My hands. This keeps me close to nature.
Tell us about who inspired you to garden.
As a child I always found comfort in the garden and learned an appreciation for tending to plants and flowers. Life is like a four-season garden as you have many opportunities to learn and fine-tune your skills.

—Mar Jennings

Hartford County
Saturday, June 15

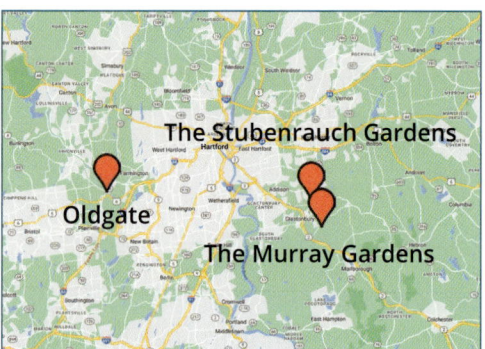

FARMINGTON
OLDGATE
NEW partial 10–4

The historic garden at Oldgate was created as a pleasure garden in the early 1900s by Anna Roosevelt Cowles, President Theodore Roosevelt's sister.

Anna's great-grandson and his wife currently maintain the acre and a half ornamental garden, which has been called a "green garden" emphasizing plant texture, shape, and character. It includes large swaths of traditional pachysandra and yew shrubs as well as newer perennial beds and the introduction of more native plantings.

As an old garden, some of the trees on the property are Connecticut notable trees, giving the garden strong bone structure. Spring is a beautiful time in New England and to visit our garden–please come and enjoy it.

This garden's estimated size is 1½ acres.

NEW 5 10 20 95 Year  No Photography  Accessibility  Nibbled Leaf Garden

GLASTONBURY
THE MURRAY GARDENS
 10–4

This property is a two-acre collection of gardens carved out of a woodland setting punctuated by unusual and native trees.

The front yard features three long blooming perennial borders, a hydrangea bed, and a small pond with a weeping maple water sculpture that gently rains all day. Also in front is a bank of Carpet Flower roses, as well as a naturalized woodland garden, where you can enjoy a myriad of shade and woodland plants and sculpture surprises with soft music in the background.

The backyard has several gardens built into the pool deck and a formal triangle garden containing Knock Out roses, Oriental lilies, and coleus inside a boxwood border. Daylily beds run along an old stone wall beside a large perennial garden and patio. Curved steps ascend from there to a 50-foot rose bed.

Finally, the sunken garden features a waterfall running from a little upper pond to the fishpond below, surrounded by a spectacular Heptacodium tree, several large Japanese maples, and a collection of miniature conifers. Watching over the pond is a six-foot frog sitting on a stone bench.

This garden's estimated size is 2 acres.

THE STUBENRAUCH GARDENS
♿ partial   10–4

The Stubenrauch gardens flow naturally around the property under the high shade of mature oaks and white pines, with highlights of Glastonbury ledge.

Areas range from bright light to deep shade, with the understory of small trees, shrubs, and perennials adding both vertical and horizontal dimensions. Evergreen and exfoliating deciduous plantings add year-round interest. The broad selection of plants also extends to bulbs, vines, ferns, ground covers, and container plantings, all of which provide both foliage and color all season long, attracting birds, bees, butterflies, and some less desirable mammals.

While much of the garden is well established, having grown for more than twenty years, it is constantly expanded and renewed. The paver-block driveway and patio were added to better blend the hardscape with nature.

Native and exotic plants look equally at home in the landscape, and small and large treasures have found a home in this plant-lovers garden, which delights at every turn of the winding pea stone and grass pathways.

Fairfield County
Saturday, June 22

FAIRFIELD
GARDEN OF KATHRYN HERMAN
♿ partial   🖊 10–4

Part of the original Pepperidge Farm estate, the gardens, created by landscape designer Kathryn Herman, surround the charming 1920s groom's cottage and chauffeur's quarters.

There are a custom Alitex greenhouse with adjacent garden, an extensive vegetable garden and orchard, meadows, beehives that produce honey, a water-feature garden, and a swimming-pool garden with the original gamecock house.

A 114-foot double herbaceous perennial garden, original yew "muffins" dating back to the 1920s, sculptural evergreen plantings, and many mature deciduous trees complete the picture, all on six acres.

This garden won the 2016 Stanford White Award and the 2019 Palladio Award, and the house won the 2008 Palladio Award.

The gardens have been featured in *Architectural Digest* and *Gardens Illustrated*.

This garden's estimated size is 4 acres.

💬 **TROWEL TALK**

One of my favorite plants in my perennial garden is *Datisca cannabina*. It is by far the tallest plant in the garden, topping out close to 10 feet. It has a wonderful presence with its size and is well behaved.

—Kathryn Herman

GREENWICH
SLEEPY CAT FARM
 10–12, 12–2, 2–4

This garden is open twice this year: June 22 and October 5.

The 13 acres of Sleepy Cat Farm have evolved over the last 25 years in close collaboration between the present owner and Virginia-based landscape architect Charles J. Stick.

The landscape bordering Lake Avenue includes an extensive greenhouse and potager. "The Barn," distinguished by its half-timbered French Normandy vocabulary, is surrounded by thyme-covered terraces, providing an elegant stage set for a fine collection of garden ornament, sculpture, and boxwood topiary.

The visitor's experience of the garden unfolds as pathways lead from garden room to garden room in a carefully orchestrated series of discoveries. The central portion of the garden is distinguished by two parallel garden spaces; the first is dominated by a long reflecting pool, terminated on the north end by a wisteria-covered arbor, and on

---

NEW    Year   🚫 No Photography   ♿ Accessibility   🖊 Nibbled Leaf Garden

the south end by a pebble mosaic terrace and fountain basin. One of the great surprises of the tour is the adjacent garden space. Bordered by a precisely clipped hornbeam hedge, the green architecture of this room is meant to frame the view to the Chinese pavilion (or "ting"—a place to stop and take in the view) positioned on a small island in the middle of a pond teeming with koi.

The north end of this garden is terminated by an impressively scaled statue of Atlas. The heart of the original 6 acres is most joyfully experienced along the "Golden Path," a granite dust pathway that leads from the main house and formal terraces on top of the hill, out into the New England landscape. As it winds through the oak and beech woodland, one encounters fountains, statuary, an iris garden traversed by a Japanese spirit bridge and planted with 10,000 Japanese iris, and finally a rustic stone grotto.

The woodland stream is bordered by native azaleas and a collection of spring flowering trees and bulbs, all planted for enjoyment throughout the year. The most recent additions to the property include a limonaia used for the winter storage of citrus trees, a new fruit orchard, and a sacred woodland grove that is enjoyed from a series of pathways radiating from a newly planted meadow. The southern expansion of the property over the past three years has added a new dimension to the overall landscape experience of Sleepy Cat Farm.

Another recent addition to the garden is an English-style perennial border directly across from the koi pond and, directly below, a viewing path framed by a wisteria arbor. This border is surrounded by decorative stone walls covered with hydrangea, climbing roses, clematis, and boxwood. It consists of four linear beds around a central axis of lawn pathway and features a mixed shrub and perennial border containing a succession of blooms through the seasons.

During the 2020 visitor hiatus, we updated several garden areas. The iris garden was completed, with many more Japanese iris cultivars added, as well as a winding bamboo railway path leading to it, featuring a fragrant Korean spice viburnum border interspersed with spring bulbs and fall-blooming kirengeshoma.

The garden is now bordered by a ring of bright red *Cornus* 'Arctic Fire' against a backdrop of *Ilex glabra* topiaries. In addition, seven new pieces of art have been installed in various spots along the paths.

This garden's estimated size is 13½ acres.

Litchfield County

Sunday, June 23

Additional gardens are open nearby:
Dutchess County, NY
   Dappled Berms–The Garden of Scott VanderHamm, Poughkeepsie, NY
   Garden of Helen Bodian, Millerton, NY
   Shekomeko Hillside Garden, Millerton, NY
See page 268.

CORNWALL BRIDGE
GARDEN OF DEBBY AND BART JONES
⑤   partial   10–4

In 2000, when Debby and Bart bought their classic Greek Revival house, built by Colonel Dwight Wellington Pierce circa 1836, there were jagged topless spires of 50-foot spruce trees behind the house that had been ravaged by the tornado of 1989. These used to shade a small existing garden.

Debby, a painter with strong feelings about order and geometry, knew little about gardening but cobbled together a "loose" plan for the space. Bart cleared away the vast overgrown riffraff of multiflora rose and wild honeysuckle blanketing the backyard, and together they created gentle meandering paths out of flat stones collected from the adjoining field and circled them around the unsightly stumps, camouflaging them as well as they could with climbing roses, lilacs, magnolias, and fragrant English cottage garden perennials: clematis, foxgloves, delphiniums.

Each year they try to add a new project: a stonewall fountain, long beautiful beds of teeny spring narcissi, followed by summer nepeta, a crab apple allée, a wisteria-covered pergola, and a topiary barberry alligator, to name a few.

Across the street is an orchard, a small kitchen garden, and an old dairy barn that is listed on the Connecticut Register of Historic Places.

This garden's estimated size is 1 acre.

💬 TROWEL TALK

It seems that every time a plant crops up I think it might be my "favorite" plant (with the exception of the weeds of course). I love hellebores because they are early, have no diseases, and play well in the garden with others, causing no problems whatsoever.

But I also adore roses and clematis, which are total problem children needing special attention every time I look at them. One of my favorite garden "musts" is my Gardener's Hollow Leg which attaches to my waist and is a receptacle for weeds, which saves trips back and forth to my wheelbarrow.

—The Gardeners

FALLS VILLAGE
GARDEN OF BUNNY WILLIAMS

   partial 10-1, 1-4

Interior designer and garden book author Bunny Williams' intensively planted 15-acre estate has a sunken garden with twin perennial borders surrounding a fishpond, a seasonally changing parterre garden, a year-round conservatory filled with tropical plants, a large vegetable garden with flowers and herbs, a woodland garden with meandering paths, and a pond with a waterfall.

There are also a working greenhouse and an aviary with unusual chickens, an apple orchard with mature trees, a rustic Greek Revival-style poolhouse folly, and a swimming pool with eighteenth-century French coping.

This garden's estimated size is 12 acres.

SALISBURY
THE SHILLINGFORD GARDEN

  10-1, 1-4

Inspired by the English Arts & Crafts movement, where the garden is seen as an extension of the house, this garden was started from a completely blank canvas in 2013 by its owners, two English transplants who found themselves living in the NW corner "if not quite by mistake, then never by design."

The garden is first and foremost a family garden, home to children and a pack of dogs. The aim has always been to re-create the atmosphere of the owner's grandmother's garden, with perhaps different plantings but the same effect of exploding borders within a year-round formal framework of hedges, boxwood, and trees.

Divided into a series of garden rooms leading out and away from the house, with areas gradually becoming less formal to blur with their boundaries, the garden now includes mass spring bulb plantings, late spring, summer, and fall perennial borders, and the use of trees to create extraordinary seasonal displays. There is also a large vegetable and flower garden, supporting a thriving cut-flower business.

The design, the majority of the planting, and all subsequent maintenance have been undertaken by the owners. The garden is still very much a work in progress.

This garden's estimated size is 3 acres.

NEW 5 10 20 '95 Year   No Photography   Accessibility    Nibbled Leaf Garden

SHARON

GARDEN OF LEE LINK

  10–4

Three stone walls climb up a hillside, at the top of which is a greenhouse containing a wide spectrum of succulents and tropical plants.

Within the last few years, the former perennial border was replaced with a new hardscape and three kousa, or Korean dogwoods set off by a hardscape of gravel and cobblestones. A perennial border is now behind the greenhouse consolidating all the hard work.

A woodland garden edges the ridgeline. Throughout there are a lot of potted plants from the greenhouse in the courtyards. One level has a fishpond, which reflects a winter conservatory attached to the house.

This garden's estimated size is 2 acres of garden on a 15-acre property.

WASHINGTON

BRUSH HILL

   10–4

Take a virtual tour of Brush Hill Gardens at brushhillgardens.com for a preview of many different areas, including the Moon Garden planted in yellows and purples, the Rose Walk, the Peony and Wheelbarrow borders, the Serpentine Garden with its garden folly, and up through the Arch into the Woodland Walk with its series of cascading pools and rills. Each area is adorned with structures designed and built by Charles.

The garden has been featured in many articles and books, including Rosemary Verey's book *Secret Gardens*, and the HGTV series *A Gardener's Diary*. Barbara's new book, *Heroes of Horticulture: Americans Who Transformed the Landscape*, and her first book, *Rosemary Verey: The Life and Lessons of a Legendary Gardener*, will be available for sale.

This garden's estimated size is 10 acres.

💬 TROWEL TALK

My new book will just be out, and it recounts the story and evolution of this garden, titled *Gardening, A Love Story: Creating Brush Hill*.

—Barbara Paul Robinson

NEW 5 10 20 '95 Year

THE SUMACS

  10–4

Set on 9 sprawling acres, The Sumacs features a stately home designed by Ehrick Rossiter and built in 1894. Rock outcroppings, specimen trees, boxwood hedges, and gardens surround the house. Within the gates, you will find a formal potager enclosed by a hedge of yews, a cutting garden, orchard, and perennial gardens that make an elegant nod to the classic English garden.

The modern elements are brought to life with sculpture, a putting green, and a folly made of wood from the property. Walk through a hidden woodland trail that includes a continued array of specimen trees, shrubs, and shade-loving perennials.

The landscape holds interest throughout the four seasons: spring brings an extensive bulb collection that transitions into a meadow under the apple trees, elaborate tropical planters on the terrace in the summer, and fall is ushered in with a colorful dahlia collection.

This garden's estimated size is 10 acres.

TROWEL TALK

Favorite plants are peonies and dahlias. My first garden was a rock garden when I was a child in New Jersey. I have never had luck with mountain laurel—the Connecticut state flower.

—Barbara

WEST CORNWALL

GARDEN OF JANE GARMEY

  10–4

Surrounding an 1827 house and situated next door to the historic eighteenth-century North Cornwall Meeting House, this garden belongs to garden writer Jane Garmey, whose most recent book is *City Green: The Public Gardens of New York*.

Shielded from the road by a row of huge 250-year-old sugar maples and bordered by stone walls, the garden, designed by its owner, has evolved gradually over time.

Its features include a formal boxwood parterre, a rill and fountain bordered by a high hornbeam hedge, two long flowerbeds planted for drama and height, an enclosed picking garden intersected by brick paths, a preponderance of container plantings, and a birdhouse village that floats above a glade of giant *Petasites japonicus*.

This garden's estimated size is 1 acre.

TROWEL TALK

What inspired me to garden?

Necessity—moving into a house surrounded by a field.

Desperation—if not me, who else?

Ignorance—no idea how much time this would take.

Results—dirt behind my nails, occasional burnout, constant pleasure.

— Jane Garmey

NEW Year

110 Connecticut   Register online: gardenconservancy.org/opendays

MICHAEL'S WEST CORNWALL GARDEN
   10–4

This intimate Old World-style garden is replete with cobbled paths, terraced gardens, raised perennial beds, and reflecting pools. Overlooking the Housatonic River, the property has a distinct French/Italian flavor.

Windham County
Saturday, July 13

ASHFORD
MY GARDENS OF SERENITY
NEW 10–4

We were NEVER going to have gardens. We built our geothermal home in 2003 and rationalized that since we lived 600 feet off the road in the woods, and mostly because of the deer, nobody would even notice our blank canvas. Little did we know and through circumstances beyond our control, we now have massive gardens that have become our daily joy.

We live on 5 acres in the woods. There are beautiful stone walls that surround our property that were built decades ago to hold pens for livestock. Together, we added a stone wall with two arbors across the front of the house. Between the house and the rock wall, there are raised beds and steps made of stone. All the rocks were harvested from our woods and carried by hand or wheelbarrow. Certainly, a labor of love.

There are flowers that bloom from early spring (peonies, poppies, and bulbs) to late fall (canna lilies, dahlias, and purple salvia) which provide vivid colors throughout the yard. There is also a large organic garden and blueberries and figs that provide a year-round bounty.

An arbor from the driveway leads to a cozy setting in the backyard where a 20 × 24 patio and gardens were created with our love of the Italian countryside in mind. There are multiple seating areas, surrounded by our stately houseplants, and beautiful blue ceramic pots with flowering annuals. The gardens and patio are a welcoming site for all types of birds and bees, enjoying all that summer has to offer. It is common to have hummingbirds buzzing around throughout the day, and mother birds going to feed their young in the many bird nests around the patio.

We have chosen July to give our tours because our gardens are at their most vibrant colors, with the widest number of annuals and perennials in full bloom, and our vegetable gardens, their most productive. We look forward to sharing it all with you.

TRANQUIL REFUGE
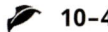 10–4

A 1,000 foot unpaved driveway leads through the woods to my passive solar home and gardens. Surrounded by trees, the clearing was farmland long ago.

Because the front yard is unprotected deer candy, it is made up of mostly ornamental grasses, shrubs, perennials, and annuals deemed not especially tasty to deer. Of course, even these plants are sometimes chosen as treats by the more adventuresome and/or hungry animal life on our road. My mainly organic vegetable garden is also situated here.

Since we had the house built in 1984, the trees have grown considerably taller. The vegetables don't receive as much sun as they would prefer. The backyard, protected by a 900-foot fence hidden among the trees, includes a butterfly garden, herb bed, "tropical dreams" circle garden, and multiple paths through sun/shade gardens. Stone walls built from the remains of old stone walls on the property enclose the area.

Usually by mid-July I enjoy blooms from lacecap hydrangea, astilbe, aruncus, crocosmia, beebalm, rodgersia, amsonia, spigelia, echinacea, salvia, canna lilies, calla lilies, butterfly bush, coreopsis, heliopsis, as well as assorted daylilies and annuals.

This garden's estimated size is ½ acre.

💬 TROWEL TALK

It is as difficult to name a favorite plant as it is choosing a favorite sister or friend. Throughout the seasons, I enjoy different gardens in different ways. In early spring, the hellebores, foam flower, wild ginger, bleeding hearts, lamium, Japanese painted fern, and hosta area under the maple tree is my favorite place to bring a cup of coffee in the morning.

In June, I especially like the path behind the Murry Rock (named for a fluffy stray cat who liked to sun himself on the warm rock). Only at that time of year is the heuchera foliage so rich in chocolate and red hues and striking against the yellow grasses.

Midsummer, the deep blue of the lacecap and bright red and white of the astilbe become my favorite view. At the same time, I love watching hummingbirds feed on the canna. Butterflies abound on the butterfly bush, lantana, and coneflowers. The giant white trumpet-like datura presents a daily surprise.

My family always had vegetable gardens. As a child, I often grabbed a few carrots from my grandmother's garden, wiped the dirt off on my dungarees, and enjoyed a delicious snack. The garlic in my garden are the descendants of the bulbs my grandmother brought from Italy when she came to America.

When I finally owned my own home, I scattered flower beds haphazardly about. Flower gardens were not a family tradition as they were not edible and considered superfluous. In 2000, I hired a landscape architect to create a basic design in order to tie together my little patches. Over the years, I added more intimate spaces by adding pathways and ended up changing about 90 percent of her original plant scheme.

Gardening is a passion and a never-ending learning process. The beauty they bring nourishes my soul. The work is satisfying and therapeutic. Each year I transplant old friends, discover new ones, and forever attempt to create perfection, knowing, and needing constant reminding all the while, that goal is unachievable, and the excitement and pleasure truly comes from the continual journey.

—Fiddlehead

New Haven County

Saturday, July 20

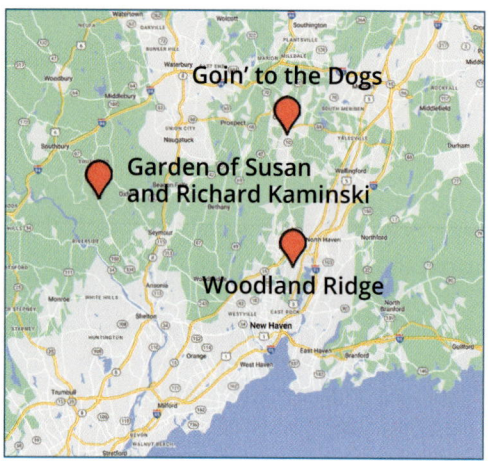

CHESHIRE
GOIN' TO THE DOGS
NEW　partial　10–12, 12–2, 2–4

More than 40 years ago we moved to Cheshire. I didn't like the house, but the yard called to me—not the area where there was a doghouse and dog run; it was the trees that beckoned. And the pattern of the yard; it was surrounded by tall trees on the north and east.

The chain-link fence on the west gave way to a bird-loving viburnum hedge. And the dog run morphed into a meadow! The dirt pile from the kitchen construction blossomed into a dogwood/redbud thicket. Walking into this "garden" is like walking into another world—a calming yet very much alive world where a woodchuck might walk near you and meadow grasses move gracefully with the breeze.

This garden's estimated size is ½ acre.

NEW　5　10　20　'95　Year　　No Photography　　Accessibility　　Nibbled Leaf Garden

💬 TROWEL TALK

I was a teacher who after a day of talking to second graders in a schoolroom welcomed the peace of the backyard with its trees, flowers, and birds. Even watching the "squirrel brothers" chasing each other far up in the trees was fun.

My small spade, its handle now replaced, is my tried-and-true companion—it digs, it chops, it stands at the ready—close to Stan, the "statue" made from car parts. The "garden" hosted a wedding, several anniversaries, picnics, and birthdays. I think that Channel 3 came to look-see one spring.

Inspiration? My mother gardened for years and sold flowers to the Red Lion Inn. I headed in another direction—one that lets nature do a lot of planting on her own. And I can give away many small trees to fellow gardeners.

—JRSCHESANOW

HAMDEN
WOODLAND RIDGE
NEW   ♿   🍃   10-4

This woodland shade garden is enhanced by mature trees creating a park-like ambiance. As a master gardener, I started pulling together unfinished garden beds and removing turf to expand gardens eight years ago when we bought the property.

The low stone wall that now separates shade beds and a stone fire pit area, completed five years ago, creates restful garden rooms. Stone steps on the right lead to a series of garden beds filled with shade-loving, primarily native, plants that end in a "bird corner" of winterberry, viburnum, and cornus for our resident and migratory birds. The flowers and shrubs were selected with an emphasis on supporting pollinators and their life cycles. Our garden is a pesticide-free zone.

Ornamental evergreens and a large specimen magnolia in the front of the property welcome visitors, but the magic is in the back!

This garden's estimated size is ½ acre.

💬 TROWEL TALK

A challenge with a shade garden is planting around all the roots encountered, so plugs are good, patience is better.

My favorite flower is the 'White Swan' echinacea which I grow on the property but not in the shade gardens. I love its elegance. Echinacea in general is the host plant for the silvery checkerspot butterfly, and we see them in one of my gardens.

I also manage a pollinator garden for master gardeners at the Hill-Stead Museum in Farmington, CT, and I encourage all the gardeners to pay attention to and protect the insects in a garden. Insects open up a new world to us.

With a sharp pruner and a hori-hori knife there is not much else a gardener needs to spend a day among plants in one's garden.

—*Pat Sabosik*

NEW 5 10 20 '95 Year   📷 No Photography    Accessibility    Nibbled Leaf Garden

OXFORD

GARDEN OF SUSAN AND RICHARD KAMINSKI

  10–4

All aboard! The OSP&C (Old Swimming Pool and Compost) garden railway is ready to bring back some train memories.

We run three trains simultaneously along with a trolley, and it's one of many gardens we have on our property. We rebuilt almost all of the gardens over the last several years following a serious illness and last year added two more gardens, including a meadow.

We think the garden has something to interest just about anyone. It starts with several roadside gardens and a welcoming topiary.

If the railroad is your final destination, be sure not to miss the perennial beds, fairy garden, and goldfish pond in front of the house. Then proceed past the rose and vegetable gardens to the backyard, where there are more perennial beds. Pass into and through the pergola, keeping an eye out for the old men chiseled into the stone wall.

Stop and visit the large goldfish pond; it should be easy to spot the fish, but the frogs are more difficult as they are masters of camouflage. The gazebo stands ready to offer you a rest and a bit of refreshment.

You can go directly to the OSP&C by walking over the bridge or walking around the pond. If you go around the pond, another 2023 garden addition is behind the espalier apple trees. When you get to the OSP&C, check out the various railroad scenes and let your imagination go wild.

We only ask one thing from our guests: please enjoy yourself.

This garden's estimated size is 1 acre.

💬 TROWEL TALK

Hydrangea and *Acer palmatum* jump out as favorites. After a several year hiatus, we tried lupine again. I'll know in the spring if the streak of bad luck is broken. I actually enjoy weeding but would not attempt it without my trusted Birkenstock kneeler.

—*The Gardeners*

NEW 5 10 20 '95 Year

Hartford County
Sunday, July 21

BURLINGTON
GARDEN OF ROBIN LENSI
 10–4

The garden of Robin Lensi (aka lensi designs photography) and Tom Zabel in Burlington, CT started as a blank slate six years ago. Every landscape is first seen through her lens.

Robin was a photographer for the Garden Conservancy a few years ago, and a member of the Connecticut Daylily Society, and those many wonderful spaces inspired this one. This creative yardscape is intertwined with color explosions and architectural structures spanning months of viewing beauty incorporating all the possibilities into a personal landscape that creates "magic" and infuses one with a calm zen-like feeling.

Enamored of all types of plants and with a background in interior design, garden design, and horticulture, Robin was given tons of ideas and a blank slate to begin. The challenges here: the heavy clay soil, a windy site, exceptional water runoff down the mountain, rabbits, and voles.

We all know gardens are never stagnant but a constant work in progress, and this one's no different. As with her passion for cooking, she views the landscape like a layer cake combining large trees and shrubs for color, texture, height, bird habitat, and structure. Then the filling: the perennials that change with the seasons, ending with the icing: the annuals like herbs, dahlias, and zinnias that thrill all summer. Finally, hundreds of bulbs like alliums, tulips, and daffodils that prepare us to be excited when spring beckons us outside again.

This true four-season garden is a passion, including a wide variety of daylilies, hydrangeas, dahlias, roses, grasses, and hostas scattered throughout. Springtime here is for peonies, lilacs, roses, bleeding hearts, nepeta, magnolia, irises, amsonia, spireas, viburnums, and hawthorn trees as the later blooming plants start waking up. Through this diversity the landscape changes daily—and who knows what next year will reveal, since only Mother Nature will decide? —but they will keep trying to intervene and influence.

This garden's estimated size is ¾ acre.

THE SALSEDO FAMILY GARDEN
  10–4

Our gardens enjoy a unique location: a hilltop, 1,000 feet above sea level, with a magnificent view of 4,000 acres of watershed and state forest.

Beginning in 1977, physical transformations have resulted in stone-walled terraces that render this acre-plus site usable. The last big change, in 1995, added an expanded backyard terrace with a pool, post-and-beam gardener's tool shed, dwarf conifer collection, vegetable garden, and a collection of hardy chrysanthemums.

The front yard features low-maintenance lawns punctuated by beds of native and exotic trees, shrubs, and perennials. The emphasis here is sustainability with a focus on low maintenance and minimal water requirements.

CANTON
SUDDEN DELIGHT
 partial 10–4

Through the curves of the tree-shaded pathway, up past the stately house and around the corner, you'll be surprised to find this lovely storybook garden with its richly variegated hosta hill, cedar arbor, custom chicken coop, and native perennials, all set against the backdrop of a spectacular red New England–style barn.

Meander along the walking paths, stop to watch a yellow finch sip at the birdbath, spy a hummingbird flitting among the roses, or take a secret route through the various tall grasses to the barn.

Sudden Delight garden welcomes you to relax and reflect.

THE MARSTED'S GARDEN OF WHIMSY
 10–4

In 1969 we began transforming a bland landscape into a "Garden of Whimsy." Pine grove and clothesline became terrace and swimming pool.

Perennial and heather borders and a fieldstone retaining wall topped with a field of wildflowers fringed the northern edge. To the east, a pool house and purple greenhouse completed the circle.

Separate small gardens now greet visitors. The Frog Pond with lilies and shade plants and Giverny, begun with seeds from Monet's garden, are separated by stone steps to the Secret Garden, behind a vine-covered fence. The Hosta Necklace weaves the southern lawn. Well-placed sculptures, mirrors, and benches invite the visitor to explore.

GLASTONBURY

THE MURRAY GARDENS
 10–4

This property is a two-acre collection of gardens carved out of a woodland setting punctuated by unusual and native trees.

The front yard features three long blooming perennial borders, a hydrangea bed, and a small pond with a weeping maple water sculpture that gently rains all day. Also in front is a bank of Carpet Flower roses, as well as a naturalized woodland garden, where you can enjoy a myriad of shade and woodland plants and sculpture surprises with soft music in the background.

The backyard has several gardens built into the pool deck and a formal triangle garden containing Knock Out roses, Oriental lilies, and coleus inside a boxwood border. Daylily beds run along an old stone wall beside a large perennial garden and patio. Curved steps ascend from there to a 50-foot rose bed.

Finally, the sunken garden features a waterfall running from a little upper pond to the fishpond below, surrounded by a spectacular Heptacodium tree, several large Japanese maples, and a collection of miniature conifers. Watching over the pond is a six-foot frog sitting on a stone bench.

This garden's estimated size is 2 acres.

Nearby Counties

- **FAIRFIELD**
- **LITCHFIELD**

Saturday, July 27

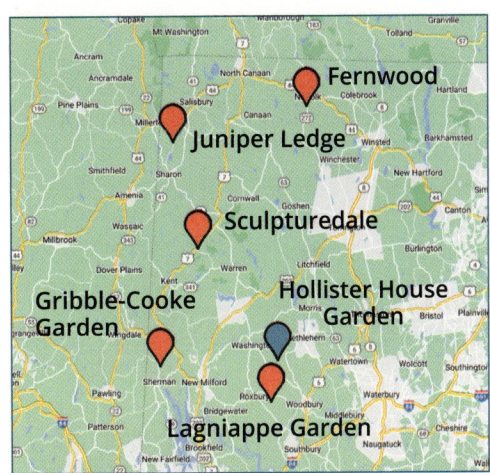

Dutchess County, NY
Highgrove Cottage, Millerton, NY
Lithgow Cottage Garden, Millbrook, NY
See page 286.

Berkshire County, MA
Garden of Jeffrey A. Steele, Ashley Falls, MA
See page 168.

FAIRFIELD COUNTY
SHERMAN
GRIBBLE-COOKE GARDEN
NEW 10–4

Our garden began when Catharine designed our home, built in 2001, on fifteen acres. About 3–4 acres are gardened. With all gardens, it is an ongoing process of growth, change, mistakes and rearranging.

NEW 5 10 20 95 Year   No Photography    Accessibility   Nibbled Leaf Garden

As we get older, we are transitioning to more shrubs and specimen trees. As you come up the drive there is a south facing meadow (designed by Mother Nature, encouraged and edited by us), and to your right is the start of a Rhododendron Dell.

Behind the house is a formal crescent garden hedged with trimmed linden trees, and rock gardens are up the hill to the west. Vegetable gardens lead to a pea gravel dining area with a pergola and fire pit. Beyond there and years ago, Ian created a grass amphitheater and a sunken spiral garden with no-mow grass which finishes off the northern boundary.

Behind the "stage" we are trialing some new cultivars of hydrangeas - as professionals, we need to know if the hype is real! Plenty of sitting areas with long views offer restful contemplation or, after a long day of gardening, the outdoor bathtub nestled in the rockery is a joy! A general map, tree list, and refreshments will be available.

LITCHFIELD COUNTY
KENT
SCULPTUREDALE
 5   partial   10-4

Sculpturedale is a garden of 4 acres surrounding a house built in 1776 with barns and outbuildings. After the usual brambles had been cleared in successive years starting in 1993, the land indicated what would best suit its various natural areas: sun, shade, wet, dry, hilly, rocky, etc.

Each area has been planted around existing features of walls, stumps, banks, buildings, rocks, marsh, woods, pond, lawn. Originally designed to showcase sculpture made here, the garden has developed distinct interest in its own right, where a large variety of perennials, shrubs, and trees are planted to enjoy in all seasons.

No deer fencing and no irrigation mean natives and organics rule. All work is done by the owners. Visitors are invited to walk the paths established throughout, to enjoy the life-size steel sculpture, and to visit the studio where the art is constructed.

Among many areas to enjoy are the primrose path, woodland walk, fern ramble, pollinator patch, wetland wander, conifer corner, shade bank, sun border, Carter Creek, and Fiji Island. In the later summer garden there is angelica, clethra, ligularia, hydrangea, cardinal flower, kirengeshoma, nicotiana, and many more highlights of unusual plants. A very unique treehouse is not to be missed.

This garden's estimated size is 4 acres.

💬 TROWEL TALK

Denis and Barbara had a career in teaching around the world, so have lived and gardened in the tropics, the desert, the British Isles, and the Mediterranean.

On return to their native New England, aspects of these various climes are woven into Sculpturedale's property. "Hardscape" has a different meaning when the "Big Five" wander through this Connecticut land!

—*Barbara Curtiss*

NEW    Year   No Photography   Accessibility   Nibbled Leaf Garden

LAKEVILLE
JUNIPER LEDGE
♿ partial   10–4

Juniper Ledge garden faces south on a gently sloping hillside. It's a garden for meandering; one is often presented with choices of going this way or that way.

There are benches along the way for resting and appreciating the views, sometimes of distant hills. A tennis pavilion is a larger, shaded rest spot. There's even a secluded meditation garden hidden away.

Recent changes include eliminating areas of lawn, replacing it in front with mixed shrubs and flowering plants, and, in a quarter-acre south of the residence, with a tended, but natural, meadow. An experiment with NoMow grass in the lilac walk has been successful, so we are extending its use to several other areas.

We've further provided privacy for swimmers and loungers with planted berms. Invasives on the way to the guesthouse are being replaced with mostly native shrubs, defining a pathway.

This garden's estimated size is 3 acres.

💬 **TROWEL TALK**

My first garden came with a house I bought in New Jersey. While the rose garden was then in heavy shade, it had prosperous knotweed. Luckily I have none in Connecticut. I do have acanthus, which I found at the Beatrix Farrand garden in Hyde Park. Many visitors have not seen it before.

— *The Gardener*

NORFOLK
FERNWOOD
♿ partial   10–4

The garden was originally designed when the house was built in 1908. Both are in the English Arts & Crafts style. The garden was an early design by Marian Coffin. We have an early working plan dated 1908, as well as photographs of the garden that were published in the magazine *Country Life in America* in 1922.

Virtually everything had been lost and we based our re-creation on the original layout, but we have taken some liberties. It appears that the large double border was never executed, but we have attempted one, in addition to reinstalling the smaller square upper part of the garden.

ROXBURY
LAGNIAPPE GARDEN
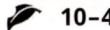 10–4

This 25-year-old informal garden, designed to flow with the Connecticut hillside contours of an old cow pasture and stone walls, has densely planted borders on winding pebble paths.

Beyond the Greek Revival–style house's patio, the main garden curves toward a classical temple folly surrounded by the vegetable beds and the cutting garden.

Uphill is the apple orchard; downhill, a *Nyssa sylvatica* allée with a *Mazus reptans* path ends with a Sissinghurst-inspired stone sofa.

Below, the garden opens to a field with specimen trees: *Taxodium distichum* (bald cypress), *Oxydendrum* (sourwood), *Cercidiphyllum japonicum* (katsura), and

---

NEW 5 10 20 '95 Year    No Photography    Accessibility    Nibbled Leaf Garden

Chionanthus virginicus (white fringetree).

This garden's estimated size is 1½ acres.

💬 **TROWEL TALK**

We learned that we needed perennials, shrubs, and small trees to establish the loose, full look we wanted. Formal Greek Revival house, informal floriferous gardens!
—The Lagniappe Gardener

**PRESERVATION PARTNER
PUBLIC GARDEN**

HOLLISTER HOUSE GARDEN

**300 Nettleton Hollow Rd
Washington, CT 06793**

Beautifully situated on a sloping, terraced site, Hollister House Garden is an American interpretation of such classic English gardens as Sissinghurst, Great Dixter and Hidcote, formal in its structure but informal and rather wild in its style of planting.

Begun in 1979 by George Schoellkopf, the garden since that time has evolved under George's direction into a unique synthesis of the formal and the natural, the right angles of paths, walls and hedges melting seamlessly into the lush surrounding landscape, which forms a magnificent backdrop to the garden's exuberant plantings.

Although the garden is in no way a recreation of an eighteenth-century garden, it was nevertheless planned to complement the old house, and antique or hand-made materials have been used wherever possible in its construction.

The garden unfolds in successive layers of space and color with delightful informal vistas from one section to the next. Eight-to-ten-foot walls and hedges with dramatic changes in level define the progression of garden spaces—"rooms" as the English like to say—and create a firm architectural framework for the romantic abundance of the plantings.

f facebook.com/hollisterhousegarden

📷 instagram.com/hollisterhousegarden

🌐 hollisterhousegarden.org/

NEW   Year   Nibbled Leaf Garden

Fairfield County
Saturday, August 24

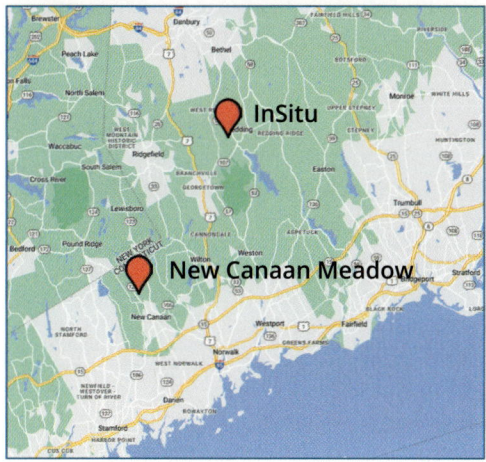

NEW CANAAN
NEW CANAAN MEADOW
NEW  10–4

Over the last five years, we have been replacing turfgrass and planting a variety of native flowering plants and grasses. We also did a great deal of work to transform a flooding problem into a stream we constructed that ends in a small pond.

The goal has been to create an environment conducive to wildlife ranging from birds to butterflies and fireflies.

REDDING
INSITU
10 10–4

Nestled in the pastoral countryside of Redding, CT, surrounded by 300 protected acres of rock ledges, dense forest, grasslands, and meandering streams, InSitu is a 24-acre sculpture garden where nature and art dramatically intersect.

Owner Michael Marocco, actively involved with the skillful team of designers, craftsmen, and plantsmen, has created a richly composed showcase of architecture, horticulture, and sculpture, harmoniously woven together in a series of 27 garden rooms.

The stone, cedar, oak, and rich palette of deep reds and browns integrate InSitu's houses and outbuildings seamlessly into the landscape. The sequence of distinctive garden rooms artfully incorporates native meadows, deciduous trees, flowering plants, grasses, arbors, water features, berms, and terraces, all elegantly connected by lawn, stone, and woodland pathways.

Marocco's internationally curated sculpture collection flourishes in concordance with these masterfully styled spaces. Two unique structures—The Sanctuary, a striking stone, chapel-like space emerging from the side of a hill, and Pulpitum, a sculptural observation tower—offer sweeping vistas of the inspiring oasis.

The gardens at InSitu were designed in collaboration with Richard Hartlage. They were installed and are meticulously cared for by John and Andrew Kuczo.

InSitu has been featured in numerous publications, including the Garden Conservancy's book *Outstanding American Gardens: A Celebration: 25 Years of the Garden Conservancy* (2015), a portrait of 50 of America's most beautiful gardens.

This garden's estimated size is 25 acres.

Fairfield County
Saturday, September 14

WESTON
FRANCES PALMER'S GARDEN
  10–4

Adjacent to Frances Palmer's pottery studio is her large cutting garden, which supplies myriad blooms from early spring through frost.

Frances grows *Alice in Wonderland* flowers. They inspire her ceramics and photography. Her garden is especially known for its dahlias; she plants more than 100 different shapes-from the smallest "pom" to the largest dinner plate varieties. Colors and textures abound, dahlias interweave with tomatoes, zinnias, amaranth, sunflowers, and herbs.

September is the height of the garden's abundance.

This garden's estimated size is ¾ acre.

💬 TROWEL TALK

Of course, my favorite plants are dahlias, and I have never had any luck with orchids. My gardens bring me great joy though they are neither elegant nor beautifully organized plots.

I embrace the volunteer seedlings that pop up from the previous year's flowers and I add something new to my gardens each year.

—*Frances*

WELLS HILL FARM
♿ partial   10–4

Wells Hill Farm strives to model sustainability and the best organic growing practices for small family farms.

Companion herbs and flowers are integrated throughout our production gardens. We grow produce intensively on one-third of an acre and use our remaining 13 acres of pastures and woodlands for rotating two mobile chicken coops, one sheep house, and a rabbit hutch—all of which fertilize our pasture, add to our rich compost, control pests, and keep weeding around the property to a minimum.

Our two livestock guardian dogs keep the animals safe from predation. We do all farming by hand and do not till our soil. Additionally, we grow through four seasons in a 125-foot-high tunnel.

Wells Hill Farm sells to restaurants in Fairfield County and New York City, runs a small CSA, and holds farming classes for children and adults.

All inputs are carefully considered, and almost all of the farm's garden structures

---

NEW 5 10 20 '95 Year    No Photography   ♿ Accessibility    Nibbled Leaf Garden

and architectural elements are built from downed trees and rocks found on the property.

💬 TROWEL TALK

Just one? I need two because there is the edible garden and there is the surrounding landscape that supports the beneficial insects and pollinators we need to farm as organically as possible.

In my garden, Red Burgundy Okra (*Abelmoschus esculentus*) is one of my favorite crops. It reminds me of my childhood in the South. Both as an edible and ornamental, this striking plant in the mallow family has edible flowers, leaves, and pods and grows 5–6 feet tall.

In the landscape, *Quercus* (oak trees) are my favorite tree because of their incredible ecological value. They are the kings of biodiversity, supporting more than 4,000 species, including even bacteria and microorganisms. They are the cathedrals of the natural world.

My first garden was built as a first grader outside my backyard fence in the local park in New Jersey. I found a little grassy corner and planted flowers and tomatoes. I can't seem to get brussels sprouts right, and they are my favorite vegetable. I need to cover my brassicas with Agribon fabric to deter cabbage moths and whiteflies, as I won't use any pesticides on the farm. They grow a little too tall for proper covering, and the wind always blows the fabric off the crops!

My favorite garden tool is the Harvest Broadfork from Johnny's Selected Seeds. My garden is entirely no-till, and the tool allows me to gently aerate the soil while not disturbing its layers that organisms call home.

My great-grandmother, an immigrant from Hungary, was a farmer. She never learned to drive a car after arriving through Ellis Island and living in NYC in 1914, but she always drove her tractor around her farm in Port Jervis, NJ.

I grew up running around her meadows and streams, eating berries from her brambles, and picking cherries and apples from her orchard.

—*Farmer Michelle*

WESTPORT
PROSPECT GARDENS WESTPORT
♿ **partial**   🍃 **10–4**

This garden is open twice this year: June 8 and September 14.

Prospect Gardens Westport dates back to the 1812 original Victorian farmhouse and surrounding acres of the Wakeman onion farm.

Through a series of abutting property acquisitions over the last twenty-plus years, the property is now a contiguous arboretum-style garden of almost 9 acres featuring planting collections, gardens, open lawns, and winding pathways leading from one area to the next, allowing the visitor a three-dimensional experience of being "in" the gardens.

Mature deciduous and evergreen trees create a sweeping canvas and provide a sense of scale, shape, and texture reflective of the owners' contemporary style and sense of design.

Some of the property's key features include a Mediterranean graveled entry garden, two orchards, a three stone–tiered

Fairfield County
Saturday, October 5

vegetable garden, berry houses (blueberry, raspberry), beehives, a sunny perennial garden, a shady perennial woodland walk, a conifer collection, numerous flowering shrub and grass borders, a Japanese-inspired meditation garden and maple collection, red-clay tennis court, two pools, containers featuring citrus and cacti, a glasshouse, an internationally renowned sculpture, and a 1-acre perennial/native wildflower meadow.

Most recently added is a four-tiered amphitheater with a stone-medallioned stage.

This garden's estimated size is 8 acres.

GREENWICH
SLEEPY CAT FARM

 10–12, 12–2, 2–4

This garden is open twice this year: June 22 and October 5.

The 13 acres of Sleepy Cat Farm have evolved over the last 25 years in close collaboration between the present owner and Virginia-based landscape architect Charles J. Stick.

The landscape bordering Lake Avenue includes an extensive greenhouse and potager. "The Barn," distinguished by its half-timbered French Normandy vocabulary, is surrounded by thyme-covered terraces, providing an elegant stage set for a fine collection of garden ornament, sculpture, and boxwood topiary.

The visitor's experience of the garden unfolds as pathways lead from garden room to garden room in a carefully orchestrated series of discoveries.

NEW 5 10 20 95 Year    No Photography    Accessibility   Nibbled Leaf Garden

The central portion of the garden is distinguished by two parallel garden spaces; the first is dominated by a long reflecting pool, terminated on the north end by a wisteria-covered arbor, and on the south end by a pebble mosaic terrace and fountain basin.

One of the great surprises of the tour is the adjacent garden space. Bordered by a precisely clipped hornbeam hedge, the green architecture of this room is meant to frame the view to the Chinese pavilion (or "ting"—a place to stop and take in the view) positioned on a small island in the middle of a pond teeming with koi.

The north end of this garden is terminated by an impressively scaled statue of Atlas. The heart of the original 6 acres is most joyfully experienced along the "Golden Path," a granite dust pathway that leads from the main house and formal terraces on top of the hill, out into the New England landscape. As it winds through the oak and beech woodland, one encounters fountains, statuary, an iris garden traversed by a Japanese spirit bridge and planted with 10,000 Japanese iris, and finally a rustic stone grotto.

The woodland stream is bordered by native azaleas and a collection of spring flowering trees and bulbs, all planted for enjoyment throughout the year. The most recent additions to the property include a limonaia used for the winter storage of citrus trees, a new fruit orchard, and a sacred woodland grove that is enjoyed from a series of pathways radiating from a newly planted meadow.

The southern expansion of the property over the past three years has added a new dimension to the overall landscape experience of Sleepy Cat Farm.

Another recent addition to the garden is an English-style perennial border directly across from the koi pond and, directly below, a viewing path framed by a wisteria arbor. This border is surrounded by decorative stone walls covered with hydrangea, climbing roses, clematis, and boxwood. It consists of four linear beds around a central axis of lawn pathway and features a mixed shrub and perennial border containing a succession of blooms through the seasons.

During the 2020 visitor hiatus, we updated several garden areas. The iris garden was completed, with many more Japanese iris cultivars added, as well as a winding bamboo railway path leading to it, featuring a fragrant Korean spice viburnum border interspersed with spring bulbs and fall-blooming kirengeshoma.

The garden is now bordered by a ring of bright red *Cornus* 'Arctic Fire' against a backdrop of *Ilex glabra* topiaries. In addition, seven new pieces of art have been installed in various spots along the paths.

This garden's estimated size is 13½ acres.

SOUTHPORT
THE GOULD GARDEN
NEW 10–12, 12–2, 2–4

This garden is open twice this year: June 8 and October 5.

I started to think about a garden in 2002, but it took several years to figure out what I wanted to achieve. Since my red brick house was built as a boys' club, it has an assertive presence on a street facing a river, a golf course, and Long Island Sound.

I decided that pastel colors wouldn't be swallowed by the house scheme of orange, purple, chartreuse, and deep red, for the south-facing garden which sits well above the street. This colorful garden has become a destination for monarchs and hummingbirds.

Southport is a unique waterside destination and a great walking town. A brick wall faces the street, and to honor my grandmother, we planted a mix of peach, orange, and dark pink climbing roses and many varieties of clematis on the street level. This location is a perfect microclimate. The May–June bloom has become a "go see" legend in Southport when it is in its full blooming glory.

The backyard is the shade garden, featuring an *Ulmus americana*. This elm is well over 90 years old and has been listed with The Notable Trees Project sponsored by the Connecticut Botanical Society, The Connecticut College Arboretum, and the Connecticut Urban Forest Council.

This garden's estimated size is ½ acre.

TROWEL TALK

My favorite plants are tithonia which attracts Monarchs, ricinus 'Red Spires' as it looms over the fall garden, and *Trycirtis hirta* that is so delicate and whimsical. *Rosa* 'Climbing Polka' is my favorite rose.

I had my first garden at the age of five. It was a school plot. We grew carrots—I was so proud of my bounty. My grandparents loved to garden, and my grandmother's roses were the best in her neighborhood.

I met Tom when my beloved late husband decided we needed a garden at our new weekend house in Greenwich. My husband and Tom got along so well that when we decided to move to Southport, the one to call was Tom—23 years ago.

My gardens evolved over time to become the colorful fall garden it is today. It has been documented and was accepted into the Smithsonian Archive of American Gardens.

—*The Gardener*

New London County
Saturday, October 12

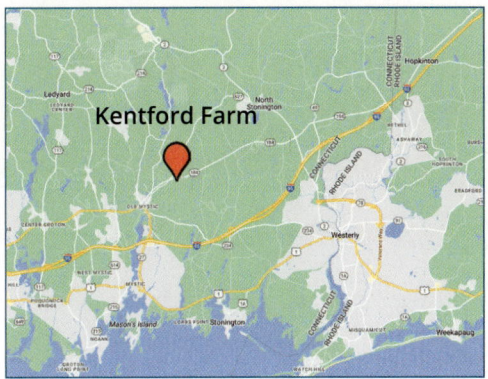

STONINGTON
KENTFORD FARM
10 ♿ partial ⚐ 10–4

This garden is open twice this year: May 25 and October 12.

Kentford Farm is a perennial farm in the making. For 25 years, Paul Coutu and William Turner have been creating grass pathways and planting beds.

The farm dates back to 1727, and the previous owner started planting in 1945. Fifty-foot weeping cherries, a Norway spruce, copper beech, and blue Atlas cedar, to name a few, dot this 6-acre garden. There is a walk-in root cellar built into the hillside, and stone walls surround the whole property.

For more information, visit: kentfordfarm.com

This garden's estimated size is 6 acres.

Thistle - Wilmington, DE
Photo: the Garden Host

Delaware

Open Days dates and times by County, Town, and Garden

NEW CASTLE

Wilmington
Old Oaks on Owl's Nest Rd.
Saturday, June 15, 10–4
Peggy Anne and Dan's Home Garden
Sunday, June 23, 10–4
Thistle
Saturday, May 11, 10–4

Register online: gardenconservancy.org/opendays   Delaware   131

DELAWARE

New Castle County
Saturday, May 11

An additional garden is open nearby:
Delaware County, PA
   WynEdyn, Chadds Ford, PA
See page 313.

WILMINGTON
THISTLE
NEW   10–4

plants, deciduous rhododendrons, alpines, and bulbs are in peak bloom in mid-spring. A variety of primulas and cypripediums are in bloom through May.

A special treat awaits those who venture into the "magic wood." On warm and sunny spring days, the lucky visitor may see trolls and fairies at play deep in the forest.

This garden's estimated size is 2 acres.

"'Thistle" is sited on nearly 2 acres in North Wilmington and is located where the Coastal Plain transitions into the Piedmont Plateau (Garden Zone 7).

An Asian aesthetic weaves together numerous gardens, including a Japanese courtyard, rock and trough garden, small ponds, and a secluded woodland. Native

NEW 5 10 20 95 Year   No Photography    Accessibility    Nibbled Leaf Garden

New Castle County
Saturday, June 15

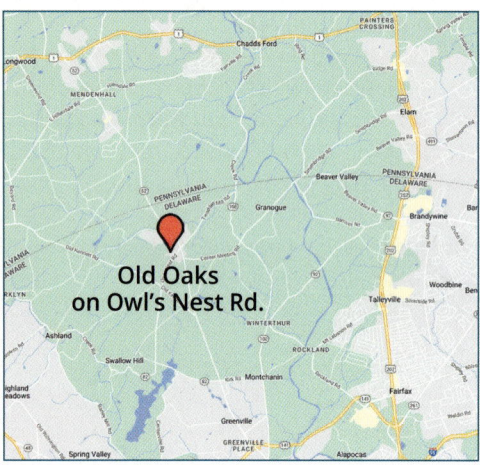

Additional gardens are open nearby:
Chester County, PA
  The Garden of Donald Pell, Phoenixville, PA
Delaware County, PA
  Nature's Flow, Chadds Ford, PA
Montgomery County, PA
  Lenbury West, Wyndmoor, PA
  Vickie's Garden, Flourtown, PA
Philadelphia County, PA
  Home Place Garden, Philadelphia, PA
  Garden of Patty Redenbaugh, Philadelphia, PA
See page 314.

WILMINGTON
OLD OAKS ON OWL'S NEST RD.
NEW 10–4

On 9 acres in Centreville, DE, surrounded by world-class gardens (Winterthur, Mt. Cuba, Longwood), Bill Duncan started landscaping 40+ years ago on property in his family for four generations.

The original oak/tulip poplar/beech forest on part of the land has been enhanced with uncommon trees and shrubs that Bill picked up in his landscaping business. Hardscaping and water features abound. When Bill divided the property, Meg Spurlin fulfilled her lifelong gardening passion and snapped up No. 19, adding flower borders and other grace-notes to this superb, mature landscape.

💬 TROWEL TALK

Meg's vivid, early memories are of the natural world, and flowers especially rolling in a mossy bank covered in Quaker Ladies. With two gardening parents, green genes came out strongly by age 6 or 7, when she took over a corner of the large vegetable garden for her patch of potatoes and bachelor buttons. At age 11, when she fell in love with blueberries, she saved up to buy ten plants to add to the family's big orchard.

She has gardened practically everywhere she lived, including Burma, and most extensively on a 35-acre farm on the historic register near Shepherdstown, WV.

She also travels and visits gardens around the world and is delighted to live now in the garden-rich Brandywine Valley.

—Meg Spurlin

New Castle County
Sunday, June 23

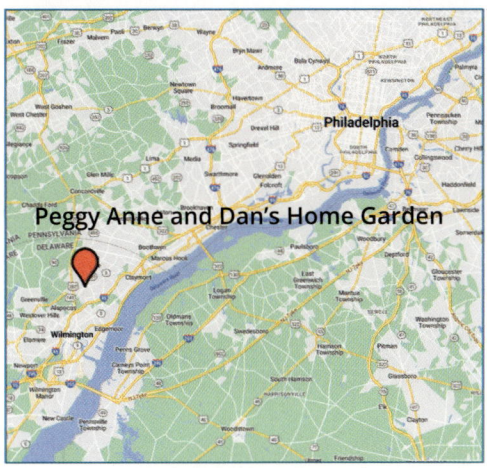

Additional gardens are open nearby:
Delaware County, PA
  Belvidere, Swarthmore, PA
  Hedgleigh Spring, Swarthmore, PA
See page 318.

WILMINGTON
PEGGY ANNE AND DAN'S HOME GARDEN
NEW   10–4

Dan Benarcik and Peggy Anne Montgomery's garden is a testament to their shared passion for horticulture and landscape design.

Their modest home is sited well forward on the property, leaving an ample space in the back for guests to wander from room to room; a carved-out grotto, a gravel garden, sunny pollinator borders, a "Little Minnesota" fire pit area, and a secret garden at the very back for the littlest visitors, softened with moss-covered paths.

Many of the plants on the property were gifts from friends brought back from plant-hunting trips around the globe. The stories of their friends and the origins of the plants are the heart and soul of the place and dearest to the couple. Guests will be invited into the Fort Dan built for Peggy Anne so they can spend their evening outdoors free of mosquitoes and entertain their friends and family.

The gravel garden was featured on the cover of Kelly Norris's book, *New Naturalism*. More recently, they were honored to be included in *American Roots* by Allison and Nick McCullough, along with Teresa Woodward.

This garden's estimated size is 1 acre.

💬 TROWEL TALK

Dan is currently enjoying the cultivation of broad-leaf evergreens, and moss gardening.

Peggy Anne is slowly learning to step back from gardening a bit and enjoying other pursuits.

—*Peggy Anne and Dan*

Highland Park Residence - Highland Park, IL
Photo: Tony Soluri

Illinois

136 Illinois

Open Days dates and times by County, Town, and Garden

COOK

Highland Park
Highland Park Residence
   Saturday, July 27, 10–4

Mettawa
Mettawa Manor and Kurtis Conservation Foundation
   Saturday, July 27, 10–4

DUPAGE

West Chicago
The Gardens at Ball
   Saturday, August 3, 10–12, 12–2, 2–4

LAKE

Lake Forest
The Cottage
   Saturday, July 27, 10–4
The Gardens at 900
   Saturday, July 27, 10–1, 1–4

Register online: gardenconservancy.org/opendays   Illinois 137

ILLINOIS

Chicago Area
Saturday, July 27

HIGHLAND PARK
HIGHLAND PARK RESIDENCE
5 partial 10–4

A sweeping driveway and naturalistic planting of bold masses of spirea and hydrangea creates a subtle plinth for this refined white Georgian house set on a raised knoll in a quiet sun-dappled neighborhood.

A hint of classic English formality is established around the architectural details and access points of the house. Boxwood hedges, juneberry, espaliered crab apple, pachysandra, and dimensioned bluestone paths lead you through each garden room. Sweeping and undulating lawn panels layered with purpleleaf wintercreeper create a solid composition along with sequence of spaces unified by a clear sense of movement and vistas terminating into modern and antique focal points that include garden benches, a fountain, staddle stones, and classically inspired raised urns dripping with seasonal annuals.

Taking advantage of the existing change in elevation, a raised bluestone terrace frames a screened pavilion for entertaining. Stone walls and wide graceful steps lead down to a formal allée of Armstrong maples accented and framed by white lattice panels and perennial gardens, creating a playful contrast to the surrounding landscape borders.

Long and short sight lines and axial line movement clearly articulate and frame a garden that displays "art in harmony with Nature."

NEW **5** **10** **20** **'95** Year   No Photography   Accessibility   Nibbled Leaf Garden

LAKE FOREST

THE COTTAGE

  10-4

This garden was constructed on the site of one of Lake Forest's early farms. The forecourt is of special interest, and boxwood, yews, and vinca were used to create a green tapestry wall. This was a favorite of Rosemary Verey, the English landscape designer who worked with Dorothy Hebert of Gardens In Progress on the design of this garden. Mrs. Verey's book *The Garden in Winter* is a reminder of winter being the longest season in our Midwest gardens, so as we followed her advice, you will see heavy planting of boxwoods and yews for outlining the deep perennial beds on the property.

The use of plants with strong architectural interests such as the hawthorn hedgerow, Japanese tree lilac allée, and willow grove are all interesting additions to the winter landscape. Spring is another special season for this garden. Fifteen thousand bulbs bring in the seasons, all with traditional bulbs being used. The favorite of the owners are the fritillaria, which are found in great abundance on the property.

The iron gate in the stone wall leads to a white shade garden. Note the climbing hydrangea used as ground cover for edging the bed of Solomon's seal, lily of the valley, *Tricyrtis*, roses, phlox, *Leucojum*, sweet woodruff, and trillium. The old Chicago park bench in the shade garden provides a place for passersby to rest and enjoy the view.

Of special interest are the garden objects you will find throughout the property that represent the work of American and British designers working during the Arts & Crafts period. Enjoy.

THE GARDENS AT 900

 partial 10-1, 1-4

The Gardens at 900 are a sensitive renovation and interpretation of the original entry building complex and gardens of the historic Elawa Farm.

Originally designed by architect David Adler in 1917 for A. Watson and Elsa Armour, the buildings had been abandoned for nearly a decade before being acquired by Craig Bergmann and Paul Klug. Used as both private residence and the design offices for Bergmann and Klug, the buildings and garden areas regard the history of the site, while also fostering creativity.

Formal borders, a shade garden with a 2022 greenhouse addition, an orchard laden with old roses and a panicle hydrangea collection, a swimming pool garden, and a motor court constitute the garden today.

A relatively young garden (2010), the Gardens at 900 is an excellent example of how quickly a landscape can be transformed with a focused, collaborative vision. The property has been designated as a State of Illinois historic landmark.

This garden's estimated size is 2 3/4 acres.

NEW   Year    No Photography    Accessibility    Nibbled Leaf Garden

METTAWA
METTAWA MANOR AND KURTIS CONSERVATION FOUNDATION

 10–4

Both homes on the 65-acre property were built in 1927 as part of a family estate. The current owners, Bill Kurtis and Donna LaPietra, are only the second in its history, and they have been working since 1990 to restore native ecosystems and create a series of formal garden rooms with more than 30 distinct areas to visit.

The centerpiece is a walled English-style garden with two perennial borders framing a sunken lawn, that leads to a spring walk and rose room. Outside the east gate is a golden garden and an orchard bordered by the fenced cutting garden and circular herb garden.

The property has two ponds, a prairie, a parkland of specimen trees, and a reclaimed oak-hickory forest. The owners have also created a silver garden, a bronze garden, a lily pool, an aqua-theater, and a fern garden. Other sites worth exploring are the pine forest reflection garden, a gravel garden and succulent collection around the pool house, and a shrubbery.

The day also includes a honey tasting from their hives, a Club Car tour of the prairie in bloom with Bill, a photographic and video exhibit in the Kurtis Conversation headquarters house, and a stop at the Kids Fun Table on the Lily Pond Terrace for frog watching.

This garden's estimated size is 65 acres.

Dupage County
Saturday, August 3

WEST CHICAGO
THE GARDENS AT BALL

 partial   10–12, 12–2, 2–4

Guests will enjoy the opportunity to visit The Gardens at Ball, usually reserved for the wholesale customers of the 118-year-old Ball Horticultural Company, a world leader in the breeding, production, distribution, and marketing of horticultural products.

With more than 15 acres of gardens, including sun, shade plantings of annuals, perennials, and containers with more than 500 varieties, Ball features the top new introductions from recent years. Also featured are a growing collection of home garden vegetables. Ball is an All-America Selections evaluation trial site as well.

Guides will be available throughout the day to give garden tours and answer questions. This is a once-a-year opportunity to visit the historic Ball Horticulture Garden not generally open to the public. The company's motto is "Color the World!"

This garden's estimated size is 15 acres.

NEW   5 10 20 95 Year    No Photography    Accessibility    Nibbled Leaf Garden

Butterfly Alley - Hollywood, MD
Photo: the Garden Host

Maryland

142 Maryland

Open Days dates and times by County, Town, and Garden

ST MARY'S
Hollywood
Butterfly Alley
Saturday, June 1, 10–12, 12–2, 2–4
Leonardtown
Dragonfly
Saturday, June 1, 10–12, 12–2, 2–4
Lexington Park
Allen's Heirloom Homestead
Saturday, June 1, 10–12, 12–2, 2–4

MARYLAND

St Mary's County
Saturday, June 1

HOLLYWOOD
BUTTERFLY ALLEY
NEW 10–12, 12–2, 2–4

Butterfly Alley has a native plant demonstration garden. The garden was created because of my love for butterflies and the realization that to have butterflies we need host plants.

I'm a self-taught experimenter surrounding myself with as many native host and nectar plants in a residential garden as I can squeeze in. It's always evolving. Please stop in. Success is measured in caterpillars!

This garden's estimated size is 3,000 sq. ft.

LEONARDTOWN
DRAGONFLY
NEW 10–12, 12–2, 2–4

Dragonfly is a 30-year-old waterfront garden in St. Mary's County. What started out as a half-acre landscape project led to purchasing the adjoining 1½-acre lot to expand the garden. Full sun natives along with trees and shrubs welcome visitors to the eternity sculpture garden.

The side gardens and waterfront areas are in semi shade. Visitors can meander along paths to view a host of shade-loving plants with Cherry Cove in the background.

This garden's estimated size is 2 acres.

TROWEL TALK

My favorite plant is the perennial cranesbill due to its year-round interest, mounding effect for a ground cover, and lovely raspberry blooms.

—Kathy G.

LEXINGTON PARK
ALLEN'S HEIRLOOM HOMESTEAD
NEW 10–12, 12–2, 2–4

Frank has been plant collecting and gardening for more than 70 years; Christina has been Kitchen Gardening for more than 40 years. We have lived at this farm/homestead, of about 10 acres, for 28 years, where we grow a huge variety of our own foods, year-round.

I grow about 1,500 feet of salad greens a

NEW   Year

year, lots of sweet potatoes, many fruits (including pomegranates, hardy kiwi, watermelons, cantaloupes, berries, pears, apples, Asian pears, Asian persimmons, blueberries, etc.).

We have sheep, chickens, and rare breed turkeys that are integral in our system of totally natural pest control. A lot of flowers go in our kitchen gardens to encourage beneficial insects, as well as for beauty and some unusual crops for this area like eucalyptus tree, tea camellia (for black tea), and colored cotton for spinning into yarn.

We grow several rare varieties of ornamental flowers, shrubs, and trees. It is an example of a healthy, diverse, working homestead farm.

This garden's estimated size is 10 acres.

💬 TROWEL TALK

Frank has been gardening since he was 3 years old. He followed his grandmother around her garden, so his mother got him some tulip bulbs to plant. He joyfully planted them and dug them up every day to see how they were growing! Of course they died.

He says he has been successfully killing plants since then

—*Frank and Christina*

PUBLIC GARDEN
ANNMARIE SCULPTURE GARDEN & ARTS CENTER

**13470 Dowell Road
Solomons, Maryland 20688**

An affiliate of the Smithsonian Institution, Annmarie is a located in scenic Solomons, Maryland, where the Pautxent River meets the Chesapeake Bay. The sculpture garden features a walking path that meanders through the forest, past permanent and loaned sculpture, including more than forty works on loan from the Smithsonian Institution and the National Gallery of Art.

The garden also presents a variety of special events, gallery shows, and engaging public art programs throughout the year. The Studio School offers creative classes taught by a talented faculty. The award-winning Murray Arts Building is a 15,000 sq.ft. museum-grade exhibition space that includes two large galleries, a gift shop, the artLAB, and a sunny patio that offers lovely views of the outdoor sculpture.

Our Mission:
Annmarie is committed to connecting people to art and nature. Through a wide variety of engaging exhibits, programs, classes, public projects, and annual events, Annmarie opens

up opportunities for creativity, collaboration, and reflection.

By providing opportunities for visitors to experience and engage in imaginative activities, Annmarie seeks to nurture the human spirit and contribute to a healthy society.

 facebook.com/annmariearts

 instagram.com/annmariearts

 annmariegarden.org/annmarie2

PUBLIC GARDEN
HISTORIC SOTTERLEY

**44300 Sotterley Lane
Hollywood, Maryland 20636**

A National Historic Landmark and a UNESCO Site of Memory for the Routes of Enslaved Peoples, Historic Sotterley is one of the oldest museums of its kind in the United States, with a history dating back to the turn of the eighteenth century.

Through the preservation of the site's historic structures and natural environment and the use of powerful stories to educate and bring American history to life, the organization strives to foster a better understanding of our world today by providing a living link to America's complex history and legacy of slavery.

One of Historic Sotterley's most stunning features is a Colonial Revival Garden, which is maintained by our Garden Guild. The garden is approximately 1 acre and host to a wide variety of plants that flower throughout the warm months.

 facebook.com/historic.sotterley

 instagram.com/historicsotterley

 sotterley.org

Andrew Grossman's Garden - Seekonk, MA
Photo: Andrew Grossman

Massachusetts

148 Massachusetts

Mayflower
Epigaea regens

Open Days dates and times by County, Town, and Garden

BERKSHIRE
Ashley Falls
Garden of Jeffrey A Steele
 Saturday, July 27, 10–4
Richmond
Black Barn Farm
 Saturday, May 4, 10–4
West Stockbridge
Kingsmont
 Sunday, July 28, 10–4
Walford
 Sunday, July 28, 10–4

BRISTOL
Seekonk
Andrew Grossman's Garden
 Saturday, September 14, 10–4

ESSEX COUNTY
Manchester
Highgarden/High Contente
 Saturday, May 18, 10–4
Marblehead
Ticehurst
 Saturday, July 20, 10–4
Salem
Renaissance Italy Comes to River Street, Salem
 Saturday, July 20, 10–4

FRANKLIN
Greenfield
Mary Chicoine's Garden
 Saturday, June 29, 10–4
Phoenix House Gardens
 Saturday, June 1, 10–4
Leverett
Earthworks Garden
 Saturday, June 29, 10–4
 Saturday, September 28, 10–4
Sunderland
Maples of Silver Lane
 Saturday, June 1, 10–4
Swampfield
 Saturday, June 1, 10–4
 Saturday, October 19, 10–4

HAMPDEN

Holyoke
Rock Valley Paradise
Saturday, August 3, 10–4
Saturday, October 19, 10–4

Springfield
A Country Garden in the City
Saturday, August 3, 10–4
Our Color-Filled Retreat
Saturday, June 1, 10–4
Saturday, August 3, 10–4

West Springfield
Suburban Garden in Transition
Saturday, June 29, 10–4

HAMPSHIRE

Amherst
Kinsey-Pope Garden
Saturday, May 11, 10–1, 1–5
Saturday, June 29, 10–1, 1–5
Saturday, October 19, 10–1, 1–5
Flying Pig Farm
Saturday, June 1, 10–4

Florence
Culver's Garden
Saturday, June 1, 10–4

MIDDLESEX

Carlisle
Gardens at Clock Barn - Home of Maureen and Mike Ruettgers
Saturday, September 14, 10–4

Groton
Garden of Pepe and John Maynard
Sunday, May 11, 10–4

Pepperell
The Stone Sphere
Saturday, June 15, 10–4

Stow
Glenluce Garden
Saturday, May 18, 10–4

Weston
Spencer-Scott Garden
Saturday, May 18, 10–4

WORCESTER

Boylston
Berry Garden
Saturday, May 11, 10–4

Petersham
Swift River Farm
Saturday, May 11, 10–4

Worcester
Garden of Matt Mattus and Joe Philip
Saturday, May 11, 10–4

150 Massachusetts   Register online: gardenconservancy.org/opendays

MASSACHUSETTS

Berkshire County
Saturday, May 4

An additional garden is open nearby :
Columbia County, NY
   Wombat Crossing, Hillsdale, NY
See page 237.

RICHMOND
BLACK BARN FARM

    10–4

After being greeted by a pair of fantastical topiary birds, guests pass by the East Terrace entry with its collection of container plantings and espaliered Fuji apple.

Proceeding past the collection of dwarf evergreens and through the doors of the first hedged room with its gazing-ball–capped topiary columns, stroll down the allée of 'Wyman' crabs, on the right of the allée, see the 80+ mature hornbeam topiaries, the only ones you will see in the United States.

Progress through the Chinese red gates to the Pool Garden, where containers of tropicals decorate the Neoclassical pavilion, with its collection of furniture inspired by branch coral. A new addition is the bronze fountain *Sculpture Andata, Sculpture Storna*, a unique collaboration between Italian artists Enzo Cucchi and Sandro Cucchi. Leaving the pool you can stroll through a collection of large topiary in several stages of development. Look for the elephant, the ibis, a rhino, and more fantastic animals among the more traditional geometric topiary forms. As you head toward the rustic pergola and tea house, surrounded by boxwood topiary large and small, take a peek into the woods at the Stumpery which features a collection of toxic and poisonous plants; our Garden of Discomfort is an homage to the end cycle of life.

The Ornamental Hermit Hut is a new addition. The pergola leads into the main kitchen garden, enclosed by a mature beech hedge, which provides fruit and vegetables for the owners and friends. As you pass by the moss-covered garden shed don't miss the West Terrace ahead, which features raised bluestone and steel beds planted with vegetables and herbs close to the kitchen. The beginnings of a hornbeam maze, now nearly ten years old, are shaping up nicely.

This garden's estimated size is 3 acres.

NEW 5 10 20 '95 Year    No Photography    Accessibility    Nibbled Leaf Garden

Nearby Counties

- **HAMPSHIRE**
- **MIDDLESEX**
- **WORCESTER**

Saturday, May 11

HAMPSHIRE COUNTY
AMHERST
KINSEY-POPE GARDEN
NEW   10–1, 1–5

This garden is open three times this year: May 11, June 29, and October 19.

This is a garden begun by my late husband and me (both academics with no formal garden training) soon after we moved here in 1978, working and learning together for twenty years.

I have been the primary garden designer from the beginning, and designer and gardener for another twenty years, now recently with some wonderful garden help. It is a landscape of many uncommon trees with strikingly beautiful bark and a wide variety of textures, flowers, berries, and great autumn color; many shrubs with more than one season of beauty; perennials flowering in three seasons; ground covers of unusual dramatic effect covering all beds during all seasons; and in winter offering a wide palette of interesting shapes, lovely bark, and many evergreen trees and shrubs.

In addition, there are three bridges over a stone-lined swale, a hand-built screened gazebo and curved top arbor, a charming little pond, many benches and Japanese stone lanterns, large-stone walkways and stone walls, and a Japanese inspired fence surrounding all of the ½-acre garden.

💬 TROWEL TALK

I have no formal training in garden design, but when my husband was diagnosed with cancer, I quit my academic job to spend more time with him and began reading everything about gardens and garden design. We then made the task of creating our garden a major focus together for the five years of time he eventually had.

During that time, friends and colleagues began asking for my design help, and I suddenly became a garden designer with many clients. When my husband was diagnosed with cancer, he was allowed to give up tasks other than teaching and meeting with students. So, we had more time together, and I began reading all sorts of garden books, especially Michael Dirr's excellent tomes, and my husband and I worked and focused constantly in/on the garden. Later we met the Dirrs here in Amherst and were invited to come visit them in Georgia, which we did.

NEW | 5 10 20 95 Year | No Photography | Accessibility | Nibbled Leaf Garden

In 1998, my husband passed away. In 2000, Michael (along with Allan Armitage) came for a weekend of fundraising events and talks at Amherst College to benefit a memorial garden I had designed for my husband that was installed at our local library by me, his grad students, colleagues, and our friends and family. All this to explain, that most of what I know about gardening started with Michael's and Allan's books and expanded via many more garden books for years thereafter.

—*Carol Kinsey-Pope*

MIDDLESEX COUNTY
GROTON
GARDEN OF PEPE AND JOHN MAYNARD

  10–4

Our place, currently about 25 acres, was originally part of a much larger property, most of which was placed under conservation in 2006. We were attracted to it by the sweeping views to the west and the protection offered by hundreds of acres of surrounding fields and woodland, all protected from development.

Starting in the nineteenth century, successive large country houses had been built on the site, surrounded by the formal, high-maintenance gardens of the day.

The last of these rather grand houses was demolished in the 1960s. The succeeding generation of the previous owning family was more interested in breeding Black Angus than in horticulture. As a result the formal gardens had succumbed to neglect, bittersweet, and browsing deer by the time we purchased the property in 2007. At that time we had no interest in restoring formal gardens.

Our first steps were to plant an allée of small sugar maples along the lane leading to our barn, and to fence a small nursery area where we could stockpile plants and grow them safe from deer.

We dithered about building a deer fence around more of the property, fearing it would interfere with the view, but finally fenced about 15 acres. The fence enabled us to begin planting to create informal, naturalistic grounds using native plant material as much as possible. While the nursery is now empty and the maples in the allée have reached 8 inches in diameter, all the plantings are still young and have only begun to mature. Nonetheless we believe the grounds have grown in enough to reward unhurried exploration with a wide variety of trees and shrubs, and, in the spring, extensive plantings of daffodils and other bulbs.

The surrounding areas under conservation are open for walks, and a few remaining Black Angus add interest to the landscape. In the summer of 2020 an energetic couple working for us decided to clear out a small formal garden neglected for 25 years and overgrown to the point of invisibility. An exceptional stonemason rebuilt the dry stone walls over the winter and we began replanting in the early summer of 2021. An exceptionally wet summer helped to get new perennials established.

This garden's estimated size is 10 acres.

WORCESTER COUNTY
BOYLSTON
BERRY GARDEN
10–4

The Garden began as an open hayfield in 2021, and everything in the garden was planted by the owners. So much time and energy has been lavished on it that it has the feel of an established garden.

Many layers lead the visitor past a marvelous array of trees, shrubs, and herbaceous plants. The owners' great passion for plants is infectious. Parts of the garden are still evolving.

This garden's estimated size is 2 acres.

PETERSHAM
SWIFT RIVER FARM
  10–4

When Bruce and Gus acquired this 87-acre property in north central Massachusetts in 1998, there wasn't even the hint of a garden to be seen.

Over the next few years, an orchard of heirloom apple varieties was planted, stone walls built, and the first of several perennial gardens was installed.

A woodland garden filled with spring ephemerals, epimediums, hellebores, mukdenia, hostas, and small flowering trees and shrubs now stretches from the front of the house down along the north side of the property to a bed of tree peonies. There is also a large rock garden, a spring garden with primulas, and spring bulbs.

I

n 2010, Gordon Hayward created a master plan designed to unite the gardens, adding a water garden, a large pollinator meadow garden, an oak walk, and gravel paths allowing easy access between different areas.

Since 2012 Helen O'Donnell, garden designer and plantswoman extraordinaire, has been consulting on planting design and new garden projects.

WORCESTER
GARDEN OF MATT MATTUS AND JOE PHILIP
♿ 10–4

Matt's garden is a mature, third-generation family property in a suburban neighborhood. It contains many tall trees (now more than 90 feet tall) planted in the 1920s by his grandfather and father.

"The garden is an ongoing restoration project" says Matt. "I've never opened it up for tours as I've always believed that it was more of a small collector's garden than one that is 'tour-worthy', yet I know that most visitors enjoy the casual atmosphere, and the 'down the rabbit hole-ness' of a true collector's garden!"

Expect to see collections of interesting plants and greenhouse projects, sweet peas, stone and gravel paths, boxwood and hornbeam hedges, garden rooms, and even a small 100-year-old goldfish pond.

Charming and picturesque as a small English garden and as horticulturally interesting as a botanic garden, this 1½ acres is essentially a home garden, yet one that has recently been featured in *Martha Stewart Living*, *Better Homes and Gardens*, and other magazines.

154 Massachusetts   Register online: gardenconservancy.org/opendays

Matt Mattus, whose blog is Growingwithplants.com, is the author of *Mastering the Art of Vegetable Gardening* (2019) and *Mastering the Art of Growing Flowers* (2020).

Nearby Counties

- ESSEX
- MIDDLESEX

Saturday, May 18

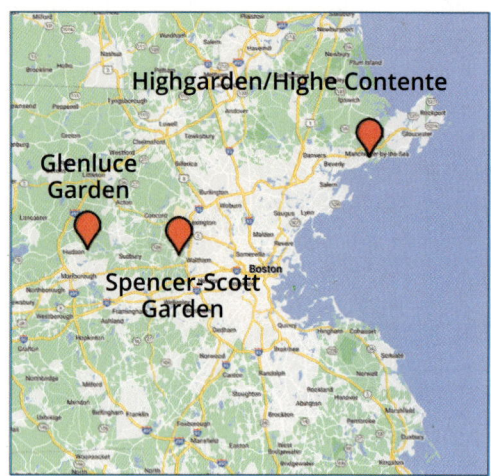

ESSEX COUNTY
MANCHESTER
HIGHGARDEN/HIGHE CONTENTE
NEW   🖋 10–4

The house was built in 1883 by Henry Lee Higgenson, founder of the Boston Symphony. The garden, designed by Fletcher Steele between 1931-1977, is a hilltop garden with ocean views, sculpture, and reflecting pool.

The garden was expanded by Catherine Hull between 1967-2005. I am in process for an application for the National Registry of Historic Places for the estate.

This garden's estimated size is 1 acre.

NEW 5 10 20 95 Year    No Photography    Accessibility    Nibbled Leaf Garden

💬 TROWEL TALK

I enjoy fine art, poetry, bonsai, design, and history, and ideally focusing on topics that involve all of the above. I love a story. The visual arts have always been a passion for me, focusing on many different mediums such as painting, photography, and sculpture.

My garden has been my "work in progress" for eight years. I am trained as an Interior Designer and Visual Artist, but I want to learn about horticulture from the members of the Garden Conservancy for the restoration of this garden.

—Paul R. Stremple

MIDDLESEX COUNTY
STOW

GLENLUCE GARDEN
  10–4

Glenluce Garden is a small, personal, and romantic garden. Entering by the western gate, you will find yourself on a mound with green paths beckoning in seven directions.

Explore these paths to discover a grove of paperbark maples, an island of tree peonies, or a border of fragrant native azaleas. A pergola covered by climbing roses leads to a frog pond shaded by heptacodium and a courtyard with raised vegetable beds.

Magnolias, rhododendrons, peonies, and roses abound in Glenluce Garden.

This garden's estimated size is 2/3 acre.

💬 TROWEL TALK

When the peonies or the roses bloom, it really doesn't matter if the flower beds are edged nicely or if the pergola has been pruned. But when the truly spectacular flowers are spent, then quieter beauties can also shine. I love them all!

—Katy

WESTON

SPENCER-SCOTT GARDEN
  10–4

Having been blessed with a sun-drenched site with deep loam, we set out to create a garden to satisfy our varied interests in flowering trees, shrubs, vines, ground covers, perennials, and bulbs. We designed, created, and maintain the garden. Included are rock gardens, partial shade gardens, dwarf evergreens, and perennial beds with walking paths, all set against an open meadow.

Of special interest are many varieties of peonies, species of old roses, iris, hardy geraniums, alliums, lilies, wildflowers, clematis, daylilies, azaleas, and rhododendrons.

It is amazing to us that we have collected more than 1,500 varieties over the years. Our efforts have been rewarded with delights for all our senses.

NEW 5 10 20 95 Year    No Photography    Accessibility    Nibbled Leaf Garden

156 Massachusetts   Register online: gardenconservancy.org/opendays

Nearby Counties

- **FRANKLIN**
- **HAMPDEN**
- **HAMPSHIRE**

Saturday, June 1

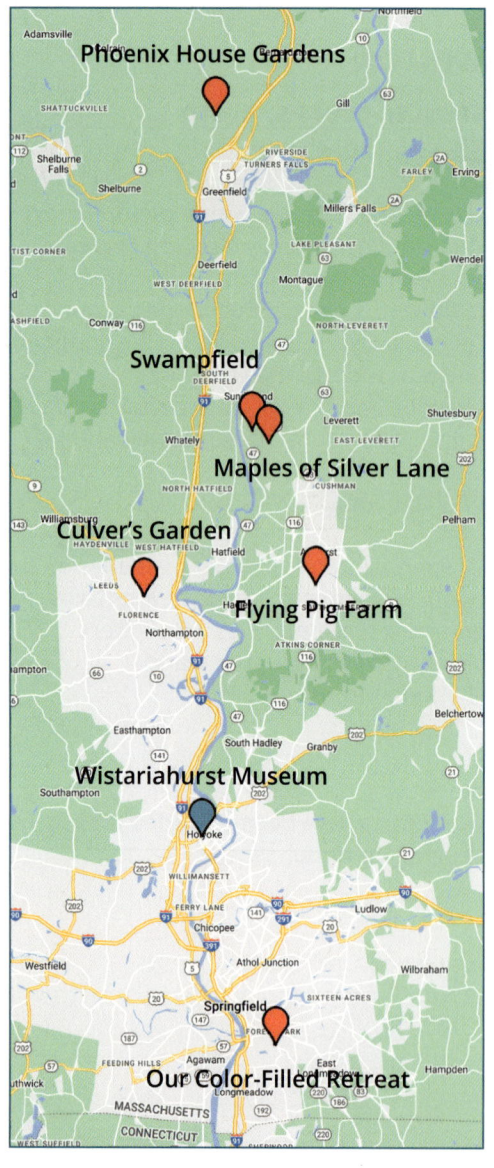

FRANKLIN COUNTY
GREENFIELD
PHOENIX HOUSE GARDENS
NEW   10–4

In 2008 I moved from the woods of Michigan to 2½ acres in the city of Greenfield. I had a relatively blank slate to work with.

I had trees and shrubs planted as a barrier next to the busy street. Then I created an 80-foot labyrinth with gardens leading up to and surrounding the center gazebo which holds a large, hollowed-out tree trunk with a seat and many carved animals. There is a small streambed with a Japanese bridge, and a back deck with a built-in water feature.

Behind an ancient and huge ash tree, I planted a berry patch and a vegetable garden, while off to the side are a variety of fruit trees and a grapevine. My desire to create a pollinator home for our many small-winged creatures was central to my thinking as well as creating a quiet refuge for myself and my friends.

Unfortunately, many small, four-legged creatures were drawn to this space as well, and I feel like the voles have a subway system underneath the whole property! Gardening is a vibrant and challenging love affair whose reward is a living connection to the earth.

This garden's estimated size is 1½ acres

💬 TROWEL TALK

My mother's Phoenix House Garden is the newest in a long series of gardens. At 89, she has been a gardener for a very long time. She was a member of

---

NEW 5 10 20 '95 Year    No Photography    Accessibility    Nibbled Leaf Garden

the Massachusetts Horticulture Society as a young housewife and helped with the annual flower show exhibitions. I remember during clean-up my brother and I were allowed to take the coins from the water features until it was decided that there was quite a bit of money in there, and suddenly children were not allowed to take them!

Elise's gardens were featured in *Better Homes and Gardens* along with the gardens of two friends of hers in town when we lived in Princeton, MA. She was horrified to see them cutting flower stems and moving them around for a better photo.

Newly divorced, Elise moved to the woods in Michigan in the 1980s and helped build her own house, creating gardens around the home and carving out a vegetable garden to feed the many people who came to the retreat center she helped run. Elise is not afraid to cut out plants that no longer work, as she did with the lilacs that had gotten overgrown around her deck here in Greenfield. Her keen sense of design and color makes her gardens a pleasure to explore. We look forward to your visit!

—*Elise's daughter Laura*

SUNDERLAND
MAPLES OF SILVER LANE
NEW   10–4

Maples of Silver Lane is my version of a contemporary Japanese stroll garden. It contains almost 80 Japanese maples (only a handful of repeats) amidst dwarf conifers and an enormous bed of hostas, all in a private zen-like setting. The ten-year-old garden, with rocks, a Japanese walkway, and a modern tearoom, was laid out to take advantage of an odd-shaped lot.

This garden's estimated size is ½ acre.

💬 TROWEL TALK

My first garden here was a cottage garden—it was an utter failure! Today there are hardly any flowers in my garden.

Instead, it's a garden filled with leaves of varying shapes, sizes, colors, and textures. Although some of my plants are more temperamental than others, I have no favorites and love them all equally.

As a novice gardener, it took me quite a while to recognize that plants will do their own thing, come what may: early frost/late frost, too much rain/too little rain, too much heat/perfect conditions, etc. Rarely does a tree grow quite the way I would like. Yet, I find it difficult to walk away from a Japanese maple or a conifer at a nursery. I want to take them all home even though I have completely run out of garden space.

I have also finally accepted that the daily imperfection of my (somewhat) crowded garden is perfection itself.

—*The Gardener*

SWAMPFIELD
NEW 10–4

This garden is open twice this year: June 1 and October 19.

When we moved here in 2015, the property was a blank slate. Since then, we have added 7,000 sq. feet of perennial border, in a mixture of sun and shade.

Our sunny borders are filled with classic cottage garden plants and many natives. While there's a playful exuberance, the color palette within each season is relatively limited—creating a sense of harmony and continuity as you explore the property. The two woodland gardens are lush, with towering actaeas and tiny primroses and everything in between.

The garden crescendos in the fall as mums, asters, sedums, and more explode alongside scores of ornamental grasses and shrubs—just as their foliage begins to take on exciting hues. Welcome to Swampfield!

This garden's estimated size is 7,000 sq. ft.

💬 TROWEL TALK

I didn't realize I was a gardener until I was 30 years old. Gardeners who have inspired me include Piet Oudolf, Nan Ondra, my mother, and my grandfather. Some of my favorite plants are hydrangeas, amsonias, actaeas, english primroses, and baptisias.

Because my soil is heavy clay, I struggle with any plant that requires sharply draining soil.

—*Bill Hodgeman*

HAMPDEN COUNTY
SPRINGFIELD
OUR COLOR-FILLED RETREAT
NEW   10–4

This garden is open twice this year: June 1 and August 3.

Half an acre overflowing with Itoh and tree peonies, scores of hydrangeas and David Austin roses, multicolor coneflowers, daisies, rudbeckia, and hundreds of other flowering plants and bushes surrounding multiple seating areas: pavilion, patio, fire pit pergola, teak Thai bench, and multilevel decks.

This garden's estimated size is ½ acre.

💬 TROWEL TALK

Vana has dirt in her veins growing up on a farm, and Al was inspired by the fields of tulips at the Keukenhof.

When they retired, they were determined to create a garden that provided many different views, meandering paths, and endless delight.

—*Vana and Al*

NEW   Year 🚫 No Photography ♿ Accessibility  Nibbled Leaf Garden

HAMPSHIRE COUNTY
AMHERST
FLYING PIG FARM
NEW   10–4

A rambling informal garden of quirks and delights, Flying Pig Farm (no pigs, no farm) has taken shape through twenty years of trial and error. The landscape has evolved to work with the natural contours left by the clay and ledges of the ice age.

There are colorful, manicured beds close to the eighteenth-century farmhouse, an incline of viburnums and azaleas, an enhanced meadow, and wandering woodland paths. Find a seat and enjoy views of the farm pond or the meditation garden

This garden's estimated size is 9 acres.

💬 TROWEL TALK

There is a small wooded area on our property. Twenty years ago it was a impenetrable mass of multiflora rose, poison ivy, and bittersweet which pulled and warped young volunteer trees. Over the years, the invasives have been tamed.

Although there are still scars from the vines, many trees are now fine, gracious New England specimens.

—*The Gardener*

FLORENCE
CULVER'S GARDEN
NEW   **10–4**

Together, we spent 70 years working the gardens and grounds of Smith College, which nurtures an old botanical garden. Our garden includes trees and shrubs started from seeds obtained through a global Index Seminum trade. Those plants are now 25 years old.

We have raised beds, perennial borders, a shade garden area, and spring ephemerals. Fruits, vegetables, herbs, roses, clematis, hellebores, peonies, lilies, and a chicken coop, too.

This garden's estimated size is ¼ acre.

💬 TROWEL TALK

My family moved to a small rural town a few minutes away when I was three. Our next-door neighbor was a lovely elderly woman with gorgeous gardens. I met her after I had wandered into her yard and pulled all the heads off of her tulips, and then offered them to her bunched up in my skirt.

She decided I was meant to be a gardener and became a mentor, walking me through our woodlands and introducing me to the natives. Her name was Emma Stuart, and she sparked a passion in me that survives now into my own old age.

—*Tracey Atwood Putnam, the name I had when I met Emma Stuart.*

160 Massachusetts   Register online: gardenconservancy.org/opendays

PUBLIC GARDEN
WISTARIAHURST MUSEUM

238 Cabot St
Holyoke, Massachusetts 01040

Wistariahurst is a cultural and educational center owned and operated by the City of Holyoke and supported by The Wistariahurst Foundation. Wistariahurst is dedicated to preserving Holyoke's history and inspiring an appreciation of history and culture through educational programs, exhibits and special events.

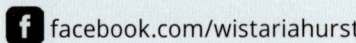
facebook.com/wistariahurst

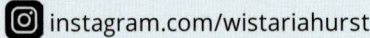
instagram.com/wistariahurst

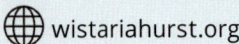
wistariahurst.org

Middlesex County
Saturday, June 15

Additional gardens are open nearby:
Hillsborough County, NH
　The Garden on Briarwood, Nashua, NH
　Hollis Village Edible Garden, Hollis, NH
　Lakeside Retreat, Hollis, NH
　New Shire Gardens, Manchester, NH
See page 191.

PEPPERELL
THE STONE SPHERE
NEW   　　10–4

This tranquil recuperative sanctuary stands as a mini arboretum meticulously designed, maintained, and cherished by its proprietor—an undertaking spanning a quarter century. This metamorphosis has seen the conversion of a cow pasture originally associated with the Nichols estate into ornamental gardens that grace the Cape-style domicile.

NEW 5 10 20 '95 Year    No Photography   Accessibility    Nibbled Leaf Garden

The Stone Sphere, a central hallmark of this garden, was skillfully fashioned by the owner, drawing inspiration from the Knockan Crag Globe in Scotland. This emblem also lends its name to the proprietor's recent literary offering. The circular motif embodies the concepts of self-integrity, cohesion, and spirituality. This abstract artwork assumes the role of a therapeutic instrument, echoing the sentiments of John Ruskin, who opined that "fine art is that in which the hand, the head, and the heart of man go together."

The gardens include a crab apple allée, New England stone walls, a farmer's pond, and a larger body of water. Taxus and boxwood hedgerows, meticulously groomed, partitioning the spaces in the various rooms, invite exploration.

A European-style vegetable garden, a contemplative Zen berry garden, a water feature, teak benches, beckoning to rest or convene. A formal bluestone patio and deck with pergola offer optimal vantage points to survey the undulating landscape and aqueous expanse.

This garden's estimated size is 2 acres.

💬 TROWEL TALK

I am profoundly fond of peonies, magnolias, conifers, Japanese maples, and the exquisite presence of stone within the garden. This garden marked the inauguration of my initial foray into the realm of gardening.

Despite my initial lack of expertise, I embarked on this endeavor with fervent enthusiasm that, in retrospect, resulted in an inadvertent mess of the canvas. A turning point arrived when a series of vivid dreams seemingly impelled me to enroll in a certificate program offered through Tower Hill Botanical Garden of five years of night classes. This period was defined by a dedicated pursuit of knowledge, wherein I honed my skills in garden design with a particular focus on my cherished property.

The genesis of the gardens was not solely grounded in personal preference, but also stirred by a higher source. They emerged as a conduit for processing traumatic stress, channeled through arduous physical exertion. Moreover, the nurturing cocoon of nature provided a therapeutic sanctuary for emotional healing.

My journey was a masterclass in creative adaptation, as I learned to harmonize my artistic inclinations with the natural contours of the land and the available resources at hand.

—*Suzanne Greco*

162   Massachusetts   Register online: gardenconservancy.org/opendays

Nearby Counties

- **FRANKLIN**
- **HAMPDEN**
- **HAMPSHIRE**

Saturday, June 29

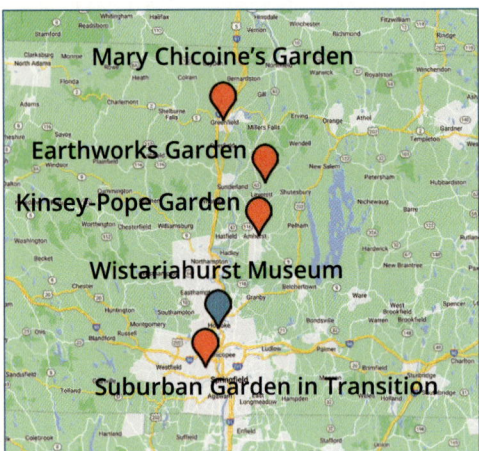

FRANKLIN COUNTY
GREENFIELD
MARY CHICOINE'S GARDEN
NEW   10–4

This in-town homestead on two-tenths of an acre of land is a testament to getting the most bounty and beauty out of a small property. Located along a busy street, the house and gardens are often admired by passersby, some who ask for help identifying an eye-catching plant and others who might leave with an armful of rainbow chard or some tender young squash.

More than ten years in the making, this property was transformed from lawn and hedges to an abundant mix of fruit trees and shrubs, perennial beds, and more. A goshen stone patio with a pond provides a place of rest in otherwise riotous full-sun front and side gardens; large trees edge the property behind the house, providing a shady respite in the summertime.

This garden's estimated size is ⅛ acre.

💬 TROWEL TALK

I love walking out into my gardens in the early midsummer mornings, while the air is still cool, and dew is still sparkling on flower buds. I seek out ingredients for breakfast—Japanese eggplant, some poblano peppers, a Wethersfield red onion.

Once the just-picked vegetables are sauteed and served on tender steaming rice, we sit at our window-side dining room table and gaze out on our gardens, watching mourning doves visit the pond and bees tumble in the hot pink blooms of our rugosa roses. Life is good.

—Mary C

LEVERETT
EARTHWORKS GARDEN
NEW   10–4

This garden is open twice this year: June 29 and September 28.

The Earthworks Garden is 4 acres carved onto a steep, rocky, southwest-facing hillside at the bottom of Rattlesnake Gutter. The garden was begun in 1984.

From the first the aim of the garden was design enhanced with sculpture. We have mature trees and shrub plantings anchoring all levels of the garden. We

NEW   5 10 20 '95 Year   No Photography   Accessibility   Nibbled Leaf Garden

feature a 135-year-old revamped Lord and Burnham greenhouse, numerous sculpture sites, and three garden buildings to gather and party in!

This garden's estimated size is 4 acres.

💬 **TROWEL TALK**

My favorite garden tool is an Excavator! When you come you will understand why!

—Michael B. Mazur

HAMPDEN COUNTY
WEST SPRINGFIELD
SUBURBAN GARDEN IN TRANSITION
NEW ♿ 10–4

We moved six years ago to a garden I referred to as lollipop trees, bonbon shrubs, and boring lawn. The plants had been constantly clipped so tight that all the flowering shrubs such as azaleas and rhododendrons did not flower for two years; the blue hollies produced no berries until the third year.

As the garden transitioned, numerous obstacles familiar to many home gardeners had to be dealt with: beautiful but overgrown shrubs, deer, moles, and voles, plants in the wrong place, poor soil, large trees, and being adjacent to wetlands.

Rather than tearing out the plants that were there we choose to work with them; changing their size when possible, moving them when necessary and adding interesting and unusual plants to highlight the garden.

The current garden is changing slowly to a mixture of natural forms, perennials, and flowing shrubs.

This garden's estimated size is 15,000 sq. ft.

💬 **TROWEL TALK**

My friends say I'm a plant addict and they are probably correct. I never met a perennial, shrub, or tree that I didn't want to try in my garden. Perennials are probably my favorites, but any plant with interesting color such as variegation or shape such as yucca will make it onto my wish list.

I buy and plant them where they should grow but don't baby them—my version of tough love. I am a fearless transplanter who hates to throw out anything that's in the wrong place or not doing well. I have been known to move a perennial, shrub, or small tree two and three times to give it its best chance of flourishing, but in the end, it's up to the plant to survive.

There are certain plants I have repeatedly tried in a number of different garden settings which always eventually die. These include hellebores, Epimedium, coreopsis, and astilbe. On the other hand, my clematis vines flower continually, hostas grow from seeds, and 'Bloodgood' Japanese maple and kousa dogwood seedlings have to be weeded out of planting beds they grow so thickly.

My previous gardens emphasized native plants, natural forms, informal plantings, and water features. These characteristics have not been as easy to implement in my current garden as I had originally thought they would be. I keep working in that direction.

In recent years I've acquired a substantial collection of various orchids and semitropical and hardy bonsai. These

---

NEW 5 10 20 '95 Year  No Photography ♿ Accessibility  Nibbled Leaf Garden

keep me busy in the winter months while I wait for the garden to awaken in the spring. In the summer they move outside onto the deck for their vacation.

I love working in my garden, especially hand-pruning my shrubs and trees. I find it mentally challenging as I make decisions on where to trim but relaxing as well.

As opposed to many gardeners, I don't mind weeding as long as I have my Cape Cod hand weeder in hand. My least favorite chore is dealing with landscape fabric and rock "mulch" which were used extensively in my current home.

—Paula V.

HAMPSHIRE COUNTY

AMHERST

KINSEY-POPE GARDEN

NEW   10–1, 1–5

This garden is open three times this year: May 11, June 29, and October 19.

This is a garden begun by my late husband and me (both academics with no formal garden training) soon after we moved here in 1978, working and learning together for twenty years.

I have been the primary garden designer from the beginning, and designer and gardener for another twenty years, now recently with some wonderful garden help. It is a landscape of many uncommon trees with strikingly beautiful bark and a wide variety of textures, flowers, berries, and great autumn color; many shrubs with more than one season of beauty; perennials flowering in three seasons; ground covers of unusual dramatic effect covering all beds during all seasons; and in winter offering a wide palette of interesting shapes, lovely bark, and many evergreen trees and shrubs.

In addition, there are three bridges over a stone-lined swale, a hand-built screened gazebo and curved top arbor, a charming little pond, many benches and Japanese stone lanterns, large-stone walkways and stone walls, and a Japanese inspired fence surrounding all of the ½-acre garden.

💬 TROWEL TALK

I have no formal training in garden design, but when my husband was diagnosed with cancer, I quit my academic job to spend more time with him and began

NEW 5 10 20 '95 Year   No Photography   ♿ Accessibility   🍃 Nibbled Leaf Garden reading everything about gardens and garden design. We then made the task of creating our garden a major focus together for the five years of time he eventually had.

During that time, friends and colleagues began asking for my design help, and I suddenly became a garden designer with many clients. When my husband was diagnosed with cancer, he was allowed to give up tasks other than teaching and meeting with students. So, we had more time together, and I began reading all sorts of garden books, especially Michael Dirr's excellent tomes, and my husband and I worked and focused constantly in/on the garden. Later we met the Dirrs here in Amherst and were invited to come visit them in Georgia, which we did.

In 1998, my husband passed away. In 2000, Michael (along with Allan Armitage) came for a weekend of fundraising events and talks at Amherst College to benefit a memorial garden I had designed for my husband that was installed at our local library by me, his grad students, colleagues, and our friends and family. All this to explain, that most of what I know about gardening started with Michael's and Allan's books and expanded via many more garden books for years thereafter.

—Carol Kinsey-Pope

PUBLIC GARDEN
WISTARIAHURST MUSEUM

238 Cabot St
Holyoke, Massachusetts 01040

Wistariahurst is a cultural and educational center owned and operated by the City of Holyoke and supported by The Wistariahurst Foundation. Wistariahurst is dedicated to preserving Holyoke's history and inspiring an appreciation of history and culture through educational programs, exhibits and special events.

facebook.com/wistariahurst

instagram.com/wistariahurst

wistariahurst.org

Essex County
Saturday, July 20

MARBLEHEAD
TICEHURST
NEW 10–4

This is a young garden, about 3–4 years old. It was previously a lawn with a small patch of perennials that has been transformed into an oasis. It is dynamic and changing with the seasons—creating privacy using organic forms.

I love the combination of trees, shrubs, flowering perennials, bulbs mixed with the smattering of annuals we choose each year. It is mostly native plants, very low maintenance and a haven for birds, bees, butterflies. It brings us so much joy—every day.

💬 TROWEL TALK

My first garden was a small strip of colorful flowering perennials that I picked randomly because I liked the flower color. This garden is like an ever-changing painting or symphony- it all works well together and different plants come in and out of focus depending on the month. It always looks beautiful even in the winter months; it is sculptural.

—Mimi, Henry, and Larry!

SALEM
RENAISSANCE ITALY COMES TO RIVER STREET, SALEM
NEW 10–4

Nestled among the dense period homes located at the northern edge of Salem's famed McIntire Historic District, this delightful urban garden of only 2049 square feet immediately transports the visitor out of eighteenth-century Salem into Renaissance Italy through the use of interlocking garden rooms; multiple east/west and north/south axes and changes of levels; tall arborvitae bushes; dense hedging; ingenious brick and granite paving throughout; water features with vintage millstone fountains; a 6,700-pound, four-foot-diameter brownstone column base from an early nineteenth-century Greek Revival Salem Theater (which forms the centerpiece of one of the garden rooms); and a profusion of vintage cast iron and terra cotta building fragments providing accents of instant antiquity, punctuated by the owners' collection of antique Italian terra cotta pots bulging with flowers throughout.

 All in all, a magical space for alfresco dining, entertaining, reading, relaxing, or quiet introspection!

This garden's estimated size is 2,050 sq. ft.

💬 TROWEL TALK

Though redolent of age and antiquity, one truly amazing aspect of this garden is that it is less than 25 years old, and was created only after the demands of raising the owners' three sons.

Another is that the garden was designed by the owners themselves without professional landscape advice or help, all the more remarkable because the owners are entirely self-taught, and that everything you see, both hardscape and plantings, were created either by the owners themselves, or with the help of friends and neighbors.

Take a moment to experience the rest of the street, of which this house and garden is such an integral part. When the owners purchased their circa 1788 home on May 16, 1973, River Street looked very differently than how it looks today. Most of the structures on the street, then as now all located directly on the sidewalk, were predominately multi-family, absentee-owned, and in such deplorable condition that many of them seemed about to implode. One eighteenth-century dwelling had been abandoned and another didn't even have modern indoor heating or an indoor bathroom as late as 1977.

Fortunately, the owners were followed by an influx of other new young owners who also recognized the underlying value and potential of the street as a family-orientated urban neighborhood of great period charm and human scale.

Since 1973, one by one, through the tireless efforts of those new families who were also willing to take on the challenge and risk of buying and restoring their own homes—mostly using their own sweat equities—River Street was transformed into the historic residential urban oasis that you see today.

The neighbors themselves installed the brick sidewalks lining both sides of the street, bought and planted all of the trees, created the raised planting bed at the head of the street, and envisioned and had installed the compass rose imbedded in the brick sidewalk, the first in the city of Salem to commemorate their sidewalk achievement.

The owners maintain that their garden will never be completed, and that is as it should be, not least because their continuing garden efforts give them such joy and contentment, and keeps them young, or at least as young as one has a right to feel at their age!

—*John and Carol Carr*

NEW 5 10 20 '95 Year    No Photography    Accessibility    Nibbled Leaf Garden

Berkshire County

Saturday, July 27

Additional gardens are open nearby :
Dutchess County, NY
  Highgrove Cottage, Millerton, NY
  Lithgow Cottage Garden, Lithgow, NY
See page 286.

Litchfield County, CT:
  Sculpturedale, Kent, CT
  Juniper Ledge, Lakeville, CT
  Fernwood, Norfolk, CT
  Lagniappe Garden, Washington, CT
See page 117.

ASHLEY FALLS
GARDEN OF JEFFREY A. STEELE
10–4

The garden has been created over the last twenty-five years, with many changes along the way, to complement a small Greek Revival house. No master plan was ever drawn, the garden (all self-maintained) evolving according to whim, available time, and, of course, funds.

The intent was to make an attractive and interesting garden to be in and wander through, with views and focal points throughout and from the house. The result is a series of seven connected circles, with both formal and informal side gardens of favorite plants, particularly hostas and daffodils.

This garden's estimated size is 2½ acres.

💬 TROWEL TALK

Over the years I have created a daffodil (my favorite flower) woodland, with about 500 varieties planted in clumps or drifts of 25 to 200 bulbs of each variety. There is something truly wonderful about sitting with my dogs and a mug of tea in the early morning quiet, watching the spring sun rise and kiss the tops of the daffodils.

A foggy morning makes it purely magical. It is my favorite part of the garden. Having planted all the daffodils individually with a simple hand trowel, it is therefore my favorite gardening tool.

—*Jeff Steele*

Berkshire County
Sunday, July 28

Additional gardens are open nearby:
Columbia County, NY
  Rockland Farm, New Canaan, NY
See page 291.

WEST STOCKBRIDGE
KINGSMONT
 10–4

Our garden is located on a 12-acre site in the Berkshire Mountains of western Massachusetts near the border with New York state. The land, once part of a summer camp, is terraced down the eastern side of Harvey Mountain, which is immediately west of the site.

We began to develop the gardens in 2010 after converting the former camp gymnasium into our home. Gardens now surround the house on all sides. We started by planting a front border made up of evergreen and deciduous trees, then moved on to other areas of the garden.

The circular drive in front of the house is surrounded by borders of flowering trees, shrubs, grasses and perennials. Since the house is stained a strong color, the plantings closer to the house (mainly mixed borders) emphasize different shades of green with varying foliage shapes and textures.

Between the house and barn is a bank with a mixed planting of trees, shrubs, perennials and floral carpet roses (Tesselaar, Amber). Adjacent to the barn is a trellised garden with raised vegetable beds and apple trees. On the north side of the barn are cutting beds of mostly annuals started from seeds. They are bordered on the north by a stone retaining wall, and a bank of hydrangeas, *Cornus mas*, and fastigiate oaks.

Behind the house and barn, a grassy bank punctuated by London plane trees runs down to a large pond flanked by mature maple, pine, oak, and spruce trees The pond, designed by Anthony Archer Wills, was built in 2017 and has provided us with a new and interesting set of gardening challenges. Continuing to the south of the pond, the banks feature beds of tall grasses and flowering shrubs. One bed surrounds an array of solar collectors. To the east the solar array is an experimental xeriscape garden (in very gravelly soil) adjacent to one naturalized meadow and overlooking another.

Coming back up the stone step path to the house level leads to a lawn that extends southward from the house between stone walls and flanking beds into the remains of an old sugar maple allée.

This garden's estimated size is 5 acres.

NEW 5 10 20 '95 Year    No Photography    Accessibility    Nibbled Leaf Garden

💬 TROWEL TALK

My husband and I began gardening in Wellesley as second owners of a Colonial Revival house built in 1905. The house needed much work and its gardens no longer existed. After years of gardening and some hardscaping, we had turned our ½-acre into a Massachusetts Horticultural Society award-winning garden featured in *Wellesley Weston* magazine and on garden tours sponsored by Mass Hort and the Tower Hill Botanical Garden.

After 30+ years in Wellesley, we moved to the Berkshires and embarked on a new gardening and landscaping challenge—12 acres that were formerly part of a summer camp—which has occupied us over the past thirteen years.

In both locations, it took us time to learn the horticultural characteristics of the land across the seasons and what plants would work there. For us, it has been a deliberate but pleasurable endeavor to create gardens.

—*Sherry and Dan Kasper*

WALFORD
NEW   10–4

We named our garden Walford because of our admiration for and strong attachment to our street, West Alford Road. Our land consists of 6 acres, most of which is meadow. The property was somewhat barren and, we were told, was initially a gravel pit.

There were hidden gems mixed in the surrounding woods along with beautiful species of trees that we cultivated, transplanted, and nurtured. We started with a small perennial garden around the house which evolved to multiple beds, a greenhouse, and a meadow full of wildflowers, milkweed, and of course, butterflies.

Some of the beds have specific themes such as catmint and Russian sage—the purple theme. Another with hydrangea and sedum with a popup of poppies to add striking colors. Also, a bed with elderberry, fringe, and cherry trees mixed with mini asters, delphinium, cosmos, roses, and several other interesting plants. There are two huge beds of echinacea which add to our beautiful palette of purples, pinks, white, and multiple shades of green with something flowering every minute throughout the season.

This garden's estimated size is 3 acres.

💬 TROWEL TALK

At one time I would have called myself a city girl. We lived in a suburb of New York, and I often complained about the "seclusion" of our little house and lack of lighting.

My first garden was in our backyard under huge oak trees, which proved quite challenging for flowers. I thought I would never have any success. Still, I became fascinated with gardens, especially after visiting Dumbarton Oaks in Washington, DC and viewing old estates on Long Island. The house we have now is the complete opposite—several open acres and tons of sun, which of course, was challenging in different ways.

We learned from tours of botanical gardens and estate visits about local flowers. We had some help, as well, from local gardeners. I love the idea of gentle

---

NEW 5 10 20 '95 Year    No Photography    Accessibility   🍃 Nibbled Leaf Garden

Hampden County

Saturday, August 3

color variation with an occasional pop of color. Beds should always have something blooming, and they should always be fun. For example, allium and drumsticks add a quirky whimsical touch, and the way they move in the wind makes the garden sing. Later, as these die off, tall verbena with its simple elegant shape coupled with meadow rue makes the garden dance with delicacy.

My husband, who helps me in the garden, primarily takes care of the vegetable garden. We also have a recent addition—our greenhouse—where he starts the annuals and his vegetables from seeds. He is an avid reader, scientist, and rule follower, understanding the chemistry of gardening, whereas I just go for the "gusto." If it works, great! If it doesn't, I change it and move on! I like to get my hands dirty, which makes my hands my favorite tool.

I love to weed and deadhead, so my garden repays me with beautiful blooms and constant inspiration. It is important to fine-tune the garden by changing plants that are too high or too low, skimpy, or poor flower producers. I am always moving plants to different beds. I also like the idea of a single flower concept.

We have two large echinacea beds; one is all pink and the other is multicolored. The multicolored bed was created by my husband and me from seeds harvested from existing plants. It was so exciting to see that we could do it. Hours of beauty and satisfaction is how the garden repays us. Thank you, dear garden.

—Lydia G

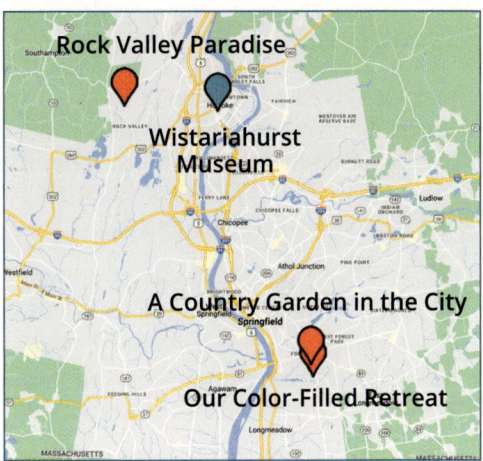

HOLYOKE
ROCK VALLEY PARADISE
NEW 10–4

This garden is open twice this year: August 3 and October 19.

The garden is my sanctuary, my activity, and my happy place. Although I do have flowers and herbs, my passion is food for the family.

The spot includes a small orchard of fifteen fruit trees, apples, peaches, plums, pears, apricots, and cherries. Our berries include blueberries, goji berries, elderberries, and black, red, and champagne currants. The concord grapes provide us with lots of juice for the winter months.

Seasonally we grow all five kinds of tomatoes, cucumbers, peppers, squash, eggplant, and all the other "regular veggies."

Our homestead also boasts two dairy goats, a dozen chickens, and a hive of honey bees. The joy I get from my hands working the soil is better than any therapy.

This garden's estimated size is ¼ acre.

💬 TROWEL TALK

I've always loved a garden with fresh veggies. When we started, I simply tilled a plot of soil and started planting. I spent all my time weeding and only received a small yield. New house = weird soil.

I decided to put in a few raised beds, and everything took off. I then became out of control with joy and excitement. We now have 22 raised beds with a ¼-acre garden area.

—I eat fresh because I can

SPRINGFIELD

A COUNTRY GARDEN IN THE CITY
NEW ♿ 🍃 10–4

When Ralph D'Amico and Bob Pellin first moved to their home, the main design element was the lawn, with a few large pine trees in the rear. Removal of those trees enabled the start of true gardens.

Lots of shade meant lots of container gardens with blasts of color from annuals. A wealth of hostas was also added.

The backyard is now divided into three small garden "rooms." Thirty-nine years of plantings means the lawn is now minimal. Specimen trees such as their favorite mimosa tree help give their yard a homey atmosphere.

A lovely weeping cherry, lost during the October 2011 snowstorm, was replaced with a "Fern Grotto" and a small brick patio.

The gardens are the summer home of their numerous houseplants, including Ralph's prize-winning *Clivia miniata*. Recent additions include a garden on the side of their home with numerous native perennials benefiting pollinators. Their hope is to establish an English Country Garden feel in their inner-city neighborhood.

This garden's estimated size is 1,000 sq. ft.

OUR COLOR-FILLED RETREAT
NEW ♿ 🍃 10–4

This garden is open twice this year: June 1 and August 3.

Half an acre overflowing with Itoh and tree peonies, scores of hydrangeas and David Austin roses, multicolor coneflowers, daisies, rudbeckia, and hundreds of other flowering plants and bushes surrounding multiple seating area: pavilion, patio, fire pit pergola, teak Thai bench, and multilevel decks.

This garden's estimated size is ½ acre.

💬 TROWEL TALK

Vana has dirt in her veins growing up on a farm, and Al was inspired by the fields of tulips at the Keukenhof.

When they retired, they were determined to create a garden that provided many different views, meandering paths, and endless delight.

—Vana and Al

Register online: gardenconservancy.org/opendays   Massachusetts 173

PUBLIC GARDEN
WISTARIAHURST MUSEUM

**238 Cabot St
Holyoke, Massachusetts 01040**

Wistariahurst is a cultural and educational center owned and operated by the City of Holyoke and supported by The Wistariahurst Foundation. Wistariahurst is dedicated to preserving Holyoke's history and inspiring an appreciation of history and culture through educational programs, exhibits and special events.

facebook.com/wistariahurst

instagram.com/wistariahurst

wistariahurst.org

Bristol County
Saturday, September 14

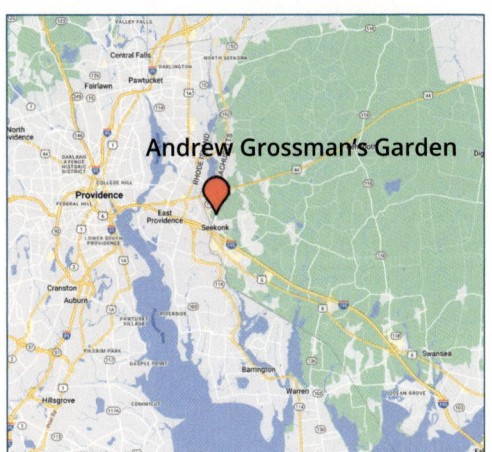

Andrew Grossman's Garden

Additional gardens are open nearby:
Providence County, RI
  College Hill Urban Oasis, Providence, RI
  The Garden at Power Street, Providence, RI
  Sycamore Farm Community Garden, Providence, RI
See page 324.

SEEKONK
ANDREW GROSSMAN'S GARDEN

5   partial   10–4

My 1-acre property, which borders the Martin Wildlife Refuge and the Runnins River, is home to a wide variety of perennials, grasses, shrubs, and flowering trees. In the spring of 2021 we completed work on a swimming pool garden, which is planted with a low maintenance assortment of predominantly summer-blooming favorites.

The remainder of the property includes a blue-and-white garden with a rectangular lily pond, a hot-colored garden with a checkerboard thyme patio, a cottage

NEW 5 10 20 95 Year    No Photography    Accessibility    Nibbled Leaf Garden

Middlesex County
Saturday, September 14

garden planted with roses and other old-fashioned cultivars, and a rustic pond surrounded by bog plantings.

There is also a cutting garden currently planted with David Austin roses, dinner plate dahlias, and sunflowers. The house and property has been featured in numerous national publications, including *Design New England*, *Old House Journal*, *Garden Gate*, *Flower*, *Country Living Gardener*, *Country Home*, and *Fine Gardening*. In 2016 the gardens were awarded first place in HGTV's Gorgeous Gardens competition.

This garden's estimated size is 1 acre.

💬 TROWEL TALK

Of all the months in the year, September is undoubtedly my favorite. After muddling through August's heat and humidity, my gardens and I breathe a sigh of relief. Cooler nights and dry, sunny days give rise to a host of late summer and early autumn blooms.

My beloved dahlias take center stage, their dinner plate blossoms accompanied by hydrangeas, grasses, asters, chelone, and of course the fluttering wings of monarch butterflies.

—Andrew

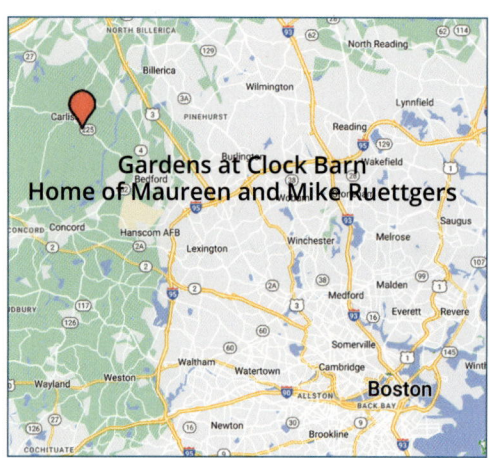

CARLISLE
GARDENS AT CLOCK BARN - HOME OF MAUREEN AND MIKE RUETTGERS
  ♿ partial   10–4

The Ruettgers family have been gardening here for nearly 40 years, although their house and drying barn date to 1790.

Entering the gardens through an arched gate, explore the old barn with trays full of herbs and flowers from the adjacent cutting garden. These trays were built as a 1930s WPA Project for drying digitalis leaves used medicinally.

East of the barn are beds of flowers, vegetables, and herbs that are rotated throughout the season. An adjacent Belgian fence espalier encloses a garden room displaying calendulas, *Verbena bonariensis*, other herbs, and ornamental vegetables. Beyond the cordon of pears is the new fall border featuring *Salvia madrensis*, tithonia, Abyssinian banana, and many dahlias.

Near the center of the property, a grape arbor leads to a walled garden with four quadrants anchored by antique roses. Mixed borders there feature sweeps of nasturtiums, 'Amistad' and 'Indigo Spires' salvia, 'Prairie Sun' rudbeckia, heleniums, and edible herbs. A second tier is flanked by two reflecting pools ringed by *Allium lusitanicum* and herbal tapestries.

The greenhouse and potting areas are filled with scented geraniums, succulents, gingers, bay, and rosemary varietals.

Beyond, a canopy of 100-year-old oaks shades woodland gardens. Favorite woodland plantings include *Paeonia japonica* and *P. obovata*, anemones, epimediums, *Kirengeshoma palmata*, and hosta from the garden of Francis Williams.

Look for the new tree fort, a koi pond, sculptures, and choice specimens of dogwood, magnolia, and maple. Pass through a hornbeam arch to the Clock Barn.

Up on the patio at the house, investigate a collection of Italian pots and troughs filled with favorite specimens, then go around the corner to discover the secret garden.

Franklin County
Saturday, September 28

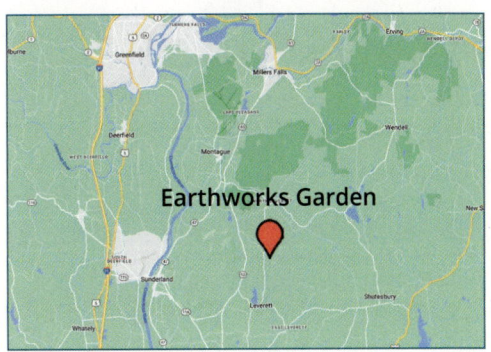

LEVERETT
EARTHWORKS GARDEN
NEW 🖋 10–4

This garden is open twice this year: June 29 and September 28.

The Earthworks Garden is 4 acres carved onto a steep, rocky, southwest-facing hillside at the bottom of Rattlesnake Gutter. The garden was begun in 1984.

From the first the aim of the garden was design enhanced with sculpture. We have mature trees and shrub plantings anchoring all levels of the garden. We feature a 135-year-old revamped Lord and Burnham greenhouse, numerous sculpture sites, and three garden buildings to gather and party in!

This garden's estimated size is 4 acres.

💬 **TROWEL TALK**

My favorite garden tool is an Excavator! When you come you will understand why!

—Michael B. Mazur

Nearby Counties

- **FRANKLIN**
- **HAMPDEN**
- **HAMPSHIRE**

Saturday, October 19

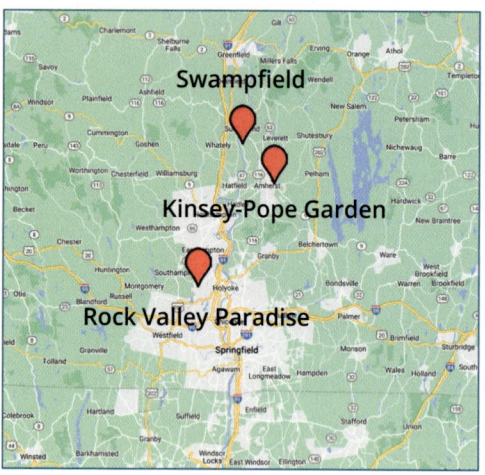

Gardens are also open this day in nearby Hampden and Hampshire counties.

FRANKLIN COUNTY
SUNDERLAND
SWAMPFIELD
NEW   10–4

This garden is open twice this year: June 1 and October 19.

When we moved here in 2015, the property was a blank slate. Since then, we have added 7,000 sq. feet of perennial border, in a mixture of sun and shade. Our sunny borders are filled with classic cottage garden plants and many natives. While there's a playful exuberance, the color palette within each season is relatively limited—creating a sense of harmony and continuity as you explore the property. The two woodland gardens are lush, with towering actaeas and tiny primroses and everything in between.

The garden crescendos in the fall as mums, asters, sedums, and more explode alongside scores of ornamental grasses and shrubs—just as their foliage begins to take on exciting hues. Welcome to Swampfield!

This garden's estimated size is 7,000 sq. ft.

💬 **TROWEL TALK**

I didn't realize I was a gardener until I was 30 years old. Gardeners who have inspired me include Piet Oudolf, Nan Ondra, my mother, and my grandfather. Some of my favorite plants are hydrangeas, amsonias, actaeas, english primroses, and baptisias. Because my soil is heavy clay, I struggle with any plant that requires sharply draining soil.

—*Bill Hodgeman*

NEW Year  No Photography  Accessibility 🍃 Nibbled Leaf Garden

HAMPDEN COUNTY
HOLYOKE
ROCK VALLEY PARADISE
NEW   10–4

*This garden is open twice this year:
August 3 and October 19.*

The garden is my sanctuary, my activity, and my happy place. Although I do have flowers and herbs, my passion is food for the family.

The spot includes a small orchard of fifteen fruit trees, apples, peaches, plums, pears, apricots, and cherries. Our berries include blueberries, goji berries, elderberries, and black, red, and champagne currants. The concord grapes provide us with lots of juice for the winter months. Seasonally we grow all five kinds of tomatoes, cucumbers, peppers, squash, eggplant, and all the other "regular veggies."

Our homestead also boasts two dairy goats, a dozen chickens, and a hive of honey bees. The joy I get from my hands working the soil is better than any therapy.

This garden's estimated size is ¼ acre.

💬 TROWEL TALK

I've always loved a garden with fresh veggies. When we started, I simply tilled a plot of soil and started planting. I spent all my time weeding and only received a small yield. New house = weird soil. I decided to put in a few raised beds, and everything took off. I then became out of control with joy and excitement. We now have 22 raised beds with a ¼-acre garden area.

—*I eat fresh because I can*

HAMPSHIRE COUNTY
AMHERST
KINSEY-POPE GARDEN
NEW   10–1, 1–5

*This garden is open three times this year:
May 11, June 29, and October 19.*

This is a garden begun by my late husband and me (both academics with no formal garden training) soon after we moved here in 1978, working and learning together for twenty years.

I have been the primary garden designer from the beginning, and designer and gardener for another twenty years, now recently with some wonderful garden help. It is a landscape of many uncommon trees with strikingly beautiful bark and a wide variety of textures, flowers, berries, and great autumn color; many shrubs with more than one season of beauty; perennials flowering in three seasons; ground covers of unusual dramatic effect covering all beds during all seasons; and in winter offering a wide palette of interesting shapes, lovely bark, and many evergreen trees and shrubs.

In addition, there are three bridges over a stone-lined swale, a hand-built screened gazebo and curved top arbor, a charming little pond, many benches and Japanese stone lanterns, large-stone walkways and stone walls, and a Japanese inspired fence surrounding all of the ½-acre garden.

💬 TROWEL TALK

I have no formal training in garden design, but when my husband was diagnosed with cancer, I quit my academic job to spend more time with him and began

---

NEW   Year   No Photography    Accessibility    Nibbled Leaf Garden

reading everything about gardens and garden design. We then made the task of creating our garden a major focus together for the five years of time he eventually had.

During that time, friends and colleagues began asking for my design help, and I suddenly became a garden designer with many clients. When my husband was diagnosed with cancer, he was allowed to give up tasks other than teaching and meeting with students. So, we had more time together, and I began reading all sorts of garden books, especially Michael Dirr's excellent tomes, and my husband and I worked and focused constantly in/on the garden. Later we met the Dirrs here in Amherst and were invited to come visit them in Georgia, which we did.

In 1998, my husband passed away. In 2000, Michael (along with Allan Armitage) came for a weekend of fundraising events and talks at Amherst College to benefit a memorial garden I had designed for my husband that was installed at our local library by me, his grad students, colleagues, and our friends and family. All this to explain, that most of what I know about gardening started with Michael's and Allan's books and expanded via many more garden books for years thereafter.

—*Carol Kinsey-Pope*

Ilona's Garden - Williamstown, MA
Photo: Brian Jones

Become a Garden Host or a Regional Ambassador

See page 374 or contact us at **opendays@gardenconservancy.org** to learn more.

Fernwood Botanical Garden - Niles, MI
Photo: the Garden Host

Michigan

182 Michigan Register online: gardenconservancy.org/opendays

Apple blossom
Pyrus coronaria

COMING SOON

This year, we are pleased to have the Open Days program return to Michigan for the first time since 2006.

Enjoy this extraordinary opportunity to visit several of the area's finest gardens, presented in partnership with Fernwood Botanical Garden.

Berrien County

Date and details are forthcoming.

Michigan 183

**NONPROFIT PARTNER
PUBLIC GARDEN**

FERNWOOD BOTANICAL GARDEN

13988 Range Line Rd
Niles, Michigan 49120

Fernwood's mission is to enrich people's lives by awakening and deepening their appreciation of nature. The garden has been a natural and an educational resource in the region for nearly 60 years. Founded in 1964, Fernwood became a public garden and today offers 105 acres of cultivated gardens, an arboretum, prairie restoration, conservatory, and natural areas on the majestic St. Joseph River.

The Sims Education Center, designed by noted architects, Stanley Tigerman and Margaret McCurry, opened in 2018, and is the last project of renowned American architect, Stanley Tigerman.

Today, more than 30,000 guests visit Fernwood and may enjoy self-guided tours, lecture series, workshops, public programs and excursions, field trips and summer camps for youth, and partnerships with colleges and universities throughout Michigan and northwest Indiana.

Fernwood is just minutes to the shore of Lake Michigan and the University of Notre Dame, and 90 minutes to Chicago.

facebook.com/fernwoodbotanical

instagram.com/fernwood.botanical

fernwoodbotanical.org

NEW 5 10 20 '95 Year   No Photography   Accessibility   Nibbled Leaf Garden

Missouri Botanical Garden - St. Louis, MO
Photo: Cassidy Moody

Missouri

MISSOURI

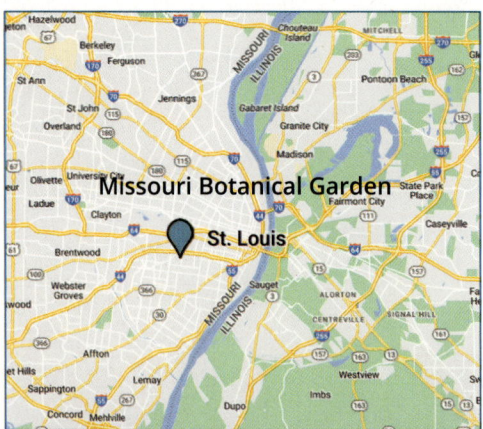

NONPROFIT PARTNER
PUBLIC GARDEN

MISSOURI BOTANICAL GARDEN

4344 Shaw Blvd
St. Louis, Missouri 63110

Founded in 1859, the Missouri Botanical Garden is the nation's oldest botanical garden in continuous operation and a National Historic Landmark.

The Garden's mission is "to discover and share knowledge about plants and their environment in order to preserve and enrich life."

The Garden is a center for botanical research and science education, as well as an oasis in the city of St. Louis. The Garden offers 79 acres of beautiful horticultural display, including a 14-acre Japanese strolling garden, historic architecture, a Children's Garden, and one of the world's largest collections of rare and endangered flora.

In addition to the Garden, the Missouri Botanical Garden has two other properties outside the city limits. The Sophia M. Sachs Butterfly House, located in Chesterfield, MO, allows visitors to mingle with more than a thousand live butterflies as they fly freely in a lush tropical conservatory.

Shaw Nature Reserve in Gray Summit, MO, features more than 2,400 acres of tall grass prairie, wetlands, and woodlands.

facebook.com/missouribotanicalgarden/

instagram.com/mobotgarden

missouribotanicalgarden.org

NEW 5 10 20 95 Year   No Photography   Accessibility   Nibbled Leaf Garden

ST. LOUIS GARDEN TOUR
Sunday, June 9, 2024

The Members' Board of the Missouri Botanical Garden is pleased to present its triennial Garden Tour, a self-guided tour of 11 spectacular home gardens at the peak of their early summer splendor. Proceeds benefit the Missouri Botanical Garden's plant science, conservation, and education work.

$65 per person | $50 for Garden Conservancy Members

Tickets on sale February 1
at mobot.org/gardentour
or (314) 577-5100.

Skatutakee Farm - Hancock, NH
Photo: the Garden Host

New Hampshire

190 New Hampshire

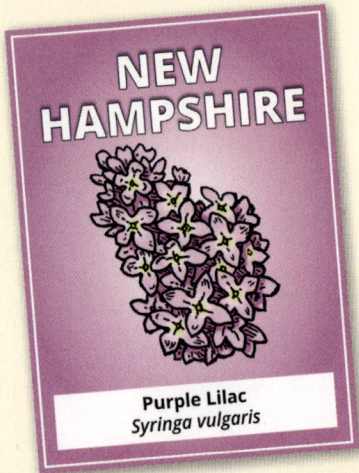
Purple Lilac
Syringa vulgaris

Open Days dates and times by County, Town, and Garden

CHESHIRE
Walpole
Boggy Meadow Farm
  Sunday, June 30, 10–4
Distant Hill Gardens - Garden of Michael and Kathy Nerrie
  Sunday, August 11, 10–4
Gilsum
Hollows End
  Sunday, August 11, 10–4
Spofford
Shooting Star Farm
  Saturday, June 30, 10–4
Westmoreland
Gardens of Ellen and Bruce Clement
  Sunday, June 30, 12–4

HILLSBOROUGH
Hollis
Hollis Village Edible Garden
  Saturday, June 15, 10–4
Lakeside Retreat
  Saturday, June 15, 10–4
Manchester
New Shire Gardens
  Saturday, June 15, 10–4
Nashua
The Garden On Briarwood
  Saturday, June 15, 10–4

MONADNOCK REGION
Hancock
Skatutakee Farm
  Saturday, August 24, 10–5
Jaffrey
The Garden of Nan Quick
  Saturday, August 24, 10–4
Peterborough
Fry Garden
  Saturday, August 24, 10–4
Michael and Betsy Gordon
  Saturday, August 24, 10–4

NEW HAMPSHIRE

Hillsborough County
Saturday, June 15

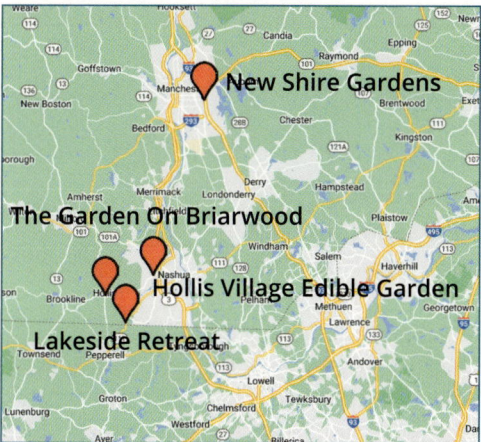

An additional garden is open nearby:
Middlesex County, MA
   Stone Sphere, Pepperell, MA
See page 160.

HOLLIS
HOLLIS VILLAGE EDIBLE GARDEN
NEW 10–4

Welcome to Hollis Village Edible Gardens, a hidden jewel on the edge of a historic New Hampshire village. This small cottage garden, lovingly curated by owners Liz and Ted Barbour, is a testament to the harmonious coexistence of creativity and "no rules" gardening.

Over 25 years this once barren canvas was transformed into a living tapestry of color, scent, and flavor, where edible and non-edible plants playfully intermingle. As you step into this ever-evolving landscape, you'll embark on a journey of inspiration and discovery, where every corner tells a story, and every visit is an invitation to celebrate the boundless beauty of gardening.

This garden's estimated size is 1/3 acre.

💬 TROWEL TALK

Nestled on the edge of the Hollis historic village, our house is one of the oldest homes in the town center.

When we moved to Hollis in 1999, our children were 1 and 4 years old. At the time, we worried about the bustling village street that ran around our home. We devised a plan to slow down traffic. We decided that if we could create a truly beautiful and interesting garden in front of our house, something that would catch the eye of the passing drivers, it might just compel them to slow down. It was a simple idea that many towns employ in their own town centers to calm traffic.

The transformation began with a blank canvas, a patch of grass and dirt that stretched out to the busy street. With each passing season, we layered landscaping elements that created a haven for both the children and the garden. The front yard became a living artwork, a kaleidoscope of colors that shifted with the changing seasons.

But this was just the beginning of our garden journey. My true passion lay in edible gardening, and as my children grew, so did my vision. I envisioned a space where beauty and function intertwined seamlessly. My edible garden would not only be a feast for the eyes but also a source of culinary inspiration in my cooking classes and garden lectures.

I began weaving fruits and vegetables, herbs, and flowers, all mingled together in a harmonious tapestry. Tomatoes ripened alongside dahlias, and basil fragranced the air beside lavender. But our garden did more than just nurture our family and students; it fulfilled our original mission to slow traffic and create a safe place that is in harmony with a village setting.

Our garden story continues to unfold. In 2020 we added a hen house that seamlessly blends into the garden landscape, surrounded by squash plants and fragrant mint. A small flock of chickens roam freely within safe wire tunnels, their gentle clucking a soothing backdrop to the garden.

More gardens are in the works and together, all the gardens will tell the story of a much-loved home and a village life that our family has cherished. We look forward to welcoming you to our Hollis Village Edible Gardens.

—Liz Barbour

LAKESIDE RETREAT
NEW   10–4

My garden has been a work in progress for thirteen years. The lot was abandoned when I first purchased it, and we experienced a microburst in August of 2022. The completion of the third rock wall in early 2024 will mark the completion of this chapter of our outdoor space. I have hosted many parties, graduations, and a wedding and am looking forward to hosting you!

This garden's estimated size is 2 acres.

💬 TROWEL TALK

My favorite plants are Peonies! One of my favorite garden tools are shears, because I like boxwoods. My late father inspired me to garden.

—*Cindi O.*

MANCHESTER
NEW SHIRE GARDENS
NEW   10–4

New Shire Gardens in Manchester is not your typical garden. It resembles an English cottage garden in a way, but it's probably best just to tell you what you will find.

Our yard includes raised vegetable beds, a pergola covered in grapes and trumpet vines, a little chicken coop with a few chickens, and tucked away in the corner is a gazebo. There is a large koi pond with a stream running down a hill, surrounded by narrow moss-covered pathways with passageways carved into bushes. A beautiful stone fire pit area sits across from a little herb garden with a few beehives.

Probably the most unusual parts of the garden have to be the parts recreated from my favorite authors' works. If you've either read the books or seen the movies of either J. R. R. Tolkien or C. S. Lewis, then you'll recognize elements from some of their stories. Kids are definitely welcome.

Finally, there is a quiet winding path in the woods to help you feel like you've left the city, at least for a few minutes. You'll need some sensible shoes to walk all the paths. With all that being said, we'll leave a few things for you to discover when you come.

This garden's estimated size is 1 acre.

💬 TROWEL TALK

I was a professional photographer for 30+ years and was intrigued by another photographer in my state who did natural light portraits outside. I had been primarily a studio photographer for my first decade and was intrigued by the idea. After becoming a homeowner, I started in the far corner of my yard to build a small garden to take pictures in. Little did I know that the love of gardening would surpass my love of photography.

I would like to say I've designed the garden, but it's more like it's evolved into what it is today. There are "many rooms" out back. For instance, the pergola would be the dining room, while the gazebo would be the living room. There are numerous places to hunker down with a good book, and while you're outside, you won't be alone.

My garden is teeming with life. Beyond the chickens, koi, and a few beehives, hundreds of birds have moved into the yard. My pergola sounds as if it's alive itself with the sound of chirping. The garden is a living, breathing thing itself, and you can feel it. There are also elements drawn from my favorite authors' works which, if you are also a fan, you'll recognize immediately. Those garden fixtures will transport you to a magical place.

I'll be endeavoring to incorporate more of my favorite authors' storylines into my garden as time permits. The joke I tell everyone is, my ideas take approximately five years to either ferment or foment in my head.

—*Guy Lessard*

NASHUA
THE GARDEN ON BRIARWOOD
NEW ♿ 🍃 10–4

This is a small inner-city, low-maintenance green garden, with not as many colorful flowers as most other gardens. We have created this garden in this way, so that we can enjoy our garden and yard in our retirement years, instead of traveling. With the assistance of professional guidance and labor, we have accomplished this goal.

This garden's estimated size is ~1 acre.

💬 TROWEL TALK

When I was younger and able to take care of the garden on my own, my favorite plant was the tea rose, preferably David Austin roses. However, in today's life, I have changed to drift roses, which require less care and are easier to maintain.

I'm inspired by my grandmother, who had a small apple orchard and fruit and vegetable garden in New York. As a young girl I would help pick apples and other fruits and make pies, jams, and jellies. My favorite garden tools are the hands attached to the professionals I have hired to create my now year-round vacation get-away in my own backyard.

—*The Lazy Gardener*

NEW  Year  No Photography  Accessibility  Nibbled Leaf Garden

194 New Hampshire   Register online: gardenconservancy.org/opendays

Cheshire County
Sunday, June 30

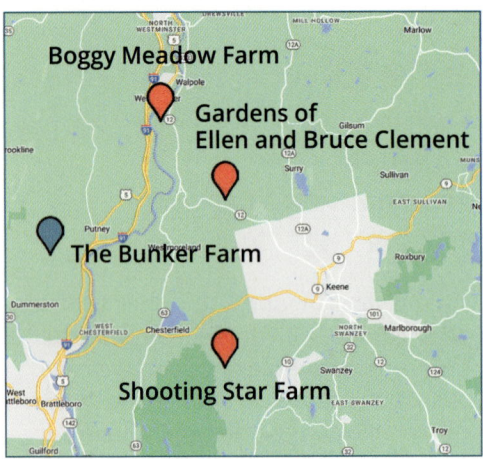

Additional gardens are open nearby:
Windham County, VT
   Garden of Gordon and Mary Hayward, Westminster West, VT
Windsor County, VT
   The Garden of Bill Noble, Norwich, VT
See page 333.

WALPOLE
BOGGY MEADOW FARM
🌱 partial   🪶 10–4

The garden is planted on a small bluff above the Connecticut River. It is an informal garden, but it has elements of an older, more formal garden planted by Miss Fanny Mason more than 100 years ago. There are English borders, a grape arbor, and a small sunken garden with a narrow ravine down to a stream, distributed over 3 acres.

This garden's estimated size is 5 acres.

SPOFFORD
SHOOTING STAR FARM
NEW   10–4

As it is with most of you, I'm sure, I'm a life-time member of Plants Anonymous. My wife and I moved our horse farm to Spofford 25 years ago, and I immediately began planting.

The challenge, of course, is having "eyes bigger than my stomach"; it's challenging keeping up with as many flower beds as I want to create.

Additionally, in August of 2023, we finished construction on a new equine facility, so we are in the midst of designing and completing the accompanying landscaping, which, so far, includes a naturalized water feature and a life-sized horse sculpture.

Having scheduled events is a convenient method of keeping us on track to finish new projects and optimize the existing beds, so we're happy to be part of the Open Days 2024 Garden Tours.

This garden's estimated size is 2 acres.

💬 **TROWEL TALK**

There are so many people who have inspired my love of gardens: From my mother's window boxes, to my great aunt Essie's conversations about lilacs, to Barbara Brown's fringe tree, to riding the bus from Keene, NH, to Boston for the Flower Show with my great aunt Avis, to helping Lily Pendleton propagate daylilies when I worked for her during high school.

Perhaps my biggest push in the last couple decades was living through colon cancer and the subsequent treatments,

NEW 5 10 20 '95 Year   📷 No Photography   ♿ Accessibility   🪶 Nibbled Leaf Garden

and deciding I want to live as many days as I can with as much beauty around me as possible.

—Scot Tolman

WESTMORELAND

GARDENS OF ELLEN AND BRUCE CLEMENT

 12–4

The year 2023 marks 50 years that we have lived, loved, and raised a family on this 20-acre hillside farm. For most of those years we raised sheep on the 15 acres of hillside pasture.

Although we always had a large vegetable garden and Ellen made some lovely small flower gardens, it wasn't until 2004 that we started to seriously turn our attention to developing a variety of gardens. They now include, in addition to our vegetable garden, a cottage garden, a conifer garden, a shade/hosta garden, a terraced rock garden, a tea house in a woodland area that overlooks a stream and small pond, an arbor with a water fountain, and quite a bit more.

Folks who have visited tell us they feel a sense of peace in our gardens. One friend calls our gardens "magical" and also says, "they have taken what most would find a challenging landscape and made it into a glorious adventure to behold." We invite you to come visit, spend some time strolling through our gardens, and see if you feel the same.

This garden's estimated size is 2 acres.

NEARBY NURSERY

THE BUNKER FARM

**857 Bunker Road
Putney, VT 05346**

The Bunker Farm is a family-run farm that produces naturally pasture-raised meats, specialty annual and perennial flowers, and award-winning maple syrup.

facebook.com/thebunkerfarm

instagram.com/thebunkerfarm

thebunkerfarm.com

Cheshire County
Sunday, August 11

An additional garden is open nearby:
Windsor County, VT
   Woodland Farms, Springfield, VT
See page 334.

GILSUM
HOLLOWS END
NEW 10–4

Surrounded by forested hills and an abundant watershed, Hollows End sits in a few acres of rolling open meadows. The recent aim of garden additions and renovations has been to better connect the house, which sits up on a rise, with the land, and vice versa.

A large sky frame that steps out and down over a terrace and deck helps that, along with plantings of native species and cultivars along with grasses. Rustic locust fences surround a barn field/dog run out front and create a backdrop for a lush border in the backyard. An old pond now sits empty, sometimes brought back by beavers and at other times, washed away by super storms.

We have finally decided to embrace the comings and goings of nature, but a large flat gazing rock is planned to allow a closer view "down in the bowl." A post and beam Summer House sits at the edge of the old pond; it's going to be lily pond and berm plantings under renovation next. A grotto featuring stone from the property awaits its next phases too, partially completed: a bog, natural stone fountain, and dipping pool.

I've learned so much by going to other people's gardens, and it's time to return the favor. While not everything is "finished" here, it's hoped that seeing some things still in process might be beneficial and even exciting.

This garden's estimated size is 1 acre.

💬 TROWEL TALK

I love, love, love foliage, and since I started off with more shade in my garden, it came easily in the form of ferns and lots more. Color is also another source of immense joy, and there are lots of yellow-foliaged plants in my garden; silvers and purples as well. Orange just became a new obsession, so we'll see where that leads!

I've always had a passion for anything creative and design oriented. In my 20s and 30s I danced, made costumes, choreographed, and performed with a troupe.

When I found collaging and gardening, I turned more of my focus there. The canvas of land and plants is mesmerizing! I was hooked! My biggest challenges are too many ideas, big ideas I can't always keep up with (during and after), and having a lot of land. I honestly sometimes wish for a small suburban lot and its limitations!

—*Catherine S.*

WALPOLE

DISTANT HILL GARDENS - GARDEN OF MICHAEL AND KATHY NERRIE

    10-4

At Distant Hill Gardens and Nature Trail, we consider the entire 58-acre property to be a garden, from the cultivated ornamentals and vegetables to the native plants of our forest, fields, and wetlands.

We use the term "garden" broadly to include the growing of any plants and believe in the importance of plants, their cultivation, and their use in the landscape to help foster an ecological balance between humans and the land.

Some of the highlights of Distant Hill include cultivated gardens with hundreds of labeled shrubs and perennials; a mile-long wheelchair and stroller accessible nature trail; a half-mile long geology trail; a large native wildflower meadow; a nature play area for the kids; a boardwalk over a floating cranberry bog; lots of beautiful stonework, including a stone circle aligned to the setting sun on the winter solstice; a storybook trail with a new children's book the first of every month; more than 3 miles of hiking trails and more!

This garden's estimated size is 2 cultivated acres.

💬 TROWEL TALK

In 1979, my wife, Kathy, and I embarked on a life-changing adventure, purchasing 21 acres of land on a hill in Walpole, New Hampshire, known as Distant Hill. The land would become a canvas for our dreams. Over the next decade, we built not just a home, but a sanctuary that celebrates the beauty of nature.

Our journey began by creating our dream homestead. We hand-crafted a timber frame home, established a vegetable garden, constructed essential outbuildings, dug a beautiful swimming pond, and restored an abandoned sugar bush on the property, yielding sweet maple syrup each spring.

Despite having no prior horticultural experience, I embraced the creative challenge of "building" a shrub garden. Armed with just the landscape design for the property and an open mind, I procured the shrubs needed and began creating our first garden. It was a revelation! I quickly realized that shrubs were not merely plants but living architectural elements, akin to lumber or stone. They provided an extraordinary opportunity for creativity, as nature worked in harmony with me, gradually shaping these living sculptures. Each shrub I planted or relocated became a brushstroke in a larger canvas of our landscape. In blending the diverse textures, shapes, and colors of these plants, I aimed to create not just a garden but a nature-based sculpture.

Each garden became a testament to the evolving collaboration between human design and the unceasing forces of the natural world. Nature played a dynamic role in this transformation, shaping

198   New Hampshire   Register online: gardenconservancy.org/opendays

rooms and concealed spaces as the shrubs matured and evolved.

As I dug into this newfound passion, I realized that I was not just planting shrubs; I was orchestrating a symphony of botanical elements, endeavoring to emulate the essence of nature itself. With each placement and every adjustment in the landscape, I sought to meld the diverse textures, forms, and hues of both plants and stones from the property into an ever-changing sculpture inspired by the natural world.

Our journey at Distant Hill, from building our home and restoring a sugar bush to creating living shrub gardens, is a testament to the transformative power of nature and the remarkable synergy between human design and the environment.

These shrub gardens, continually evolving, are more than just horticultural creations; they are a living sculpture, a testament to the beauty of nature, and a lasting legacy of our passion for artistry in the outdoors.

—*Michael Nerrie - Designer/Builder of Distant Hill Gardens*

Monadnock Region

Saturday, August 24

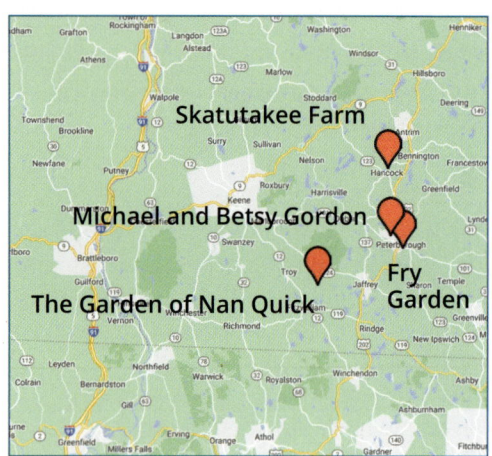

HANCOCK
SKATUTAKEE FARM

         10–5

The gardens surround Hancock's first house, built in 1776 by the town clerk, Jonathan Bennett. Since it is a farmhouse, the plantings are informal and blend into surrounding fields and woods.

On each side of the "front" door are raised beds reminiscent of colonial gardens. The real front door (never used) is flanked by plantings of old roses and nepeta. Behind the 1970 kitchen wing is a 48-foot-long koi pond designed by landscape architect Diane McGuire and planted with lotuses, irises, and water lilies. McGuire also laid out the perennial bed and woodland border. The AIA-award-winning screened porch was designed by Dan Scully.

Sculptures in the terraced vegetable

NEW   5 10 20 95 Year   No Photography   Accessibility   Nibbled Leaf Garden

garden are by Noel Grenier, and a pair of 200-year-old granite Korean rams graze on the back lawn. I followed McGuire's brilliant layout of the parallel borders but deepened the perennial bed to make a bit more room to "paint" with annuals and perennials.

The woodland border is planted with witch hazel, azaleas, snakeroot, and Rodgersia. Walking beyond the borders, one comes to a new bog garden surrounded by marsh marigolds, skunk cabbage, and sedges. A trail of cardinal flowers brightens the wetland beyond.

This garden's estimated size is 3½ acres.

JAFFREY
THE GARDEN OF NAN QUICK
NEW   10–4

In 2003, when I bought 5 acres of scrub woodland on a south-facing hill, my dream was to design a house that seamlessly integrates architecture with the hard and softscapes of surrounding gardens, and to weave together lines of sight so that outward views from every room are linked to specific garden features.

I also knew I'd eventually create eye-catchers on the farther-flung portions of my land, so that from the raised vantage point of my house, I'd have attractive, intermediate-distance vignettes to distract me from the wonderful but ungovernable wilderness of the nature preserves which surround me.

I'm also a garden historian, as well as a furniture designer whose work has been exhibited at the Chelsea Flower Show; my gardens are adorned with many of those pieces. After two decades of incessant housebuilding and land-shaping, what I initially imagined has finally taken form.

This garden's estimated size is 3 acres.

 TROWEL TALK

The world's awash with images of gorgeous gardens, but little documentation exists of how the garden-sausage is made.

To see a step-by-step account of the arduous, 4-year-long process by which my raised terrace garden came into being, visit nanquick.com, and read "How Gardens are Really Made." My diary is offered freely, to all those who love gardens.

—*Nan Quick*

PETERBOROUGH
FRY GARDEN
5   10–4

The garden consists of more than 52 garden areas connected by staircases, pebbled or grass walkways, and spread over a 9-acre site. They include level spaces and terraced areas designed to accommodate the significant elevation changes on the property.

Styles range from formal near the house to less structured closer to wooded areas, a number of water features, including numerous pools and two ponds, and a large perennial garden.

Some striking features are a 300-foot sycamore allée, a series of semicircular terraces bordered by standard Korean lilacs, an arboretum, an allée of 110 crab apples that border a 1-acre garden, and an orchard of 20 fastigiate hornbeams underplanted with European ginger.

Designers Gordon Hayward and Doug Hoerr have contributed to the design.

MICHAEL AND BETSY GORDON

 partial 10–4

This small garden in the village was designed by a plantsman to be an extension of the house. The house and garden are situated on a hill, and the garden is terraced on three levels.

The upper level was designed to be enjoyed from the street. The middle level is laid out formally using yew hedges and a century-old granite wall foundation to create a garden room. The lowest level, an informal woodland garden, has both eastern North American and eastern Asian shade-loving plants.

The garden was planted with a mixture of unusual trees, shrubs, perennials, grasses, annuals, and bulbs. Plants were selected primarily for interesting form, foliage, and texture. The garden is chronicled on Instagram @thegardenerseye.

This garden's estimated size is ½ acre.

The Mountsier Garden - Montclair, NJ
Photo: Land Morphology

204 New Jersey

Violet
Viola sororia

Open Days dates and times by County, Town, and Garden

BERGEN

Demarest
Hawks Off the Palisades
   Saturday, May 18, 10–3
Franklin Lakes
Blue Meadow Farms
   Saturday, July 13, 10–3
Lakeside Garden
   Saturday, July 13, 10–3
Ho-Ho-Kus
Lourdes and Alfredo's Garden
   Saturday, July 13, 10–3
Mahwah
Magic Mountain Sanctuary
   Saturday, May 18, 10–3
Sisko Gardens and Sculpture Site
   Saturday, July 13, 10–3
   Saturday, September 14, 10–3
Wyckoff
Janet Schulz
   Saturday, May 18, 10–3
   Saturday, July 13, 10–3

ESSEX

Montclair
Anna's Pollinator Haven
   Saturday, June 1, 10–4
   Saturday, September 7, 10–4
Cynthia Corhan-Aitken
   Saturday, June 1, 10–4
Nutley
The Mountsier Garden
   Saturday, April 13, 10–4
   Saturday, May 4, 10–4
   Saturday, June 1, 10–4
   Saturday, September 7, 10–4

HUNTERDON

Califon
Treetop
   Sunday, June 16, 10–12, 12–2, 2–4
Pottersville
Bird Haven Farm
   Sunday, June 16, 10–4
Jardin de Buis
   Sunday, June 16, 10–4
Stockton
Bellsflower Garden
   Saturday, August 24, 10–4
Pretty Bird Farm
   Saturday, August 24, 10–4
The Garden at Federal Twist
   Saturday, June 22, 10–4

MORRIS

Chester
Windance
   Sunday, June 16, 10–4

SOMERSET

Far Hills
The Hay, Honey Farm
   Saturday, May 4, 10–4
   Saturday, September 21, 10–4
Bernardsville
Mountain Top
   Sunday, June 16, 10–4

NEW JERSEY

Essex County
Saturday, April 13

NUTLEY
THE MOUNTSIER GARDEN
  ♿ partial   10–4

This garden is open four times this year: April 13, May 4, June 1, and September 7.

This month: join us to see our daffodils in bloom.

A garden for all seasons that has been created and fine-tuned for more than two decades and now encompasses 2 acres. Owners Silas Montsier and Graeme Hardie have collaborated with noted landscape designer and friend Richard Hartlage, and the result is a feast for the eyes and for the senses.

Principally a stroll garden, there are numerous focal points, small rooms, seating areas, private nooks, and impressive vistas. Drifts of variegated hakonechloa soften the strong architectural underpinnings of the garden, and many of the brilliant and original plant combinations will thrill the devoted horticulturist.

A collection of small sculptures, artworks, and commissioned pieces is interspersed throughout as accent points and disarming bits of humor. From thousands of early spring flowering bulbs to a subtle but glorious display of green on green in the early fall, there is something new to see and enjoy on every visit.

This garden's estimated size is 2-1/3 acres.

Essex County
Saturday, May 4

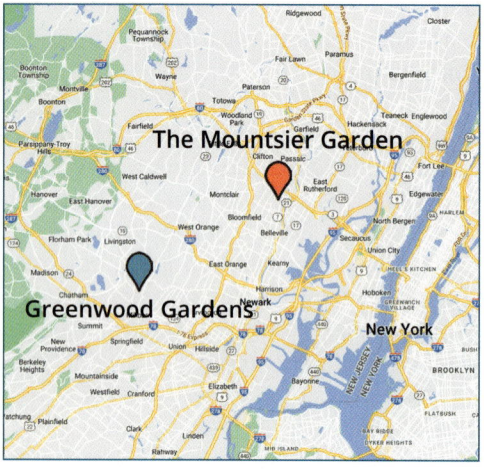

plant combinations will thrill the devoted horticulturist.

A collection of small sculptures, artworks, and commissioned pieces is interspersed throughout as accent points and disarming bits of humor. From thousands of early spring flowering bulbs to a subtle but glorious display of green on green in the early fall, there is something new to see and enjoy on every visit.

This garden's estimated size is 2-1/3 acres.

NUTLEY
THE MOUNTSIER GARDEN

  partial 10-4

This garden is open four times this year: April 13, May 4, June 1, and September 7.

This month: see our tulips in bloom.

A garden for all seasons that has been created and fine-tuned for more than two decades and now encompasses 2 acres. Owners Silas Montsier and Graeme Hardie have collaborated with noted landscape designer and friend Richard Hartlage, and the result is a feast for the eyes and for the senses.

Principally a stroll garden, there are numerous focal points, small rooms, seating areas, private nooks, and impressive vistas. Drifts of variegated hakonechloa soften the strong architectural underpinnings of the garden, and many of the brilliant and original

Somerset County

Saturday, May 4

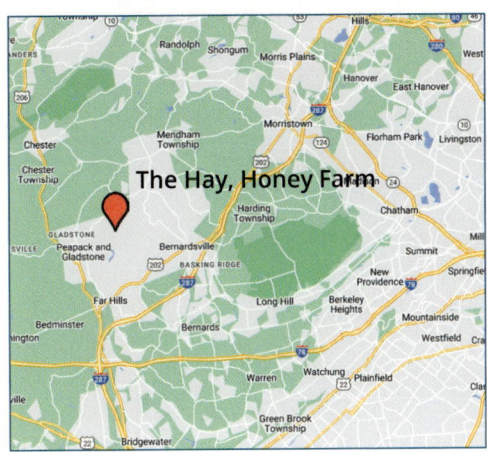

FAR HILLS
THE HAY, HONEY FARM

20   10–4

This garden is open twice this year: May 4 and September 21.

The Hay, Honey Farm's extensive gardens have been carefully added to the landscape since 1989 in a naturalistic manner, with a respect for the history and topography of the site, and consistent with the broader surrounding atmosphere of Pleasant Valley.

The plant collections reflect the diverse interests of the owners and the resident horticulturists and are set within a dwarf conifer/spring bulb garden, a walled perennial border, hosta gardens, meadow, hayfields, a kitchen garden, a woodland garden of rhododendron and companion wildflowers, and a mostly native wild garden, home to a growing assortment of

---

PUBLIC GARDEN PRESERVATION PARTNER

GREENWOOD GARDENS

**274 Old Short Hills Rd
Short Hills, New Jersey 07078**

Since the early twentieth century, Greenwood Gardens was a private retreat with formal Italianate gardens graced by colorful tiles, rustic stone tea houses, mossy-pebbled walks, and vistas stretching for miles into the surrounding wooded hillsides.

Careful preservation work and imaginative horticulture have returned much of the garden to its original Arts & Crafts design.

Greenwood Gardens is endorsed by the Garden Conservancy as a Preservation Project Garden.

 facebook.com/GreenwoodShortHills

 instagram.com/greenwoodgardensnj

 greenwoodgardens.org

songbirds.

This garden's estimated size is 12 acres.

💬 **TROWEL TALK**

Oh so many favorite plants! Collections of American holly, rhododendron, hostas, maples, dwarf conifers, oaks, and more. We also enjoy growing many plants from seed.

— The Gardener

Bergen County
Saturday, May 18

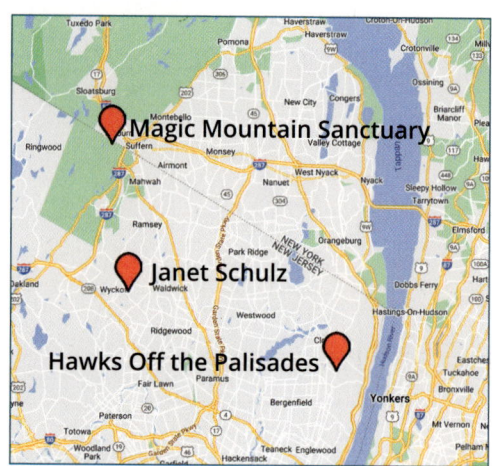

DEMAREST
HAWKS OFF THE PALISADES
♿ 🌿 10–3

Sculpted hornbeams and river birches hug, and large 'Green Giant' arborvitae and Skip laurels pronounce the front of this gated custom Mediterranean and French home.

My side yard is the largest mass of the property, which houses large 'Limelight' hydrangea trees, a smoke tree, and large decorative pine.

A quiet reflective shade garden on the opposite side houses an heirloom Japanese maple. Custom natural steps bring you to a large relaxing and private back pool and patio with many trees, roses, and garden features.

On the property are massive 100-plus-year-old trees which often house hawks and other raptors. A special viewing section has been added to capture their flight. At the front of the home are flower pollinator gardens and many rhododendrons, azaleas, weigelas, spirea, and various evergreen varietals.

My garden gives year-round interest in as natural a setting as possible. I insist on artistic use of textures in the plants chosen and blend juxtapositions within the design. We adore our trees and the birds that inhabit them.

We have a deer issue which I will discuss with anyone who inquires. This has been a huge challenge with regard to keeping the site beautiful.

This garden's estimated size is 1 acre.

💬 TROWEL TALK

The Open Days I have been to thus far were welcoming and have all had a very different feel working with the beauty around them.

The hosts were incredibly knowledgeable and had an incredible pride in their masterpieces. They let the garden show who they are and what they feel. It has inspired me to do the same. We are given different palettes to paint with the gardens we plant.

—Marie Wolpert

MAHWAH
MAGIC MOUNTAIN SANCTUARY
 10–3

Our garden was started from scratch in 2008, when we purchased our new home on a mountain. The land is surrounded by woods; the previous owner clear-cut the forest and created a vast lawn with some retaining walls.

There were no ornamental plants on the land except pachysandra. The land is beautiful and has various elevations, which made gardening somewhat challenging. Our goal was to work with the land and create a diverse, mostly self-sustaining garden which would also be a sanctuary for pollinators and wildlife.

We wanted to implement some permaculture principles and work with the land instead of against it. We also wanted to grow our own food, and so we created large vegetable and fruit/berry gardens. The property features a rock garden, Japanese garden, woodland plant collections, meandering paths, multiple ponds with koi, stone and brick patios, mixed perennial borders, fruit trees, rare and unusual edible plants and berries, tropical plants, many medicinal plants, lots of roses, and many flowering bushes and trees.

We built rustic cedar pergolas, gazebos, and wood pathways. We have a large collection of tree peonies and herbaceous peonies. The garden is a sanctuary for many species of songbirds and pollinators. We keep honey bees.

This garden's estimated size is 4 acres.

💬 TROWEL TALK

I have loved plants for as long as I can remember! As a young girl, I was playing with flowers, making tiny fairy dolls with the cosmos and calendula flower heads, weaving wreaths from dandelion blossoms, eating berries from grandma's garden, digging up tulip bulbs and obsessively collecting all kinds of seeds.

Our family didn't own land; we lived on the fourth floor of a tall apartment

 No Photography  Nibbled Leaf Garden

building, and so all my plant adventures happened in the community yard, which luckily for us was richly planted with flowers and trees.

My first "garden" was on my windowsill and my balcony. A few years later I started real gardening on my friend's property. I was happy to help out and learn from her, as she had all kinds of flowering plants and trees and a wonderful vegetable garden. I have been a passionate plant woman ever since.

My favorite plants are rose, tree peony, and primrose, and my favorite medicinal plant is elderberry. Oh there are quite a few plants I didn't have any luck with! LOL! As a young stubborn gardener, I tried to force nature's hand so I could strictly follow my design-to no avail, of course. So I'd plant something that was not suitable for my zone, like a southern magnolia or crape myrtle, or force a moisture-loving plant into a dry area...

These days I am much more attentive to these things, and I learned to follow nature's lead when it comes to finding happy habitats and stunning color combos. My favorite garden tool is a Cutco trowel! I have two of them and they are just the best, the way they fit in the hand, and the quality is outstanding, they never break or bend.

—The Gardener

WYCKOFF
JANET SCHULZ
20   partial   10–3

This garden is open twice this year: May 18 and July 13.

Although you may have visited Janet's garden on a previous Open Day, her garden always offers something new to behold. As a plant collector and enthusiast, Janet regularly adds, edits, and subtracts.

Over the years, she has created many beds consisting of hosta, ferns, and assorted shade-loving plants, many of which are natives. In 2008, due to a microburst, the primary source of shade was lost when the very large white pine came down. Janet left the trunk for the wildlife. The squirrels, birds, and insects have enjoyed this snag.

But, thanks to her neighbors' trees, hers is still primarily a shaded woodland garden receiving no more than three hours of direct sun in any one area. This gardener loves to push the envelope by attempting to grow plants that typically require more sun. It might come as a surprise to see plants that are supposed to require "full sun" thriving in her garden.

There are places to sit and view the garden from many angles, encouraging you to try each one so you can enjoy different views and perspectives.

💬 TROWEL TALK

My favorite garden tool is not a tool but a kneeler/seat. Now that I have reached a certain age, I think I can still do everything, but my body tells me otherwise. I straddle the seat, for I haven't been able to kneel for years.

—Janet

NEW   Year   No Photography   Accessibility   Nibbled Leaf Garden

Essex County
Saturday, June 1

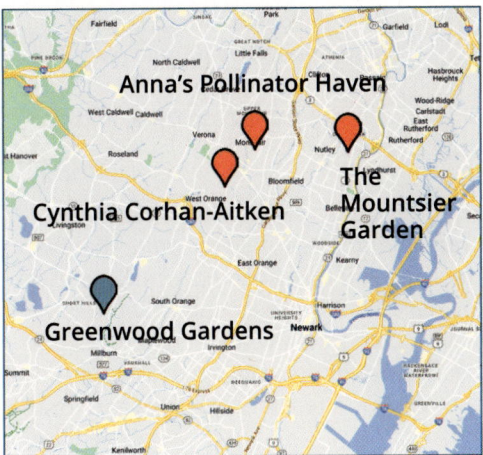

MONTCLAIR
ANNA'S POLLINATOR HAVEN
NEW 10-4

This garden is open twice this year: June 1 and September 7.

My garden is where I learned how to garden. It's full of mistakes and happy accidents. It's also home to many small trees and lots of native plants. My hope was to attract monarch butterflies and to recreate gardens I have childhood memories of. I wanted a peaceful place that feels interesting in every season and could also house some large outdoor sculptures.

Now, seven years later, it's looking like the garden I had dreamt of and is my peaceful go-to place to watch birds, butterflies, hummingbirds, and lots of bees and insects.

This garden's estimated size is ¼ acre.

TROWEL TALK

Piet Oudolf and Edie Beale! Piet Oudolf is why I garden. His gardens changed everything for me, and I dream of visiting all of the landscapes he has designed one day. Edie Beale because I'm starting to imagine myself glued to this garden as she was to Grey Gardens.

—Anna Grossman

CYNTHIA CORHAN-AITKEN
NEW 10-4

Our garden is on 1½ acres of flat land in the Estate Section of Montclair. We moved into this house ten years ago and, while the house was lovely, the garden can be best described as a bramble of overgrown shrubs, badly organized perennials, and ivy in all the beds, on all the brick walls, just everywhere.

The original house was built in 1893 and added onto in 1998, so it is a mix of old and new. I spent the whole first year pruning, moving, and ridding the property of ivy. There is a pool surrounded by original brick walls, a tennis court, and a caretaker's cottage with its own small private garden.

There is a small water feature in the back of the property, a pergola original to the house, and a grape arbor with some very old vines. It is a definite retreat for our family and friends.

This garden's estimated size is 1½ acres.

NEW 5 10 20 '95 Year    No Photography    Accessibility    Nibbled Leaf Garden

212 New Jersey

Register online: gardenconservancy.org/opendays

💬 TROWEL TALK

I grew up in Brooklyn and later in NYC. After marriage we moved to Montclair to a house which was basically a swath of lawn. The first fall my husband and I planted 2,000 tulip bulbs; that spring to our surprise they came up and it was beautiful. We got a letter from the "May in Montclair" Association thanking us for helping to beautify the town.

I was hooked. I trained and worked as a bridal gown designer, but after children I found it was all too much of a juggle and left that field. I went back to school at the New York Botanical Garden and got a certificate in Landscape Design and the rest is history.

I have been gardening for the last 25 years and continue to learn, experiment, and love what I do.

—Cynthia Corhan-Aitken

NUTLEY
THE MOUNTSIER GARDEN

20   partial   10–4

This garden is open four times this year: April 13, May 4, June 1, and September 7.

This month: enjoy the roses, iris, and Kousa dogwood.

A garden for all seasons that has been created and fine-tuned for more than two decades and now encompasses 2 acres. Owners Silas Montsier and Graeme Hardie have collaborated with noted landscape designer and friend Richard Hartlage, and the result is a feast for the eyes and for the senses.

Principally a stroll garden, there are numerous focal points, small rooms, seating areas, private nooks, and impressive vistas. Drifts of variegated hakonechloa soften the strong architectural underpinnings of the garden, and many of the brilliant and original plant combinations will thrill the devoted horticulturist.

A collection of small sculptures, artworks, and commissioned pieces is interspersed throughout as accent points and disarming bits of humor. From thousands of early spring flowering bulbs to a subtle but glorious display of green on green in the early fall, there is something new to see and enjoy on every visit.

This garden's estimated size is 2-1/3 acres.

NEW 5 10 20 95 Year    No Photography    Accessibility    Nibbled Leaf Garden

Register online: gardenconservancy.org/opendays New Jersey 213

PUBLIC GARDEN PRESERVATION PARTNER
GREENWOOD GARDENS

**274 Old Short Hills Rd
Short Hills, New Jersey 07078**

Since the early twentieth century, Greenwood Gardens was a private retreat with formal Italianate gardens graced by colorful tiles, rustic stone tea houses, mossy-pebbled walks, and vistas stretching for miles into the surrounding wooded hillsides.

Careful preservation work and imaginative horticulture have returned much of the garden to its original Arts & Crafts design.

Greenwood Gardens is endorsed by the Garden Conservancy as a Preservation Project Garden.

facebook.com/GreenwoodShortHills

instagram.com/greenwoodgardensnj

greenwoodgardens.org

Nearby Counties

- **HUNTERDON**
- **MORRIS**
- **SOMERSET**

Sunday, June 16

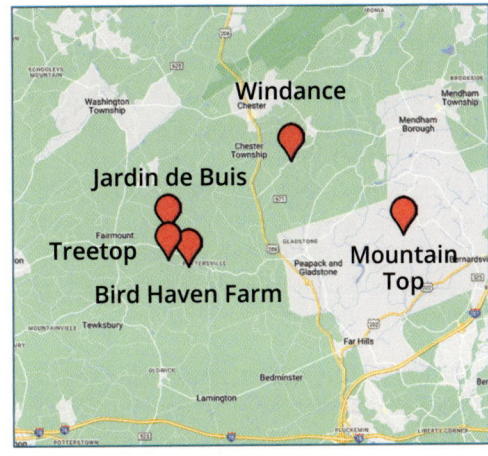

A garden is open this day in nearby Morris County, NJ.

HUNTERDON COUNTY
CALIFON
TREETOP
NEW   10–12, 12–2, 2–4

Treetop comprises 7 acres of meadows, plant beds, and trees distributed over a rolling landscape and around the owner's house, which is contemporary.

The gardens have a naturalistic aesthetic both in design and in the choice of diverse plants that support the presence of bees, butterflies, and birds. Clusters of hellebores and peonies thrive in several beds, but many native species are growing throughout the property. There is a more

NEW 5 10 20 95 Year    No Photography    Accessibility    Nibbled Leaf Garden

traditional garden in a small courtyard behind the house.

This garden's estimated size is 7 acres.

💬 TROWEL TALK

My favorite plant is probably the peony, in part because I've been successful at growing them, and because I think they are quite beautiful.

My first garden was seventeen years ago here at Treetop, which was also when I first had my own house. Frankly, there are many plants with which I've had limited success, but the one that comes to mind is the dahlia. I think they're such interesting flowers, yet I can't get them to grow in my garden.

My clippers are my favorite garden tool. I love to snip, snip, snip at plants of all kinds. My grandmother was a great gardener. I often followed her around as she worked in her beds, which spread out all around her house.

My mother was not really much of a gardener, but every year she planted lots of annuals, which I always put in for her. In this way I learned to work in the soil. I enjoyed doing it.

—*Nancy Hicks*

POTTERSVILLE
BIRD HAVEN FARM

  10–4

Bird Haven Farm is a celebration of the vision and collector's spirit of Janet Mavec and Wayne Nordberg.

The barns, outbuildings, and original nineteenth-century stone house (home of Harriet Stratemeyer Adams, creator of the *Nancy Drew* mystery stories) have been joined by a contemporary house designed by Smith-Miller + Hawkinson in the 1990s, and more recently by a guest house by Parsons + Fernandez-Casteleiro.

The garden master plan was completed in 2002 by Fernando Caruncho, lending visual clarity to the cluster of disparate elements. Hardscaping by Dale Booher added clean lines of strategically placed stone walls, evolving Caruncho's concept of a medieval village and a perfect haven for plants. With an overstory of large mature trees, the 25-acre landscape includes hay meadows, a lush orchard of heirloom apples and other fruit trees, an extensive vegetable and herb garden, and a perennial border designed by Lisa Stamm.

Other features include a meandering woodland walk with cascading ponds, a mixed shrub border, a charming pond hut, as well as a grandchildren's maze garden and elf's stump.

This garden's estimated size is 20 acres.

JARDIN DE BUIS

 ♿ partial 10–4

The gardens and landscape are part of an ongoing project begun in 1992 as a complete renovation and expansion of an eighteenth-century dairy farm on 35 acres. The original four barns and a single wooded hedgerow were all that was left of the abandoned farm in the heart of deer country.

The gardens closest to the barn/house complex were structured around three courtyards formed by the barns, stone walls, and boxwood. The stone parking court leads to the entry/west courtyard, which is adjacent to the formal sycamore and boxwood garden off the kitchen.

Continuing around the house is a thyme garden that leads to the eastern court with the pond and white garden. Moving westward away from the house, you encounter the formal French potager surrounded by privet and fence. This vegetable garden was laid out on an axis to the north side of an old cowshed and the orangery. The greenhouse was salvaged from Rutgers University and designed around an English-style orangery. It is solar powered and heated, plus the lawn and gardens are all treated organically. Behind the cowshed is a nursery of boxwood collected from around the world.

The overall aesthetic was trying to find a balance between the things we love, the French formal boxwood gardens, English borders, and the informal play of trees and allées that merge the formal grid to a much more informal sense of an American country landscape.

This garden's estimated size is 10 acres.

MORRIS COUNTY
CHESTER
WINDANCE
 10–4

The garden at Windance began 25 years ago with a formal landscape of several garden rooms around the house. Over time, more informal plantings have been added across the south-facing slope of 5 acres.

The landscape now offers surprising views, dry-laid stone walls, water features, unique garden structures, and several kinetic sculptures. Dozens of towering native trees are underplanted with a wide selection of ornamental trees, shrubs, and perennials offering four-season interest. The planting focus over the past decade has been to sustain pollinators from early spring through late fall.

Deer-resistant planting is featured in beds outside the fencing surrounding most of the property. Thousands of bulbs are planted throughout. There is also a potager, an herb garden, and a native woodland with meandering paths.

SOMERSET COUNTY
BERNARDSVILLE
MOUNTAIN TOP
NEW   10–4

Our garden was designed in the 1920's by Clarence Fowler, a landscape architect. The residence, built at that time, is a French style manor house.

The original garden still exists plus additions by our family. There are great distant views, a spectacular rhododendron allée, ending at a classical statue, hedged

---

NEW 5 10 20 '95 Year

216 New Jersey

Register online: gardenconservancy.org/opendays

lawn, a formal rose garden, a pool and pavilions, and a shade garden leading to a bridle path which leads to a large stone tower.

The property is 32 acres and is in conservation.

Hunterdon County

Saturday, June 22

An additional garden is open nearby:
Bucks County, PA
   Paxson Hill Farm, New Hope, PA
See page 317.

STOCKTON

THE GARDEN AT FEDERAL TWIST

  10–4

When we moved into a Mid-century house overlooking the woods, I immediately knew only a naturalistic garden would be appropriate to the place. The garden is hidden. You enter through a woodland garden to the side of the house, where you first glimpse the broader landscape behind: a large, sunny glade.

Federal Twist is a landscape garden, and it uses multiple intersecting paths, immersive plantings, and the surrounding tall forest trees to create an illusion of spatial immensity in a relatively small garden. The garden is intended to encourage exploration and attention to detail, and to evoke strong emotion.

Begun as an experiment to explore garden making in the challenging conditions of unimproved, heavy, wet clay, the garden is ecologically similar to a wet prairie and is maintained by cutting and burning.

Federal Twist has been featured in the *New York Times*, the *Financial Times of London*, *Gardens Illustrated*, and numerous other magazines and books, including Thomas Rainer's and Claudia West's *Planting in a Post-Wild World*, Claire Takács's *Dreamscapes*, Christopher Wood's *Gardenlust*, and *Wild* by Noel Kingsbury and Claire Takács.

Federal Twist recently appeared in the BBC television series *Monty Don's American Gardens* and in his new book of the same name. James Golden's own book on the making of the garden, *The View from Federal Twist: A New Way of Thinking about Gardens, Nature and Ourselves*, was published in 2022.

This garden's estimated size is 1½ acres.

💬 TROWEL TALK

James Golden, born in Mississippi though resident in New York City for most of his adult life, was a writer in the corporate world. Nearing retirement, and embarking on what he happily calls *la vita nuova*, he moved to a property in western New Jersey to make a garden.

It was an unusual site for a garden—little more than a derelict wood on heavy, wet clay—but he was taken with the site's emotional power and the intangible qualities of the landscape. When he began the garden, he also began a now well-known blog, *The View from Federal Twist*.

Fifteen years on, James is a celebrated garden maker and thinker whose garden, Federal Twist, has been featured in numerous publications, including the *New York Times*, *Gardens Illustrated*, *Horticulture*, *Better Homes and Gardens*, and other magazines and books.

After visiting Federal Twist for the BBC *Gardener's World* series, *American Gardens*, Monty Don, the British TV gardening guru, said, "after over 50 years of gardening and visiting gardens, it made me rethink what a garden can be and do."

James recently published a new book on the garden, *The View from Federal Twist: A New Way of Thinking about Gardens, Nature and Ourselves*.

—*The Gardener*

Bergen County
Saturday, July 13

FRANKLIN LAKES
BLUE MEADOW FARMS
 10–3

This hidden gem features two properties that complement each other offering a meandering garden, lily ponds, and mature shrubs and trees.

The 1860s farmhouse has an antique brick patio and charming koi pond and waterfall. Also present is an old horse barn that was converted into the owners' office and landscape design space. The garden adjoining is a 100-year-old Victorian home with a large tranquil lily pond with a wide variety of water lilies and marginal plants and is enjoyed as a meditative space.

The property hosts a large number of uncommon trees that are blended into the perimeter, while the rest of the garden is planted with a mix of annuals, perennials, and shrubs.

This garden's estimated size is 3 acres.

LAKESIDE GARDEN
 10–3

A native woodland overlooking the lake at the Indian Trail Club was transformed into gardens of grasses, hydrangea trees, roses, and displays of changing perennials and seasonal annuals. The beautiful annuals and perennials are interspersed between trees and bushes including azaleas, boxwood, spirea, and blue spruce among others.

The yard slopes down to the lake. The right side is lined with red everblooming roses that bloom all summer into the fall or first frost. There is a wonderful garden on the right with peonies, lilies, irises, dahlia, foxglove, astilbes, azaleas, sage, lavender, and roses. The other side of the garden consists of a pool surrounded by begonias, hydrangea bushes and trees, and several rose of Sharon bushes, salvia, and coreopsis.

As you walk up the stairs on the right side, golden halon grasses surround a crab apple tree and there are ferns, daylilies, hostas, and hydrangeas, cornflowers, peonies—perennials in that garden. Pink mandevilla encircle the stair railing, creating a stunning path to the upper deck by summer's end. Hibiscus and lilies that I winter in my sunroom are in pots against the house.

In the fall, the backyard features tropical variegated croton and tropical *Cordyline* ti plants and fire shrubs interspersed. The entire backyard is fenced. In the spring, for more than 25 years, the front of the house has featured 2,000 tulips. When the tulips fade, vinca plants surrounded by boxwoods and grasses of various heights are prominent.

During the isolation and scare of COVID-19, we were nurtured by nature while enjoying the beauty and serenity of this wonderful garden.

This garden's estimated size is ½ acre.

HO-HO-KUS
LOURDES AND ALFREDO'S GARDEN
♿ partial   10–3

Our home in Ho-Ho-Kus is on a corner, and at the time of purchase it was completely exposed to the side street. The existing landscape was very tired and there were no flowering plants to speak of.

We immediately set out to design a lush landscape using many of our favorite evergreens, shrubs, bushes, and perennials. We have a little fish pond, many potted plants that we take in during the winter months, and a wide variety of evergreens, deciduous flowering bushes, and perennials. In May we always plant numerous annuals to complement our perennials.

We pride ourselves on keeping our garden in pristine shape—pruning and changing out plants as needed—but most of all, ensuring color, flowering blooms, and bees and butterflies throughout all of spring, summer, and fall. We were featured by the Ridgewood Garden Club a few years back and by The Contemporary Club of Ho-Ho-Kus last summer.

This garden's estimated size is 10,000 sq. ft.

💬 TROWEL TALK

A garden is always changing, and as plants mature, they sometimes become too large and unruly, invading the space of other beautiful bushes, perennials, etc.

That was the case in our front garden, so last year we had to say goodbye to various old plants including two Alberta spruces (that were covering our front windows), a Hollywood juniper that had become a nightmare to prune, as well as some old ilex bushes and ground cover plants that were looking quite scruffy.

In their place we planted lovely De Runk boxwood, 'Strawberry Vanilla' hydrangeas, pink drift roses, purple dwarf butterfly bushes, green velvet boxwood, St. John's wort, and 'Spectacular' lavender. We are so happy with the way our front garden is looking!

—*Lourdes and Alfredo*

MAHWAH
SISKO GARDENS AND SCULPTURE SITE
    10–3

This garden is open twice this year: July 13 and September 14.

Paul has been working on this 3½-acre property for 37 years. The land was completely wooded within 50 feet of all sides of the original home, which years ago was a small farmhouse. Major tree removal has opened the property to sunlight and sunset views.

The fishpond and pool area are surrounded by terraced gardens from relocated stone farm walls that were on the property along with larger stones unearthed from additional construction to the home. The terraces and upper gardens have been planted with mostly perennials and numerous annuals for spring through fall color.

A new raised bed vegetable garden was added to an adjoining plot of land in 2020 which includes a ten-zone drip and spray watering system. All these gardens, as well as additions to the original home and his art studio/barn building have been developed personally by Paul. With more than 1,000 feet of installed deer fencing and electric driveway gates, the gardens are now much safer from the resident deer population that live within the surrounding forest.

Of note are the numerous contemporary metal sculptures throughout the property which were all created by Paul during his artful career and later. The Sisko Gardens and Sculpture Site is a premier example of an owner designed, constructed, and maintained sanctuary that should be seen and enjoyed.

This garden's estimated size is 3½ acres.

💬 TROWEL TALK

I started gardening about 71 years ago when my parents bought a new home in New Milford, NJ. The property was bare except for a clump of maple trees.

We worked on the parcel evenings and weekends for several years until it was up to the high standards of my parents. Nicest in the neighborhood, needless to say. They just did everything the best they could on a budget, and it looked great. I learned a lot from that time. A lot of digging, planting, raking, and lawn maintenance. Pride of ownership. Some things have to rub off on your future.

I went to college and studied Industrial Arts Education as building things was high on my enjoyment list, and it was a secure profession. Teaching would hopefully give me time when I bought a home to have a nice garden, too.

After teaching a few years I found myself designing sculptural furniture in wood and metal. After a few years of teaching, I decided to open my own business to try to sell some of my craft, which I did, but I was also experimenting with steel sculpture. I found that it was economically more profitable for me and put more effort into the metal art work. Most of my medium to larger works were being installed in private gardens as well as architectural garden sites. What a nice marriage of what is natural and what was man-made.

I continued in both fields for around 30 years and had small gardens wherever my wife, Janet, and I lived, and then we found a larger 3½-acre parcel in Mahwah, NJ. Finally, a place to build a larger studio and bigger gardens. That was 38 years ago. Taking down trees, moving more than 300 tons of stone to form the terraced gardens and merge some of the sculptures I still owned into the garden spaces.

The gardening portion of my time started taking over anything else. I joined garden clubs to learn from others and eventually took the Master Gardeners Course through Rutgers University Extension Service. More and more things to learn. Will I ever know enough to be satisfied? Probably not.

Gardening is a never-ending, life-long learning process and loaded with exercise. It's like a whole day yoga class. Interesting how much of my industrial arts building experience is necessary to create the gardens and install and maintain all the many aspects of a garden, like the watering systems, building the raised beds, varmint protection, and more. If I live to be a healthy 100, I can attribute at least a portion of that time to gardening.

—*Paul Sisko*

WYCKOFF

JANET SCHULZ

  10–3

This garden is open twice this year: May 18 and July 13.

Although you may have visited Janet's garden on a previous Open Day, her garden always offers something new to behold. As a plant collector and enthusiast, Janet regularly adds, edits, and subtracts.

Over the years, she has created many beds consisting of hosta, ferns, and assorted shade-loving plants, many of which are natives. In 2008, due to a microburst, the primary source of shade was lost when the very large white pine came down. Janet left the trunk for the wildlife. The squirrels, birds, and insects have enjoyed this snag.

But, thanks to her neighbors' trees, hers is still primarily a shaded woodland garden receiving no more than three hours of direct sun in any one area. This gardener loves to push the envelope by attempting to grow plants that typically require more sun. It might come as a surprise to see plants that are supposed to require "full sun" thriving in her garden.

There are places to sit and view the garden from many angles, encouraging you to try each one so you can enjoy different views and perspectives.

💬 TROWEL TALK

My favorite garden tool is not a tool but a kneeler/seat. Now that I have reached a certain age, I think I can still do everything, but my body tells me otherwise. I straddle the seat, for I haven't been able to kneel for years.

—*Janet*

Hunterdon County
Saturday, August 24

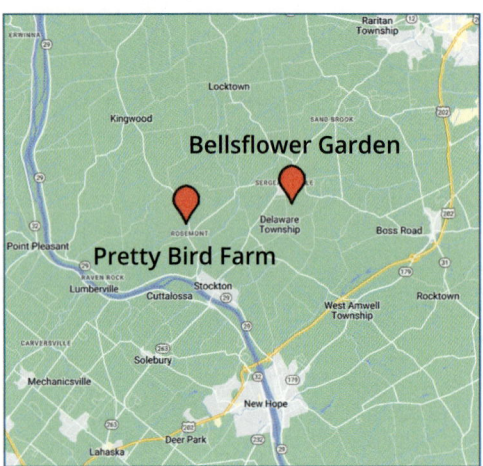

STOCKTON
BELLSFLOWER GARDEN
 ♿ partial 10–4

Bellsflower is a garden of flowers from spring through fall. In 1995, the year following our purchase of the farm, I started garden beds with little knowledge and lots of enthusiasm.

Plants were chosen for color and size and often just because they caught an eye at the garden center. Knowledge came with time. Plants that survived and thrived began to shape the garden.

Phlox subulata covers large swaths and hangs over stone walls. The pink and yellow of early catmint and alyssum signal spring. Irises, roses, and a succession of *Hydrangea arborescens*, *H. paniculata*, and *H. macrophylla* follow. July and August find crape myrtle and summer phlox in pink, blue, white, and coral.

Come September the asters begin, and the final chapter is all about blue, with tall roses adding their exclamation points and grasses flowing in the breeze. Flowering shrubs and specimen trees bloom from March through September.

As the leaves color and fall, the bright holly berries herald winter, when they feed robins as the snow flies.

💬 TROWEL TALK

Church bells from the village echoed in the garden. Moving here in 1994, their music inspired the name.

Starting with a blank canvas we filled the landscape with trees, shrubs, and flowers. Hydrangeas and crape myrtles frame the beds filled with phlox, roses, and perennials of many colors. Our garden has, as have we, matured. But we still keep planting!

—*The Gardener*

PRETTY BIRD FARM
 ♿ partial   10–4

Pretty Bird Farm is a flower and vegetable garden nestled in Delaware Township, one of the most scenic areas of Hunterdon County. Our hillside location overlooks the Rosemont Valley and allows us to be a low water use site.

Our cultivated garden is now about an acre in size and is planted yearly with more than 150 different varieties of annuals, perennials, and vegetables. While our garden has been growing over the last eight years, so has our family, and our

---

NEW 5 10 20 95 Year   🚫 No Photography   ♿ Accessibility   Nibbled Leaf Garden

Essex County
Saturday, September 7

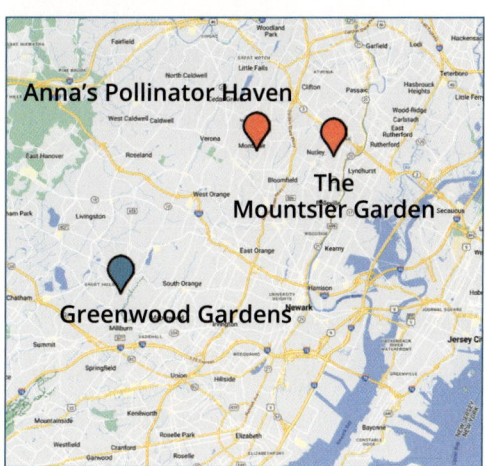

vision for the garden has also evolved over this time.

What started as a food garden for just the two of us, our half-acre garden now supports our growing small business. We sell organically grown produce and flowers to the local community and beyond. It has become a sanctuary for local pollinators and as a waystation for migrating monarchs. It has become a place for our young children to grow and learn about the natural world around them. As you wander the grass walkways you may find a secret hideout, a bit of artwork, or a lost toy.

Come visit us in June for a showcase of our Cool Flowers. These are our cut flowers that are planted the previous fall and early March of this year and tucked in under frost cloth and mulch to bring them into bloom in May—the time of year most people in our 6B hardiness zone are just planting things in the ground.

Visit in August to see the garden in full bloom! We plant thousands of milkweed plants and other pollinator host plants each year. Expect it to be full of butterflies! August is also the peak for tomatoes, and we will offer tasting of our ripe and ready heirlooms.

This garden's estimated size is 4½ acres.

MONTCLAIR
ANNA'S POLLINATOR HAVEN
NEW ♿ 🍃 10–4

This garden is open twice this year: June 1 and September 7.

My garden is where I learned how to garden. It's full of mistakes and happy accidents. It's also home to many small trees and lots of native plants. My hope was to attract monarch butterflies and to re-create gardens I have childhood memories of. I wanted a peaceful place that feels interesting in every season and could also house some large outdoor sculptures.

Now, seven years later, it's looking like the garden I had dreamt of and is my peaceful go-to place to watch birds, butterflies, hummingbirds, and lots of bees and insects.

This garden's estimated size is ¼ acre.

TROWEL TALK

Piet Oudolf and Edie Beale! Piet Oudolf is why I garden. His gardens changed everything for me, and I dream of visiting all of the landscapes he has designed one day. Edie Beale because I'm starting to imagine myself glued to this garden as she was to Grey Gardens.

—Anna Grossman

NUTLEY

THE MOUNTSIER GARDEN

 partial 10–4

This garden is open four times this year: April 13, May 4, June 1, and September 7.

This month: enjoy our lush tropicals and caladiums.

A garden for all seasons that has been created and fine-tuned for more than two decades and now encompasses 2 acres. Owners Silas Montsier and Graeme Hardie have collaborated with noted landscape designer and friend Richard Hartlage, and the result is a feast for the eyes and for the senses.

Principally a stroll garden, there are numerous focal points, small rooms, seating areas, private nooks, and impressive vistas. Drifts of variegated hakonechloa soften the strong architectural underpinnings of the garden, and many of the brilliant and original plant combinations will thrill the devoted horticulturist.

A collection of small sculptures, artworks, and commissioned pieces is interspersed throughout as accent points and disarming bits of humor. From thousands of early spring flowering bulbs to a subtle but glorious display of green on green in the early fall, there is something new to see and enjoy on every visit.

This garden's estimated size is 2-1/3 acres.

Register online: gardenconservancy.org/opendays

Bergen County
Saturday, September 14

PUBLIC GARDEN PRESERVATION PARTNER
GREENWOOD GARDENS

**274 Old Short Hills Rd
Short Hills, New Jersey 07078**

Since the early twentieth century, Greenwood Gardens was a private retreat with formal Italianate gardens graced by colorful tiles, rustic stone tea houses, mossy-pebbled walks, and vistas stretching for miles into the surrounding wooded hillsides.

Careful preservation work and imaginative horticulture have returned much of the garden to its original Arts & Crafts design.

Greenwood Gardens is endorsed by the Garden Conservancy as a Preservation Project Garden.

facebook.com/GreenwoodShortHills

instagram.com/greenwoodgardensnj

greenwoodgardens.org

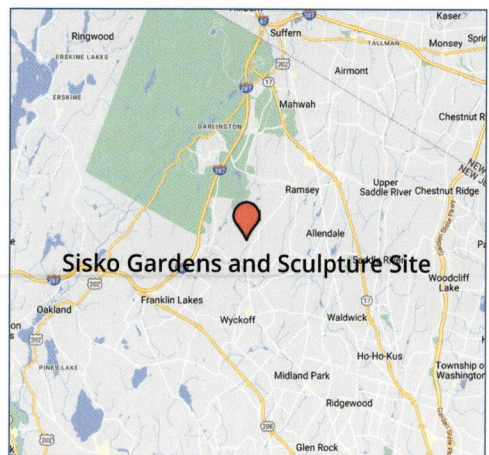

Sisko Gardens and Sculpture Site

MAHWAH
SISKO GARDENS AND SCULPTURE SITE
  10–3

This garden is open twice this year: July 13 and September 14.

Paul has been working on this 3½-acre property for 37 years. The land was completely wooded within 50 feet of all sides of the original home, which years ago was a small farmhouse. Major tree removal has opened the property to sunlight and sunset views.

The fishpond and pool area are surrounded by terraced gardens from relocated stone farm walls that were on the property along with larger stones unearthed from additional construction to the home. The terraces and upper gardens have been planted with mostly perennials and numerous annuals for spring through fall color.

A new raised bed vegetable garden was

added to an adjoining plot of land in 2020 which includes a ten-zone drip and spray watering system. All these gardens, as well as additions to the original home and his art studio/barn building have been developed personally by Paul. With more than 1,000 feet of installed deer fencing and electric driveway gates, the gardens are now much safer from the resident deer population that live within the surrounding forest.

Of note are the numerous contemporary metal sculptures throughout the property which were all created by Paul during his artful career and later. The Sisko Gardens and Sculpture Site is a premier example of an owner designed, constructed, and maintained sanctuary that should be seen and enjoyed.

This garden's estimated size is 3½ acres.

💬 TROWEL TALK

I started gardening about 71 years ago when my parents bought a new home in New Milford, NJ. The property was bare except for a clump of maple trees.

We worked on the parcel evenings and weekends for several years until it was up to the high standards of my parents. Nicest in the neighborhood, needless to say. They just did everything the best they could on a budget, and it looked great. I learned a lot from that time. A lot of digging, planting, raking, and lawn maintenance. Pride of ownership. Some things have to rub off on your future.

I went to college and studied Industrial Arts Education as building things was high on my enjoyment list, and it was a secure profession. Teaching would hopefully give me time when I bought a home to have a nice garden, too.

After teaching a few years I found myself designing sculptural furniture in wood and metal. After a few years of teaching, I decided to open my own business to try to sell some of my craft, which I did, but I was also experimenting with steel sculpture. I found that it was economically more profitable for me and put more effort into the metal art work. Most of my medium to larger works were being installed in private gardens as well as architectural garden sites. What a nice marriage of what is natural and what was man-made.

I continued in both fields for around 30 years and had small gardens wherever my wife, Janet, and I lived, and then we found a larger 3½-acre parcel in Mahwah, NJ. Finally, a place to build a larger studio and bigger gardens. That was 38 years ago. Taking down trees, moving more than 300 tons of stone to form the terraced gardens and merge some of the sculptures I still owned into the garden spaces.

The gardening portion of my time started taking over anything else. I joined garden clubs to learn from others and eventually took the Master Gardeners Course through Rutgers University Extension Service. More and more things to learn. Will I ever know enough to be satisfied? Probably not.

Gardening is a never-ending, life-long learning process and loaded with exercise. It's like a whole day yoga class. Interesting how much of my industrial arts building experience is necessary to create the gardens and install and maintain all the many aspects of a garden, like the watering systems, building the raised beds, varmint protection, and more. If I live to be a healthy 100, I can attribute at least a portion of that time to gardening.

—*Paul Sisko*

Somerset County

Saturday, September 21

FAR HILLS
THE HAY, HONEY FARM

  10–4

This garden is open twice this year: May 4 and September 21.

The Hay, Honey Farm's extensive gardens have been carefully added to the landscape since 1989 in a naturalistic manner, with a respect for the history and topography of the site, and consistent with the broader surrounding atmosphere of Pleasant Valley.

The plant collections reflect the diverse interests of the owners and the resident horticulturists and are set within a dwarf conifer/spring bulb garden, a walled perennial border, hosta gardens, meadow, hayfields, a kitchen garden, a woodland garden of rhododendron and companion wildflowers, and a mostly native wild garden, home to a growing assortment of songbirds.

This garden's estimated size is 12 acres.

💬 TROWEL TALK

Oh so many favorite plants! Collections of American holly, rhododendron, hostas, maples, dwarf conifers, oaks, and more. We also enjoy growing many plants from seed.

— *The Gardener*

New Jersey 229

Casa Nancia, Los Angeles, CA
Photo: Matt Harbicht

Become a Garden Host or a Regional Ambassador

See page 374 or contact us at **opendays@gardenconservancy.org** to learn more.

Songni Yuan - Glenville, NY
Photo: the Garden Host

231

New York

232 New York

Rose
Rosa

Open Days dates and times by County, Town, and Garden

ALBANY

Loudonville
Inspired by Italian Garden Designs
  Saturday, July 20, 10–1, 1–4

COLUMBIA

Canaan
Rockland Farm
  Sunday, July 28, 10–4
Claverack
Ketay Garden
  Saturday, June 15, 10–4
Peter Bevacqua and Stephen King
  Saturday, June 15, 10–4
Hillsdale
Wombat Crossing
  Saturday, May 4, 10–4
Hudson
Flying Pig Acres
  Saturday, June 15, 10–4
Versailles on Hudson
  Saturday, June 15, 10–4
West Taghkanic
Arcadia - Ronald Wagner and Timothy Van Dam
  Saturday, June 15, 10–4

DELAWARE

Andes
Cynthia and Charles Bonnes
  Saturday, July 6, 10–4
Mel and Peg's Rustic Cabin Cottage Garden
  Saturday, July 6, 10–4
Delancey
Clove House Farm and Gardens
  Saturday, July 6, 10–4
Delhi
West Wind Farm
  Saturday, July 6, 10–4
Hobart
Gunhouse Hill Garden
  Saturday, July 6, 10–4
Roscoe
Henderson Hollow Farm - Mermer Blakeslee and Eric Hamerstrom
  Saturday, July 6, 10–4

DUTCHESS

Amenia
Broccoli Hall–Maxine Paetro
  Saturday, May 18, 10–4
  Sunday, June 2, 10–4
Millbrook
Clove Brook Farm - Christopher Spitzmiller and Anthony Bellomo
  Sunday, June 2, 10–4
  Saturday, September 21, 10–4
Garden of Katie Ridder and Peter Pennoyer
  Saturday, September 21, 10–4
Lithgow Cottage Farm
  Saturday, July 27, 10–4
Squirrel Hall
  Sunday, June 2, 10–4

Millerton
Garden of Helen Bodian
Sunday, June 23, 10–4
Highgrove Cottage
Saturday, July 27, 10–4
Shekomeko Hillside Garden
Sunday, June 23, 10–4
Poughkeepsie
Dappled Berms - The Garden of Scott VanderHamm
Sunday, June 23, 10–4
Stanfordville
Ellen Petersen
Saturday, September 21, 10–4
Wassaic
Neverest
Saturday, May 18, 10–2

JEFFERSON
Wellesley Island
The Enchanted Edible Forest at Cross Island Farms
Saturday, May 18, 10–12, 12–2, 2–4
Saturday, October 5, 10–4

NASSAU
Glen Cove
Kippen Hill
Saturday, June 15, 10–4
Locust Valley
Garden of Carol and Jim Large
Saturday, June 15, 10–4
Port Washington
The Gardens at Sands Light
Saturday, June 15, 10–4
Roslyn Harbor
Shade Haven - Susan and Steve King
Saturday, June 15, 10–4

PUTNAM
Brewster
Rumford Hall
Sunday, June 30, 10–4

SARATOGA
Clifton Park
GrowForMe5b
Saturday, July 20, 10–4
Saratoga Springs
A Place to Nest - Moe's Garden
Saturday, June 29, 10–4
Foxglove - Sarah Patterson's Garden
Saturday, June 29, 10–4
Schuylerville
Susie and Paul's Gardens
Saturday, June 29, 10–4

SCHENECTADY
Glenville
Songni Yuan
Saturday, July 20, 10–12, 12–2, 2–4
Niskayuna
Cherie Gold
Saturday, July 20, 10–4
Garden of Gregory and Kathleen Greene
Sunday, July 20, 10–4
The Garden of M. Patricia
Saturday, July 20, 10–4
Schenectady
50 Shades of Green
Saturday, July 20, 10–4

SUFFOLK

Bridgehampton
Entwood Garden
  Saturday, June 22, 10-4
Pamela Harwood and Peter Feder
  Saturday, June 22, 10-4
East Hampton
Art House Garden of Delights
  Saturday, June 22, 10-4
Glade Garden–Abby Jane Brody
  Saturday, May 11, 10-3
Pomeroy
  Saturday, September 7, 10-2
The Garden of Dianne B.
  Saturday, May 11, 10-3
Jamesport
Winds Way Farm
  Saturday, July 13, 10-4
Mattituck
The Landcraft Garden Foundation
  Saturday, July 13, 10-4
Mt. Sinai
Tranquility
  Saturday, May 25, 10-4
  Saturday, July 13, 10-4
Old Field
Two Grey Achers
  Saturday, May 25, 12-4
Sag Harbor
Donna's Farmette
  Saturday, June 22, 10-4
The Hunting-Cooper Garden
  Saturday, May 11, 10-3
Wading River
Woodland Garden - Bill and Veronica Schiavo
  Saturday, May 25, 10-4
Wainscott
Biercuk and Luckey Garden
  Saturday, May 11, 10-3
  Saturday, September 7, 10-2

SULLIVAN

Barryville
Sally's Garden
  Saturday, July 27, 10-4
Jeffersonville
297 and 298
  Saturday, July 27, 10-4
Shady Fox Farm
  Saturday, July 27, 10-4
Livingston Manor
Old Danzer Farm
  Saturday, July 27, 10-4
Mountain Dale
Woodsndale
  Saturday, July 27, 10-4
North Branch
Grateful Beds
  Saturday, July 27, 10-4
Youngsville
Yaun Farm
  Saturday, July 27, 10-4

ULSTER

New Paltz
Ying and Yang in Tillson
  Sunday, June 9, 10-4
Saugerties
Ann Krupp Bryan
  Sunday, June 9, 10-4
Riverhill–Joe and Tamara DiMattio
  Sunday, June 9, 10-4
West Shokan
Secret Garden
  Sunday, June 9, 10-4

WESTCHESTER
Bedford
Brae Willows
Saturday, June 15, 10–4
Rabbit Hill
Saturday, June 15, 10–4
The Great Hill Schoolhouse
Sunday, April 28, 10–4
Bedford Hills
Bedford Cross Farm
Saturday, May 11, 10–4
Chappaqua
The Little Garden That Could
Saturday, May 11, 10–4
Croton on Hudson
Rivermere on the Hudson
Saturday, June 15, 10–4
Lewisboro
The White Garden
Sunday, April 28, 10–4
Mount Kisco
Rocky Hills
Saturday, May 11, 10–4
The Greneker Retreat
Saturday, June 15, 10–4
North Salem
Perrin Garden
Sunday, June 30, 10–4
The Hen and the Hive
Sunday, June 30, 10–4
Ossining
A Garden for Birds and Pollinators
Saturday, May 11, 10–12, 12–2, 2–4
Pound Ridge
James and Ellen Best's Sara Stein Garden
Saturday, June 15, 10–4

NEW YORK

Westchester County
Sunday, April 28

BEDFORD
THE GREAT HILL SCHOOLHOUSE

 10–4

The Great Hill Schoolhouse is a historic property on 2 acres that is owned by landscape designer John Holm and industrial designer Harry Allen. The original structure served as a local schoolhouse for a century until the 1940s.

Over the last twenty years, John has replaced lawn, pachysandra, and foundation plantings with (mostly) native trees, shrubs, perennials, grasses, and sedges. It's a sustainable landscape that draws inspiration from natural plant communities with great emphasis on structure, texture, and movement. In fall, plants are left to provide winter interest and to provide habitat for overwintering insects and sustenance for birds.

Much of the garden's character comes from the juxtaposition of the loose, flowing nature of the meadow-style planting against structural elements such as hedges, rock walls, and mature boxwoods. The crisp edging of the path that takes you through the garden offsets the organic elements. The house is set underneath a copse of mature sugar maples that provide shade for a woodland garden and a patio with potted Japanese maples.

There is also a crevice style rock garden with a collection of alpines, desert plants, and troughs.

This garden's estimated size is 2 acres.

💬 TROWEL TALK

John Holm's career in landscape design started at the New York Botanical Garden's School of Horticulture. In his first job out of school, he worked for Martha Stewart as head gardener on her estate in Bedford. In 2016 he founded John Holm Landscape Design and has been working on a variety of independent projects since.

— *The Gardener*

LEWISBORO
THE WHITE GARDEN
  10–4

The native oak-hickory forest provides a "sacred grove" setting for the modern Greek Revival–style house, designed by architect Patrick Naggar. The gardens, designed by Patrick Chassé, ASLA, were completed in 1999.

Nearest the house, the gardens are classically inspired, including a theater court, a pergola garden, a nymphaeum, and a labyrinth, and additional hidden gardens include a perennial ellipse, an "annual" garden, a conservatory "jungle" garden, and an Asian-inspired moss garden.

Several water features accent the landscape, and native plantings dominate in areas outside the central gardens. Many sculptures enrich this landscape, and one can visit a Temple of Apollo on an island in the main pond. In spring, more than 500,000 daffodils bloom in the woodland.

Woodland walking paths weave over a meandering brook and through a shady dell. Several glasshouses can be seen, including a new state-of-the-art greenhouse that supports the gardens. Head gardener Eric Schmidt, who ably orchestrates the rich garden plantings throughout the property, will be on hand for questions.

This garden's estimated size is 50 acres.

Columbia County
Saturday, May 4

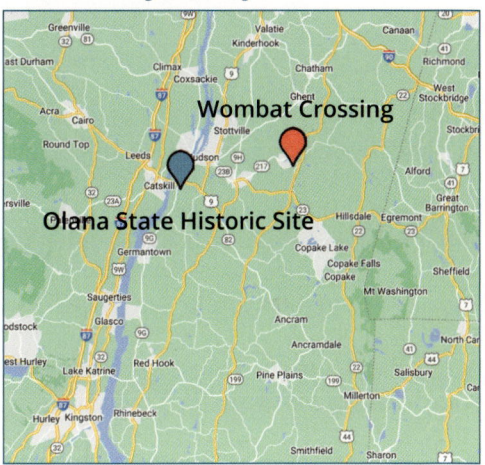

An additional garden is open nearby:
Berkshire County, MA
 Black Barn Farm, Richmond, MA
See page 150.

HILLSDALE
WOMBAT CROSSING
NEW   10–4

My husband (now deceased) and I started our garden in 1991 as complete novices. As the site was set in 25 acres of woodland containing existing mature native trees (oak, pine, hickory, maples, dogwood—a particular favorite—and a stand of grey birch) and variable topography on an escarpment, we focused on augmenting these existing features with other native plants but have not excluded exotics.

After installing a deer fence around the house and 2–3 acres, we planted many native understory trees and bushes to complement the larger trees and provide shelter and food for birds and small animals. While changing the topography somewhat to accommodate a swimming pool, we then concentrated on creating clearings and views outside the deer fence, particularly to the west where we created a large wet meadow (which had been choked with non-native honeysuckle).

In this project, we were helped by an ice storm that downed trees on our western ridge, which created a "keyhole" through which the setting sun aligns twice a year. A walk to the keyhole affords a distant western vista and a view down the escarpment to the Agawamuck Creek.

This garden's estimated size is 25 acres total, with 2 acres of gardens.

💬 TROWEL TALK

When we started gardening, both my husband and I reconnected with lovely memories of gardening with our grandfathers. It seemed that gardening had skipped a generation in our families, and we had a new sense of the men our grandfathers had been and the importance of their relationship to us.

In turn, after the death of my husband, I have found the garden to be a place full of more recent memories. I feel that the garden's foundation has been determined but that it continues to evolve in wonderful ways, especially with the expertise and taste of my gardener, Heather Grimes, and her fine team.

I think that the existing site of our garden helped us so much to see the beauty of native woodlands—how spaces flow into and out of a woodland. I love transitional spaces along the woodland edge and the plants that thrive there, especially dogwoods, redbud, and birch. The garden and the surrounding property are full of these trees. That said, I also love peonies, iris, hostas, and daffodils, so these also have a place.

I think what I love most in a garden is its flow—how your eye trips along various features or plants and finds variety and texture and color but they all seem as one integrated whole.

The garden provides me with constant amazement and surprise and delight (Did I do that? How did that bush suddenly seem so critical? Is that the setting sun hitting those berries?) and a sense of peace and serenity. I always feel very grateful to have the gift of this garden.

—*Joe Baker*

Register online: gardenconservancy.org/opendays   New York   239

**PRESERVATION PARTNER
PUBLIC GARDEN**

**OLANA STATE
HISTORIC SITE**

5720 NY-9G
Hudson, New York 12534

The Olana Partnership is a non-profit organization whose mission is to inspire the public by preserving and interpreting Frederic Church's OLANA, a New York State Historic Site and National Historic Landmark within the Hudson River Valley National Heritage Area.

facebook.com/OlanaFredericChurch/

instagram.com/olanafredericchurch/

olana.org

Suffolk County
Saturday, May 11

EAST HAMPTON
GLADE GARDEN—ABBY JANE BRODY

A layered garden planted for year-round interest has been carved in the shade of the native woodland of Springs.

From snowdrops and crocuses, wintersweet, witch hazels, and the odd camellia in January, to autumn camellias and fragrant osmanthus in December, something is flowering almost every day. After the minor bulbs and mosaic of corydalis in late winter, the ground level is carpeted with wood anemones and woodland phlox.

In early May comes a climax of primulas, hellebores, epimedium, and species peonies. The understory trees and shrubs, too, flower throughout the seasons: spring-blooming camellias, daphnes, and fragrant rhododendron are followed by a progression of hydrangeas, collections of

NEW 5 10 20 '95 Year    No Photography   Accessibility    Nibbled Leaf Garden

Japanese maples, stewartia and clethra, crape myrtles, and new treasures like the purple-leaved styrax, Chinese trumpet vine, and a gordlinia that flowers from August through November.

This garden's estimated size is ½ acre.

💬 **TROWEL TALK**

I am a plant collector, especially woodies. Botanizing in Europe, Mexico, and China. Influenced by visiting gardens and nurseries in the UK and Europe. I have been a garden columnist for the local paper for eighteen years. I work on village community gardens, including acting as curator of the Mimi Meehan Native Plant Garden.

—*The Gardener*

THE GARDEN OF DIANNE B.
  10–3

The May 11 garden should be festooned with flowers, as Dianne is now in the midst of planting her every autumn 1,000-plus bulbs.

The meadow may look a mess with the daffodils gone and all else on the come, but in the gardens, there will be various fritillary, droopy and upright trillium, lots of that spring blueness particular to ipheion and all kinds of hyacinths, plus the shocking chartreuse of epimediums and at least a few precious Jack-in-the-pulpits from this extensive collection.

A few dozen diverse Japanese maples will be in tender new leaf as will the wilds of the East Hampton Village Nature Trail which is literally next door. In this layered low-key garden, living things are mixed with symbols and sculptures from across the globe. Dianne labels herself a "garden stylist" fond of weaving together texture, accessories, color, and patterns echoing her twentieth-century career in fashion.

Her blog, *Dirtier*, diannebgardens.com, is the progeny of her '90s gardening book, *Dirt* (still available at amazon.com).

This garden's estimated size is 1 acre.

SAG HARBOR
THE HUNTING-COOPER GARDEN
NEW   10–3

The Hunting-Cooper House Garden can be entered by the driveway just off Main Street in Sag Harbor. It is a hedged town garden with lots of unusual and choice perennials set out in a series of beds flowing around the house.

The texture and color of tree, shrub, and plant foliage and their flowers are woven into a series of naturalistic vignettes in which the scale of plantings is carefully considered to create the impression of expansiveness and provide year-round interest.

💬 **TROWEL TALK**

My favorite garden tool is the dibble and the plant I would most like to be able to grow is *Glaucidium Palmatum*.

—*The Gardener*

NEW   5   10   20   '95   Year    No Photography    Accessibility    Nibbled Leaf Garden

Register online: gardenconservancy.org/opendays   New York 241

WAINSCOTT
BIERCUK AND LUCKEY GARDEN
  10–3

This garden is open twice this year: May 11 and September 7.

We designed, personally installed, and maintain our four-season garden, which shelters, under a high oak canopy, a collection of rhododendrons, camellias, azaleas, pieris, understory trees, perennials, bulbs, and in season, tropicals.

The maturing garden is adapting to changes in sunlight/brightness due to tree death and deforestation on three sides. The rear right quadrant, the sunniest space, contains a pool designed as a pond with a waterfall and is surrounded with plantings that peak mid-July through October.

Winding paths and stone walls enhance a sense of depth and elevation on a mainly flat acre. There is something in bloom every season.

This garden's estimated size is ½ acre.

💬 TROWEL TALK

Despite being a totally committed sun worshiper (my nickname is Tan Man), my preferred gardening venue is treed shaded space. I've enjoyed the opportunity to create a woodland escape, its coolness a perfect foil to a day of sunbathing. The garden, now a treed peninsula since three adjoining properties have been denuded, is a haven for birds.

—Tan Man

Westchester County
Saturday, May 11

BEDFORD HILLS
BEDFORD CROSS FARM
NEW 10–4

We purchased this 1810 farmhouse 30 years ago and have slowly been developing the gardens over the years. The 6-acre property is full of gorgeous mature native trees planted in the late 1800s when the land was used as a nursery.

As some of the oldest trees around the house have fallen, the sun has allowed us to plant more densely and intentionally. We still use the original vegetable garden (bordered by the original peonies) but have added a shade garden, pool garden, rose garden and white garden. We grow many plants from seed and cuttings and use our greenhouse for propagation and overwintering of camellias and succulents.

This garden's estimated size is 2 acres.

NEW  Year    No Photography    Accessibility    Nibbled Leaf Garden

💬 TROWEL TALK

I started gardening with my grandmother who lived next door on our dairy farm. The dairy had its own unchanging rhythms that did not much involve me, but planting sweet peas with my grandmother was just the right amount of independence, effort, and reward.

When I moved to Bedford, I struggled to replicate those wonderful sweet pea beds but now I have it down and I think of her every time I cut those heavenly smelling blooms.

—*The Gardener*

CHAPPAQUA
THE LITTLE GARDEN THAT COULD

   10–4

This modestly sized, organically maintained suburban garden won the 2007 Golden Trowel award from *Garden Design* magazine.

It features a cottage garden of bulbs and perennials, a Belgian fence espalier of fruit trees, a grape arbor, an herb garden, a checkerboard garden, and a "meadow" with naturalized bulbs, native plants, a Domenico Belli sculpture, and a greenhouse. There are many European touches, like rose arbors, window boxes, a fountain, and Anduze pots. There is also a terrace with a wisteria-covered pergola for outdoor dining.

A vertical garden of mostly ferns and heuchera, inspired by Patrick Blanc, was installed several springs ago. It has been a steep learning curve, and we are still learning! This wall has become quite the attraction.

All plant waste is composted, and rainwater is collected for watering the plants in pots. We strive to maintain a healthy ecosystem that connects with and supports the larger environment. Modest in size, our garden is rich in detail and has a great deal of visual appeal. This garden is a happy balance of keeping things natural, full of native and biologically useful plants and yet, provides the creative design elements associated with making gardens for beauty and outdoor pleasures.

This garden was featured in the 2010 "Best of" issue of *Westchester Home* magazine, and hosted a well-received "Wilding Walls, Fruiting Fences" Digging Deeper in 2021.

This garden's estimated size is ¼ acre.

💬 TROWEL TALK

When I started creating this garden three decades ago, I was deemed by most folk to be "quaint, old-fashioned, hippie-ish"—because I chose organic practices, collected rainwater, and made my own compost. Then, twenty years ago when I started converting my back lawn into a tiny meadow of native plants, the adjectives "odd" and "weird" were added.

Today, all the features and methods are current and highly recommended. I am suddenly and shockingly oh! so on trend!! All it was, was a matter of common sense and following my instincts, learning good practices from the past, applying solid science, and ignoring "fickle fashion" trends.

—*Shobha*

MOUNT KISCO

PRESERVATION PARTNER
ROCKY HILLS

  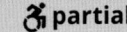 partial 10–4

At Rocky Hills, planting among the stone walls began in the 1950s by William and Henriette Suhr, whose legacy is continued by current owners Barbara and Rick Romeo.

In May and June, the forget-me-nots, which are allowed full freedom throughout the garden, appear as clouds of perfect blue flowers among an ever-expanding rock garden, through the hills and terraces, walls and paths, and fern woodlands, finding good company with self-sown Primula and Spanish bluebells along the natural brook that serves as the heart of the garden.

Tree peonies and an extensive planting of rhododendrons and azaleas compete for attention with the carpet of bulbs throughout the 13 acres.

This garden's estimated size is 9 acres within the 13 acre property.

OSSINING
A GARDEN FOR BIRDS AND POLLINATORS
NEW 10–12, 12–2, 2–4

A mostly native plant, shade/part-shade 1-acre property with an ephemeral wetland and Hudson River tributary, vegetable garden, native fruit and nut plants, and pollinator gardens and habitat. When purchased in 2004, the property was consumed by invasive plants which have now been replaced by an inventory of more than 100 native plant species.

This property was included in a four-year mulch mowing study and a 2020 pollinator study, both conducted by Cornell University. Native plant collections include clethra, ferns, grasses, and heucheras. Less common plants include *Apios americana*, *Euonymus atropurpureus*, *Ptelea trifolata*, and *Staphylea trifolia*.

This garden's estimated size is ½ acre.

💬 TROWEL TALK

I bought elderberry plants for the property only to later discover that an entire stand of elderberry plants were growing in the wetland—previously obscured by invasive plants.

—Donna S.

NEW Year  No Photography  Accessibility Nibbled Leaf Garden

Dutchess County

Saturday, May 18

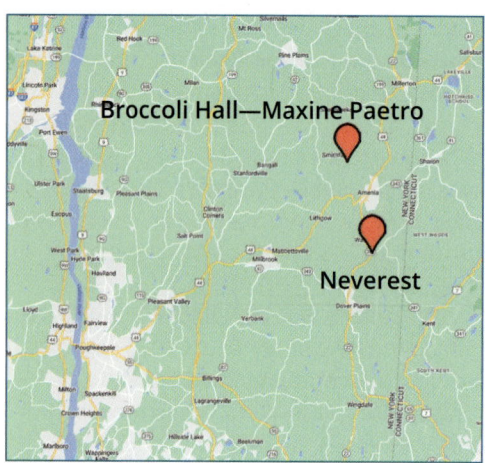

AMENIA
BROCCOLI HALL—MAXINE PAETRO
   10–4

This garden is open twice this year: May 18 and June 2.

Visitors to Broccoli Hall describe this English-style cottage garden as "incredible," "inspirational," "magical"—and they come back again and again. Starting in 1985 with 1½ acres of bare earth, Maxine Paetro collaborated with horticulturist Tim Steinhoff to create a series of enchanting garden rooms.

Broccoli Hall offers an apple tunnel; a brick courtyard; a lavish display of spring bulbs blooming with crab apples in May; an extensive border of irises, peonies, and old shrub roses flowering in June; a tree house with long views; and a secret woodland garden with a teddy bears' picnic.

We have some whimsical rustic carvings by woodsman/artisan Hoppy Quick: new bears, new stairs, new chairs, and some exceptionally charming bird feeders.

Photos and magazine stories about Broccoli Hall can be viewed at broccolihall.com. In 2010, Broccoli Hall was expanded to 5 acres, and two new mud ponds were installed. This is where we began a breeding program—but we don't sell our fish. To see the "elusive kishusui" project in progress, go to kishusui.com. We look forward to seeing you in the garden in 2024!

This garden's estimated size is 5 acres.

WASSAIC
NEVEREST
 10–2

Neverest has evolved over twenty years with the help of our neighbor and garden designer Marsha Kaufman. We found an old house with a patio, long stone wall, hemlock row, and mostly weeds. The site is shady and steeply sloped.

We built stone walls and steps to terrace the land and added a path with native woodland plants. Each spring we added perennial beds, then two fountains, a deck, fence, bluestone courtyard and walk, entry garden, screen porch, large vegetable patch (raised beds over concrete slab), a berry house, and most recently a small greenhouse.

Because of our involvement with Homegrown National Park, we have made a concerted effort to remove invasives from our property, including a very large patch of pachysandra. We will be replanting this area in the spring

NEW Year

with mostly native plants. The plants selected throughout the property feature chartreuse and purple, though there are lots of hydrangeas and a rain garden across the road.

This garden's estimated size is 4 acres.

💬 **TROWEL TALK**

After reading Doug Tallamy's book *Nature's Best Hope*, Ken joined the board of Homegrown National Park. Since then, we have become passionate about removing invasive plants and planting native trees and perennials.

—Ken and Leo

Jefferson County

Saturday, May 18

The Enchanted Edible Forest at Cross Island Farms

WELLESLEY ISLAND
THE ENCHANTED EDIBLE FOREST AT CROSS ISLAND FARMS
♿  10–12, 12–2, 2–4

This garden is open twice this year: May 18 and October 5.

Over the past eleven years Dani Baker has developed an acre of her certified organic farm as a multi-functional "Enchanted Edible Forest" garden containing more than 300 cultivars of perennial fruits, nuts, berries, flowers, and other edibles.

The garden is elegantly landscaped, including a number of native limestone patios, two small ponds, and a bridge, trellis, and gates fashioned from native white cedar. The word that visitors most often spontaneously use to describe it is "magical." Based on her experience creating this garden, Dani has written a book, *The*

NEW 5 10 20 '95 Year  No Photography ♿ Accessibility  Nibbled Leaf Garden

246 New York   Register online: gardenconservancy.org/opendays

Putnam County
Saturday, May 18

Home-Scale Forest Garden: How to Plan, Plant and Tend a Resilient Edible Landscape, a guide to help others create their own magical edible landscapes.

Learn more at enchantededibleforest.com

This garden's estimated size is 1 acre.

💬 **TROWEL TALK**

I planted several honey locusts to provide usable nitrogen to the surrounding plants. Honey locust trees are either male or female. Earlier this season I spotted some large green pods on one of the trees, and exuberantly exclaimed "It's a girl!"

—Dani Baker

DIGGING DEEPER

Power of Place at Manitoga; Garden and Home of Russel Wright
Manitoga's Landscape Collection and Conservation Staff and James Brayton Hall, CEO and President of the Garden Conservancy

Saturday, May 18
Two sessions: 10–12 and 3–5

Manitoga | The Russel Wright Design Center
Garrison, NY
$30 Members | $40 General

NEW 5 10 20 '95 Year   📷 No Photography   ♿ Accessibility   🍃 Nibbled Leaf Garden

Landscape Collection and Conservation staff lead an exploration of the "power of place" at Manitoga, the woodland garden and Mid-century Modern home of pioneering industrial designer Russel Wright and his wife Mary Wright.

Formerly a granite quarry and logging site, the name Manitoga means "Place of Great Spirit," adapted by Wright from Algonquin language. He built his house and studio directly into the quarry walls and brought stone, wood, and plants from the property inside. Wright's integrated vision blended the built elements and the natural landscape together so that each was enriched, enhanced, and transformed by the other.

Just as the house is interwoven with the site, the hillside is connected by views to its larger context of the Hudson River Valley, and the visitors themselves are involved in an intimate and unfolding relationship to place.

With a background in theater set design, Wright had an expert hand in slowly revealing the drama of the landscape. He observed how the light shifted through the trees, the spectacle of the changing of the seasons, how plant communities acted in concert, and the way the forest opened up here or there, to a clearing or to a narrow path where you felt leaves brush against your arms.

In its concept, design, and management, Manitoga unites science, culture, and nature with an ecology that is both human and spiritual. By employing the language of the forest to rehabilitate disturbed land, Wright demonstrated a sense of social responsibility and environmental sensitivity that continues to be relevant for both at-home and professional garden designers.

Photo: Rick Darke

248 New York

Register online: gardenconservancy.org/opendays

Columbia County

Saturday, May 25

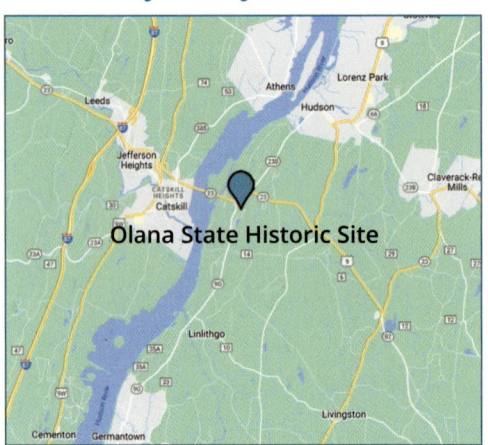

DIGGING DEEPER

Designing in Three Dimensions at Olana: A Guided Landscape Walk and Workshop

Nordica Holochuck, MA, Environmental Studies, and Chris Layman of Fox Farm Apiary

Saturday, May 25, 3–5

Olana State Historic Site
Hudson, NY
$30 GC and Olana Members | $40 General

Over the course of 40 years, the artist Frederic Church worked to create, build, and design Olana's 250-acre landscape.

With more than 5 miles of carriage roads, scenic views, a man-made lake, and native plantings, the site is both a living landscape painting and a vibrant and diverse ecosystem for native pollinators.

Join The Olana Partnership, master gardener and environmental educator Nordica Holochuck, and beekeeper Chris Layman from Fox Farm Apiary for a special walk and workshop to learn more about how to create pathways for pollinators in your own garden inspired by the legacy of Church's garden design at Olana.

During the program, participants will learn more about pollinator pathways, how Church's landscape and garden design intersected with environmental thinking, the way Olana serves as a haven for pollinator habitat, and how The Olana Partnership works closely with Fox Farm Apiary to manage beehives onsite.

The program will consist of a guided walk along 1-¾ miles of historic carriage road, participatory conversation with program guides, and culminate with wine and cheese reception in a special location outside Olana's main house. Special tastings of Olana's own honey will be provided.

Learn more at foxfarmapiary.com.

Photo: Peter Aaron

NEW    Year  No Photography  Accessibility  Nibbled Leaf Garden

Register online: gardenconservancy.org/opendays   New York 249

PRESERVATION PARTNER
PUBLIC GARDEN

OLANA STATE HISTORIC SITE

5720 NY-9G
Hudson, New York 12534

The Olana Partnership is a non-profit organization whose mission is to inspire the public by preserving and interpreting Frederic Church's OLANA, a New York State Historic Site and National Historic Landmark within the Hudson River Valley National Heritage Area.

 facebook.com/OlanaFredericChurch/

 instagram.com/olanafredericchurch/

 olana.org

Suffolk County
Saturday, May 25

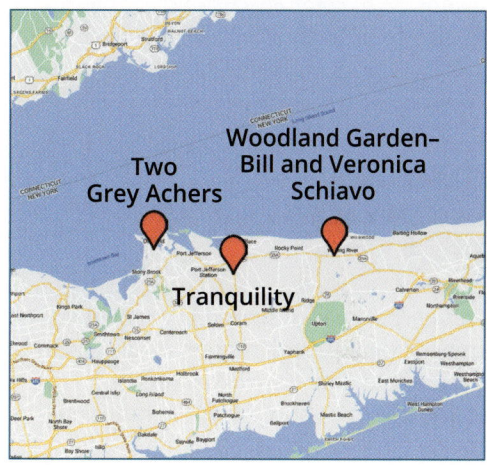

MT. SINAI
TRANQUILITY
5 ♿ partial 🍃 10–4

This garden is open twice this year: May 25 and July 13.

Hundreds of perennials, shrubs, trees, and annuals are combined with water features, lawn art, and recently relocated garden trails that allow the visitor to enter the owner's vision of an Impressionistic garden painting.

Footpaths wind through the extensive garden, allowing visitors to immerse themselves in the sights and sounds of nature and escape the general stress of modern lifestyles.

This garden's estimated size is ¾ acre.

NEW 5 10 20 '95 Year   📷 No Photography   ♿ Accessibility   🍃 Nibbled Leaf Garden

💬 TROWEL TALK

I try to create new gardens each year by moving paths and flower beds. I love explosion of color and use flowers and foliage color to create a visual display.

—The Gardener

OLD FIELD
TWO GREY ACHERS
  12–4

This garden was designed by its owners to provide beauty and interest in all seasons. Adjacent to Conscience Bay on Long Island's North Shore, the mild maritime microclimate is reflected in the broad range of taxa thriving on this intensively planted site.

A remarkable collection of choice conifers and Japanese maples, amassed over three decades, creates a year-round tapestry of color, texture, and form. Come, enjoy, and find specific ideas for stunning, hardworking woody plants to add to your own garden.

This garden's estimated size is 2 acres.

💬 TROWEL TALK

A mature landscape best described as "plants embracing plants" as they will do in advancing age. Overarching theme - the achievement year round color through the use of conifers in various types and combinations. No flowers to speak of. All planning, design and most installation done by owners.

—Bruce A. Feller

WADING RIVER
WOODLAND GARDEN - BILL AND VERONICA SCHIAVO
  10–4

Our property is a heavily wooded acre and a half comprising one large pond, three small ponds, and two streams. The main area on which our house is situated is ringed with 12- to 15-foot rhododendrons and other flowering shrubs.

The terrain was re-landscaped over time to make it both lawn-less and deer resistant, with many varieties of plants. A recently added feature is a shade and fern garden in the front woods that provides a lush setting surrounding a stone patio used for bird-watching and relaxation.

There is also a nature trail that meanders from the top of the front woods and ultimately runs parallel to the 75-foot stream and waterfall that ends by the front door. Behind the house are two ponds, the largest of which is densely surrounded by trees and ornamental grasses and highlighted by a Japanese red maple that drapes over a waterfall at the bottom of a 40-foot stream emerging from the woods.

In addition, our woodland garden is a National Wildlife Federation Certified Wildlife Habitat. The property abounds with wild turkey, deer, a wide variety of birds, and the occasional fox. The landscape design was developed with serenity, meditation, and harmony in mind.

This garden's estimated size is 1 acre.

Register online: gardenconservancy.org/opendays　　　New York　251

Sullivan County
Saturday, June 1

DIGGING DEEPER
Native Plants in the Garden
Carolyn Summers, Executive Director, Flying Trillium Gardens and Preserve, Inc.
Saturday, June 1, 2–4

Flying Trillium Gardens and Preserve
Liberty, NY
$30 Members | $40 General

Despite the recent buzz about the importance of native plants for pollinators and other wildlife, many gardeners remain unfamiliar with their wide variety.

FTGP showcases a diversity of native plants in semi-formal beds and borders, rain gardens, ponds, and meadows, including some deer resistant plantings. We hope to inspire you with new ideas for adding more native plants to your own garden.

Dutchess County
Sunday, June 2

Additional gardens are open nearby:
Litchfield County, CT
　Church House – The Garden of Page Dickey and Bosco Schell, Falls Village, CT
　Isabel and Winston Fowlkes, Washington, CT
　Japanese Gardens at Cedar Hill, Roxbury, CT
　Roxana Robinson - Treetop, West Cornwall, CT
See page 95.

AMENIA
BROCCOLI HALL—MAXINE PAETRO
[20] [95] partial　10-4

This garden is open twice this year: May 18 and June 2.

Visitors to Broccoli Hall describe this English-style cottage garden as "incredible," "inspirational," "magical"—and they come back again and again. Starting in 1985

NEW　5　10　20　95　Year　　No Photography　　Accessibility　　Nibbled Leaf Garden

with 1½ acres of bare earth, Maxine Paetro collaborated with horticulturist Tim Steinhoff to create a series of enchanting garden rooms.

Broccoli Hall offers an apple tunnel; a brick courtyard; a lavish display of spring bulbs blooming with crab apples in May; an extensive border of irises, peonies, and old shrub roses flowering in June; a tree house with long views; and a secret woodland garden with a teddy bears' picnic.
We have some whimsical rustic carvings by woodsman/artisan Hoppy Quick: new bears, new stairs, new chairs, and some exceptionally charming bird feeders.

Photos and magazine stories about Broccoli Hall can be viewed at broccolihall.com. In 2010, Broccoli Hall was expanded to 5 acres, and two new mud ponds were installed. This is where we began a breeding program—but we don't sell our fish. To see the "elusive kishusui" project in progress, go to kishusui.com.

We look forward to seeing you in the garden in 2024!

This garden's estimated size is 5 acres.

MILLBROOK

CLOVE BROOK FARM - CHRISTOPHER SPITZMILLER AND ANTHONY BELLOMO

 partial 10–4

This garden is open twice this year: June 2 and September 21.

The garden at Clove Brook Farm was started about seven years ago following a restoration of the historic Greek Revival farmhouse. The garden has quickly grown into a series of interconnected spaces, beginning with a horseshoe-shaped garden near the house that is surrounded by a clipped hornbeam hedge and anchored by a dovecote. It's this garden where we have a spectacular show of tulips and sweet peas in spring, followed by towering dahlias in late summer.

A few years ago another large garden "room" was added which centers on an oval swimming pool and Neoclassical style pool house. This garden is also bounded by a hornbeam hedge and includes perimeter beds filled with various herbaceous perennials which evolve throughout the growing season, starting with poppies in early spring, then peonies, roses, lilies, and finally dahlias.

Last year my partner, landscape architect Anthony Bellomo, designed and installed a large kitchen garden which we pack with various vegetables. We are both confirmed garden addicts, and in addition to the more formal garden spaces, continue to add informal and naturalistic plantings throughout the property. We've planted several mixed shrub borders studded with drifts of bulbs, embellished our existing orchard, and collected unique sculptures to establish focal points.

NEW 5 10 20 '95 Year    No Photography    Accessibility    Nibbled Leaf Garden

There is nothing more satisfying than tending and fostering a garden, and watching it develop and mature. It's all documented in *A Year at Clove Brook Farm* (Rizzoli, 2021, with foreword by Martha Stewart).

This garden's estimated size is 3 acres.

SQUIRREL HALL

    10–4

Squirrel Hall is a surprisingly amusing garden formally designed on a tiny village lot of less than 1 acre. The rectilinear layout emanates from a central axis defined by an allée of sixteen hornbeams with two niches.

The garden is organized into a series of rooms with features usually reserved for larger properties. Rooms include a glade/cutting garden, an apiary with a bee shed, a sunken garden with fountain, parallel hedgerows of lilac, spirea, and bulbs, a dining courtyard with fireplace, an orchid house, a hornbeam allée, a tapis vert, parterres, a petite orchard, a Neoclassic folly/hidden tool shed, a secret woodland stroll, and another folly known as "the bungalow."

A little over-the-top, a bit tongue-in-cheek, Squirrel Hall is a lot of fun!

This garden's estimated size is ¾ acre.

💬 **TROWEL TALK**

Our design dilemma is to have the elements of a 1000-acre estate installed on less than an acre village lot.
—*Squirrel Hall*

PRESERVATION PARTNER PUBLIC GARDEN

WETHERSFIELD ESTATE & GARDEN

**257 Pugsley Hill Rd
Amenia, New York 12501**

Wethersfield Estate & Garden occupies 1,000 acres in northeast Dutchess County, where it is the highest point in the region with an elevation of 1,200 feet. From that vantage point, it offers majestic views of the Berkshires, the Catskills, and the Taconic Hills.

Comprising a Georgian-style house, classical gardens, a carriage house, and a farm, Wethersfield Estate & Garden is generally considered one of the finest examples of Italian Renaissance gardens in the United States.

Founded by Citigroup heir, philanthropist, and investor Chauncey Stillman in 1938, Wethersfield Estate & Garden is now a nonprofit organization devoted to the proper stewardship of land, habitat protection, conservation, culture, and the arts.

Wethersfield hosts a diversity of formal and native-inspired garden spaces, such as an Arts & Crafts English perennial

---

NEW | 5 | 10 | 20 | '95 Year | 💬 No Photography | ♿ Accessibility |  Nibbled Leaf Garden

254 New York

Register online: gardenconservancy.org/opendays

garden, cut flower garden, hedged yew topiaries, and mature tree specimens, and 20 miles of trails for equestrian activities and hiking.

Wethersfield strives to integrate the latest horticultural knowledge to maintain a sustainable and historical garden in a changing world. Wethersfield Estate & Garden is on the National Register of Historic Places and was awarded the 2021 New York State Historic Preservation Award for Excellence in Historic Landscape Preservation.

f facebook.com/WethersfieldGarden

⃝ instagram.com/wethersfieldgarden

🌐 wethersfield.org

Ulster County
Sunday, June 9

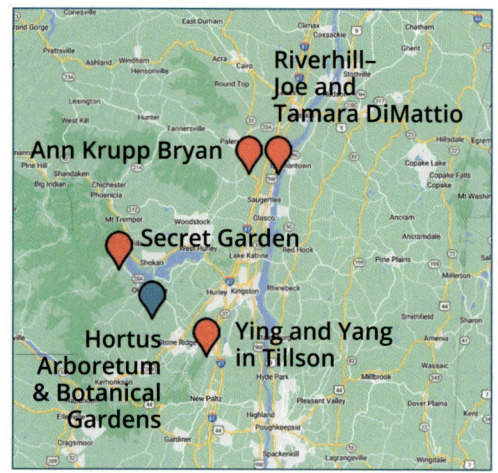

The 2024 Open Days in Ulster County are presented in partnership with Hortus Arboretum and Botanical Gardens.

NONPROFIT PARTNER
2023 GARDENS FOR GOOD RECIPIENT
PUBLIC GARDEN

HORTUS ARBORETUM & BOTANICAL GARDENS

**76 Mill Road
Stone Ridge, New York 12484**

NEW 5 10 20 95 Year    No Photography   ♿ Accessibility    Nibbled Leaf Garden

Our goal is for Hortus to be a "living textbook" of plant life that can be grown in the Hudson Valley.

We began the process of creating a botanical garden/arboretum by planting native trees, shrubs, perennials, and unusual edible plants with a focus on rare and endangered species.

In 2001 we began recording what we planted with detailed plant tags. In 2017 we received Level II Accreditation by the ArbNet Arboretum Accreditation Program and the Morton Arboretum. As a young botanical garden/arboretum, our goal is to grow the largest diversity of plant life in the Hudson Valley accessible to the general public.

This year, Allyson and Scott published *Cold Hardy Fruits and Nuts: 50 Easy-to-Grow Plants for the Organic Home Garden or Landscape* (Chelsea Green Publishing, 2022), an easy-to-use resource for growing healthy, resilient, low maintenance trees, shrubs, vines, and other fruiting plants from around the world.

chelseagreen.com/product/cold-hardy-fruits-and-nuts/

facebook.com/hortusbotanicalgarden

instagram.com/hortusgardens

hortusgardens.org

NEW PALTZ
YING AND YANG IN TILLSON
NEW 10–4

Ying and Yang in Tillson is a collaborative effort between the homeowner and Hudson River Valley Gardens. The sculpture and Zen garden is an opportunity to experience a variety of unique and artful displays in nature that will stimulate the five senses. Moss, red rock, cattails, and pottery are some of the components used to create, design, and build the garden. Ying and Yang in Tillson is a provocative juxtaposition of nature and the imagination at many levels.

This garden's estimated size is ¼ acre.

 TROWEL TALK

HRV Gardens considers many elements when designing and planning a garden similar to an artist's canvas. Space, form, function, and sustainability are contemplated in the process. In addition, the relationship to the environment and the ability to foresee the garden in four seasons as well as five, ten, or twenty years from inception. More often than not we gain knowledge from our mistakes. It is important to focus on the foundation and build from there.

—Paul Goldbacher "HRV Gardens"

SAUGERTIES
ANN KRUPP BRYAN
10 10–4

Beginning as a gravel parking lot and the grounds of a country church, the garden has developed over the past 25 years. Today, the church is a lovely house

---

NEW 5 10 20 '95 Year    No Photography    Accessibility    Nibbled Leaf Garden

surrounded by extensive sunny borders, large old trees underplanted with shade gardens, a steep hillside shade garden, and an organic vegetable garden.

Ann designed, planted, and has maintained this land, including building the stone retaining walls. During the last seven years, foliage plants have taken center stage in both sun and shade. For the past four years, Ann's newly completed sculptures have been added to the landscape each year, and a new 50-foot shrub border is just starting to come into its own.

TROWEL TALK

Every few years I fall in love with a new plant, or a new family of plants and introduce them to my garden. Some do well and stay in my garden and some don't. This means the garden changes over a fairly short period of time, and the change leads to another change but the ones that I still love remain as anchors.

—Ann Krupp Bryan

RIVERHILL—JOE AND TAMARA DIMATTIO
10-4

Riverhill is a 5-acre hillside sloping down to a rocky beach on the Hudson River. Views of the Hudson are a defining feature, as is the park-like landscape sculpted into terraces and gentle slopes. The gardens include an alpine scree, terraced perennial gardens, and an outcrop rockery, as well as extensive collections of potted succulents and alpine troughs.

Also of interest is a growing collection of homegrown ceramic sculpture and a koi canal with aquatic planting. Not to be missed are eagle spotting and watching the river flow.

This garden's estimated size is 5 acres.

WEST SHOKAN
SECRET GARDEN
NEW   10-4

My garden was created to be a very private space, a place to relax and meditate. It is walled by an 8-foot-high fence, and the space has been divided into different rooms that one gradually discovers as you walk around. The plants have been selected for their hardiness, color, and texture. The orchard adjacent to it is there to contrast its simplicity and minimalism with the abundance of plants in the garden.

This garden's estimated size is ⅜ acre.

TROWEL TALK

My inspiration has been my mother and grandmother's city gardens where I would spend many hours just hiding and observing nature. I like gardens with little nooks and places where you can sit and watch the birds and insects visit.

—Hendrik

Columbia County
Saturday, June 15

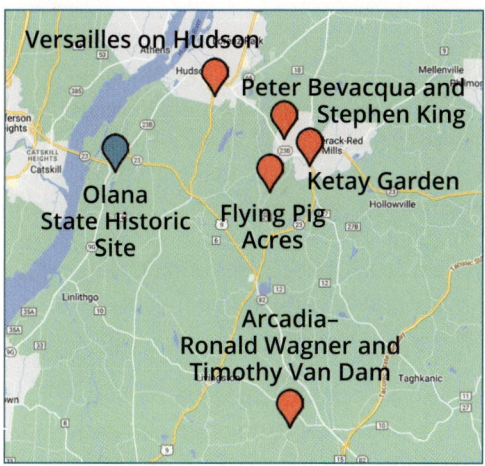

CLAVERACK

KETAY GARDEN
  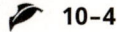 10–4

An allée of large maples and oak, bordered by meadows on either side, forms the entrance to the gardens which surround the house. A large garden in front of the house and a smaller one behind lead down to a meadow in the distance framed by views of the Catskill Mountains.

The front garden is bordered by a semicircle of forsythia that shields the garden from the road. A circular iron bench surrounds an oak tree and is a great place to sit in spring when the irises and redbud are in bloom.

The garden behind the house has a large pergola off the house, which is covered with yellow trumpet vine and looks over the garden and meadow beyond. From this garden, a curving mown path leads down the hill, through the meadow, and then along the side of the property bordered by our homage to Tuscany: a line of tall, narrow Irish juniper, which can, when you squint, look like a row of cypress. In the distance are the barn and the Catskill Mountains.

A smaller rustic pergola is set away from the house with a stone terrace to the side. Two Adirondack chairs sit there for anyone who wishes to watch the sunset or just enjoy the breeze on the meadow. The walled bocce court, with its row of Adirondack chairs added not long ago, has become a favorite late afternoon gathering spot.

This garden's estimated size is 9 acres.

PETER BEVACQUA AND STEPHEN KING
 partial  10–4

This magical garden is a private world hidden from street view in the hamlet of Claverack and has been evolving with devotion and care for the last 30 years.

The 2½-acre garden feels much larger because of its division into many garden spaces—spaces designed with a careful eye to structure, form, and texture. One area unfolds upon the next with its own sense of individuality. Among the features is the sun garden—formally laid out with topiary and surrounded by architectural yew hedges, but informally planted with billowy perennials that over the season blur the garden's green architecture.

There is a hydrangea walk, greenhouse herbaceous borders, and many unusual trees and shrubs. A boxwood cloud hedge, inspired by the work of Jacques

Wirtz, replaces an old rose border, and a border consisting primarily of shrubs and small trees was designed for ease of maintenance while meeting the objective of structure, form, and texture.

The garden continues to evolve. The addition of the ½-acre "Nearly Native Garden," with its thriving beehives, adds another unique space to the mix. The focus here is primarily on native plants, with support from non-natives, to develop a special and unique plant community.

But the thrust of the entire garden is to encourage biodiversity and habitat. The garden is featured in *Gardens of the Hudson Valley* (Monacelli Press), *Private Gardens of the Hudson Valley* (Monacelli Press), and Bevacqua is a featured designer in *Garden Design Masterclass* (Rizzoli) and the recent *American Roots* (Timber Press). The garden has been published in the *New York Times*, *Berkshire Living* magazine, *Rose and Ivy* magazine, *New York Cottages and Gardens*, and *Gardenista*.

This garden's estimated size is 2½ acres.

HUDSON

FLYING PIG ACRES
NEW   10–4

Twenty years of garden obsession! As you enter through the front gate, you'll see a formal garden with golden privet hedges and stone walls and will pass the kitchen garden with its herbs and seating where we enjoy the morning sun; opposite on the front porch, you'll see a tease of the containers and planters we have all over the property.

Walking the gravel paths surrounding the house, you'll experience shade and full sun gardens and at the back, a large entertaining space with two main features: a seating area with a vista of the open meadow and our view down the Bradford Pear Allée where a pagoda folly in traditional red and black colors will catch your eye—a perfect place for a meditation break.

Walk further on around the shipping container pool, where a small footbridge leads to the vegetable garden and greenhouse. As you come back toward the front, a small pond and stream come into view where you can sit on the squirrel bench and listen to the running water where grasses and native plants are in view.

As you end your journey, you will come to the whimsical cottage garden beds along the path where playful topiaries complement the original cedar cottage.

This garden's estimated size is 2 acres.

💬 TROWEL TALK

It is very hard to pick a favorite plant. If I had to, I would say it's my peony tree. With its vivid, hot pink petals and vibrant yellow center. Drives me wild.

My first gardens were planted twenty years ago after renovation of cottage. They started out with two beds on either side of the front door flanked by a pair of juniper topiaries. After that I was hooked, and there was no stopping me.

This is a very silly thing, but forsythia… I've tried to get it to grow on the outer edges of the garden in the woods, similar to the way you might see it growing in Asia. They've not spread out and bloom with only a few flowers.

NEW 5 10 20 '95 Year    No Photography    Accessibility    Nibbled Leaf Garden

My auger is 1,000 times better than a shovel. My father was my inspiration for gardening. He was an avid gardener himself. My gardens growing up I would say were very Italian American, a little bit of everything all mixed up together and full of color.

—Michael Tavano

VERSAILLES ON HUDSON
  10–4

We wanted to create a garden that looked as if it had been planted when the house was built in 1901. The entire land formation presented a real challenge; from the house to the bottom of the garden was a steep 30-foot drop. We needed to create an elegant way to move through the garden, so we carefully designed multi-level stone patios and easy-access stairways to guide you down to the fountain.

We chose a most unexpected plan that would take advantage of the dramatic views of the river, hills, and sunsets. By turning the garden on its axis, we created the illusion of a massive property with grand, sweeping lawns; long, flowing hydrangea and hornbeam hedges; and architectural boxwood balls. Our fountain and the hornbeam curve are the highlights of this quiet garden, complete with fish, frogs, and water plants.

In the spring and early summer, the garden is predominately green and white, and it turns ever more pink as the summer progresses. In the winter, this garden makes an equally strong statement due to its framing by many evergreens.

Versailles on Hudson offers ever-changing vistas as you walk around the property. From the upper and lower patios, the grand porch, the four staircases, to the long lawns and the bubbling fountain, this special garden always delights and soothes the soul.

This garden's estimated size is ½ acre.

WEST TAGHKANIC
ARCADIA - RONALD WAGNER AND TIMOTHY VAN DAM
   10–4

Our 1840 Greek Revival farmhouse is set in a pastoral landscape of 28 acres. An avenue of sweetgum trees lining the formal driveway is planted in a forced perspective to visually extend the approach to the house.

The gently rolling hillside behind is punctuated by a magnificent grove of black locust trees and a grove of deciduous conifers, including bald cypress, metasequoia, and larch trees. A wildflower meadow rises to the north, in which a pentagon-shaped planting of gingko trees can be reached by a mown path leading through the meadow.

Another path leads through the forest beyond. Many informal planting beds around the property include lilacs, rhododendron, mountain laurel, and hydrangea. A large pond is the focus of surrounding naturalistic plantings of Japanese primula, skunk cabbage, Japanese iris, ferns, and rudbeckia giving to views of the wetland beyond. A formal yew crescent acts as an architectural folly in contrast to the naturalistic pond.

Symmetrical terraces at the house feature

NEW 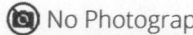 Year  No Photography  Accessibility Nibbled Leaf Garden

260　New York　　　Register online: gardenconservancy.org/opendays

a wisteria arbor over a large stone dining table on the south and a perennial border of peonies and roses on the north. A new stumpery border of ferns and shade loving woodland plants has been created to line the service drive to the south.

This garden's estimated size is 5 acres.

💬 **TROWEL TALK**

We have a very high water table in West Taghkanic. When we dug the holes to plant the avenue of sweetgum trees up the driveway, the holes filled up with water to the grass line overnight before we planted the trees.

—The Gardeners

PRESERVATION PARTNER PUBLIC GARDEN

OLANA STATE HISTORIC SITE

**5720 NY-9G
Hudson, New York 12534**

The Olana Partnership is a non-profit organization whose mission is to inspire the public by preserving and interpreting Frederic Church's OLANA, a New York State Historic Site and National Historic Landmark within the Hudson River Valley National Heritage Area.

f facebook.com/OlanaFredericChurch/

📷 instagram.com/olanafredericchurch/

🌐 olana.org

Nassau County
Saturday, June 15

GLEN COVE
KIPPEN HILL

    10–4

Kippen Hill is a twelve-year-old garden that encompasses five smaller gardens situated on 1½ acres.

The variegated garden grows 'Dragon's Eye' pine and Japanese forest grass, variegated hosta, and acuba. A formal garden of English-style borders with a central-axis bubbler fountain is the anchor to the site. An Asian garden with an aviary pagoda is home for our Asian-native egg-laying hens. Coltsfoot from the Humes Japanese Stroll Garden and black bamboo are featured here, along with a majestic centenary boulevard cedar that was planted when the house was first built in 1910.

A small vegetable garden with heirloom tomatoes hosts a collection of nineteenth-century American garden equipment. The roomy front lawn is planted with ornamental papyrus in paisley-patterned beds, surrounded by English-style borders.

A Lord and Burnham greenhouse dating to 1925 was rescued and restored from a famed Gold Coast estate about seven years ago by Dean and Jonathan. This outbuilding doubles as a site for our collection of tropicals, including bananas and orchids, as well as a dining room for guests during all four seasons.

This garden's estimated size is 1½ acres.

LOCUST VALLEY
GARDEN OF CAROL AND JIM LARGE

 partial   10–4

This garden truly reflects the personality of its owners, having been redesigned and altered over their 30 years of ownership. The bones of the original garden were designed through Innocenti and Webel in the late 1930s around a much older frame farmhouse that was moved to the site and altered in 1936 by architect Bradley Delahanty.

The property encompasses 10 acres of mature woodlands, streams, ponds, and fields placed in a framework of Long Island's signature rhododendron, mountain laurel, and azalea. There are several more formal garden areas planted with specimen woody plants, herb and perennial gardens, lawns, and terraces.

This garden's estimated size is 9¾ acres.

💬 TROWEL TALK

I am a plant lover, our garden contains plants that I have brought and bought at auctions and trips to nurseries near and

far. I am continually adding new areas of interest and making more work for myself and a project every year or two.

Particularly love sharing with other garden- and plant-loving members of my family and friends, helping my children who like to garden develop and plan their gardens. There are many rhododendron and pieris in this garden, and I particularly like mountain laurel. Although we live in a great place for growing it, I have had mixed luck in getting it to establish.

—*The Gardener*

PORT WASHINGTON
THE GARDENS AT SANDS LIGHT
partial   10–4

The Gardens at Sands Light are located on the waterfront estate of a former Vanderbilt mansion and nineteenth-century lighthouse and cottage, providing a unique and dramatic setting. The French château-inspired residence provides a grand centerpiece for the 4-acre garden, the creation of a passionate plantswoman and artist.

The garden will take you from a mixed woodland and stream to a beachside marble temple, large shrub and perennial borders to formal knot garden, and cactus garden onto a large private beach. A strolling garden, designed to provide privacy and to entertain, joins quiet alcoves as well as spacious terraces and outdoor living arrangements.

A lush summer display is achieved by the addition of more than 100 containers, sporting vibrant colored annuals and large tropicals. The extensive collections include specimen plants with unique habits and variegations, orchids, and rare tropical plants, as well as peacocks, koi, and tortoises.

This garden's estimated size is 5½ acres.

ROSLYN HARBOR
SHADE HAVEN - SUSAN AND STEVE KING
10–4

Towering oak trees provide the canopy for our 1-acre shade garden. Enter through a wrought-iron arbor and stroll through a series of garden rooms passing borders of rhododendrons, skimmia, and cherry laurels.

Nearby is a pond with a stream and waterfalls where koi and goldfish are eagerly awaiting their afternoon snack. Stacked stone walls surround shade-loving perennials, coral bark maples, and many species of hydrangeas. Follow a serpentine path to enter a woodland garden; beaded totem poles lead to a secluded area of contemplation. Pass by the colorful garden cottage with its stained glass window and walk through the arbors planted with clematis to arrive at the two-level brick patio that is bordered by lushly planted cobalt blue containers.

Visit the greenhouse filled with a wide variety of succulents. Within view are formal boxwood gardens and sweetly scented clerodendrum. These gardens have been designed, built, and maintained by the owners and their three sons over the last fifteen years.

This garden's estimated size is 1 acre.

NEW 5 10 20 '95 Year   No Photography   Accessibility   Nibbled Leaf Garden

💬 TROWEL TALK

Grass does not grow well on my property because there is too much shade. So, each year I find more and more moss. There are so many interesting varieties to discover. Happily, once moss finds a spot it likes, it grows beautifully without any care on my part and makes a soft inviting carpet to walk on.

—Susan K

Westchester County
Saturday, June 15

BEDFORD
BRAE WILLOWS

5 ♿ partial   10–4

Brae Willows, a 1-acre garden, began its infancy in June 1967 as an open, barren piece of land with three rhododendrons and a smattering of mature trees. It was completely designed and planted by the owner, who also helps with the maintenance.

The division of the property by a small seasonal creek, which winds its way through to the Mianus River bordering the back of the property, created the biggest challenge to the owner. Unifying the two sides was accomplished through careful use of trees, shrubs, and bridges.

Because of the river, the water table is in places only several feet from the surface of the ground. Careful planning was needed to use plant material that was visually stimulating without having it look like wetlands.

The varied and extensive use of conifers makes for seclusion, surprise, serenity, and year-round beauty. There is no downtime here. Meticulous attention has been paid to detail. Arbors and five natural stone garden paths leave you wondering what lies beyond. Ornate iron gates beckon your entry. A secluded patio, bird baths, and cement and decorative iron planters add to the total enchantment. Benches, strategically placed, beg you to linger awhile. Three bridges invite you across the creek. Walk under an iron arbor, down a stone path flanked by a perennial and shrub garden, open a small picket gate, and you find yourself looking at a view of the river.

Curved stone walls gently frame the two patios, and a large stone arbor welcomes you into the main part of the garden. A high tsuga hedge frames the gravel driveway. A new "hidden garden" was created in 2021. Though small in size—10 feet wide by 90 feet long—it is filled with diversified hardscape elements and tall, narrow taxus. This captivating and tranquil setting brings a sense of peacefulness. A vista of the gardens can be seen from the covered porch.

This garden's estimated size is 1 acre.

💬 TROWEL TALK

Gardening to me is a humbling experience. You must constantly accept what you cannot change or control.

Last year was no exception. The company I used to trim the hemlock hedge butchered it to the point where the front could never recover. I was devastated.

Then my wonderful, mature ash tree that was more than 150 years old could no longer hold on. This tree was an integral part of the landscape, and taking it down broke my heart. I have often said that gardening is not for the faint of heart. However, the rewards are immense. I made up a saying years ago, "If you think nothing can bring you to your knees, try gardening." I guess that's why they make knee pads.

One thing is for sure, a gardener keeps learning, you can never know everything. Content for me is when everything is weeded, watered, and pruned, at least for one day.

—Cheryl

RABBIT HILL

  10–4

Following the original garden design from Mott Schmidt's award-winning 1926 Country House of the Year, these gardens have been updated to include native plants that are of no interest to the resident deer.

Several garden rooms have been added to incorporate outdoor living spaces that open up to fields and meadows leading to the woodland walk. This family-friendly organic property allows for an informal pool garden, a classic English parterre garden, a peony garden (especially pink in early June), a vegetable garden that complements the charming greenhouse, an extensive fruit orchard, horse paddocks embracing a pollinator field, and an allée of specimen linden trees all set within an historic Georgian design.

Photos and history of the property can be accessed at MottSchmidt.com under Pook's Hill: Mr. and Mrs. Mott B. Schmidt.

This garden's estimated size is 10 acres.

CROTON ON HUDSON
RIVERMERE ON THE HUDSON
partial 10-4

The Rivermere estate overlooks the Hudson River at its widest point and has its own microclimate.

The garden offers several vantage points for peaceful reflection and meditation with serene river views: the water garden, the gazebo overlooking the stream-fed duck pond, and the lawn. A newly planted vineyard with cold hardy grapes is fed by natural water from the pond. A pergola made of natural materials provides a setting for farm-to-table eating in the vineyard.

The waterfall garden contains native plants, tropical plants, ayurvedic herbs, and vegetables with medicinal properties. A small experimental rooftop garden for greens sits atop the peacock house. Flowering trees, daffodils, and seasonal plantings round out the collection.

This garden's estimated size is 2 acres.

MOUNT KISCO
THE GRENEKER RETREAT
 10-4

This 1925 home in Mount Kisco is one of five designed and built by Lillian Greneker, whose works are now curated in Harvard's Arthur and Elizabeth Schlesinger Library on the History of Women in America. Her husband, C. P. Greneker, was then director of publicity for the Shubert Theater.

This 2-acre property has meandering woodchip trails, two streams, seven small bridges, two "secret" gardens, and a wonderful grove of 24 'Heritage' river birch trees. It includes a natural fern garden and other beautiful perennial gardens, created by the owners, that contain astilbe, roses, statuary, a kitchen stone garden, and other whimsical features. The home on this undulating property is enchanting.

This garden's estimated size is 2 acres.

POUND RIDGE
JAMES AND ELLEN BEST'S SARA STEIN GARDEN
  partial 10-4

This ecological restoration by Sara Stein, the native plant pioneer, spans 5½ acres and includes upland and wetland meadows, woodlands, and thickets.

Documenting her planting experiences in her books (*Noah's Garden*, *Planting Noah's Garden*, *My Weeds*), she included many native species important to wildlife but not often used in landscaping. Other features include a stone terrace planted with grasses and sedges, an herb garden within openings in a brick patio, and a planted moss garden and path around the pond.

266 New York

Register online: gardenconservancy.org/opendays

There are numerous paths through the various habitats, all showing a viable, sustainable alternative to the conventional suburban landscape design. Ellen and James Best acquired the property in 2007 and have been maintaining it since then.

This garden's estimated size is 5½ acres.

💬 **TROWEL TALK**

Our challenges have included managing the dense tree canopy by pruning trees and mature native plants that Sara Stein planted almost 50 years ago.

When adding plants, we often lean toward edible natives and are increasingly collecting seeds and propagating the native plants we already have to share, and we also add to the species that seem most well adapted and/or resistant to invasive plants that are increasingly a problem.

—*James and Ellen Best*

Suffolk County
Saturday, June 22

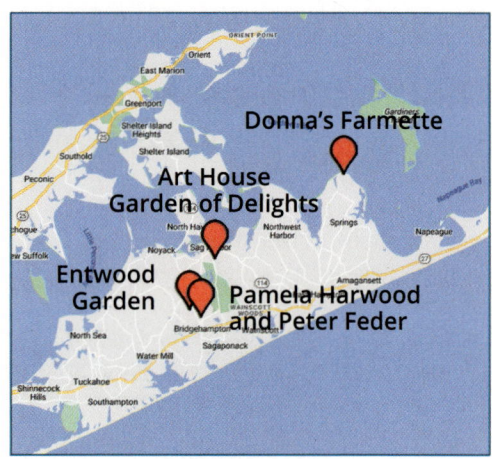

BRIDGEHAMPTON
ENTWOOD GARDEN

    10–4

Entwood is a 7-acre, park-like walking garden developed over 25 years from a flat potato field into a series of garden rooms, expansive views, specimen plants and trees, and features intended to make it difficult for adults and children to stay inside by providing a sense of peace, wonder, and fun.

Entering through an intimate, densely planted, English-style cottage flower garden, the visitor proceeds under an arbor past the owner's 1860 cottage to view a small, Japanese-style garden and koi pond. A second koi pond lies ahead hidden by a grove of cedars of Lebanon.

Crossing north through the pond on stones set in the water, the visitor enters a large arboretum of unusual cultivars of magnolia, dogwood, sweetgum, Japanese maple, redbud, dove (handkerchief) trees,

NEW 5 10 20 '95 Year   🚫 No Photography   ♿ Accessibility   🍃 Nibbled Leaf Garden conifers, and many others.

From shaded paths and shade gardens around the perimeter, views reveal a contoured landscape, a gazebo in the distance, and two large ponds. Looking down from the bridge crossing the first, you notice a wide variety of mature koi, a few of which can be hand fed if you request some koi food from Ed, who has designed and maintained these ponds.

Past the bridge, you will approach the gazebo which is set in a circle of maples and surrounded by a secret path intended to delight those young at heart. Turning right you step onto a zigzag bridge through the "monkey jungle," to the back entrance to the garden.

Turning right on the gravel driveway, you will pass dogwood and rhododendron shaded by native black cherry and red cedar. Following the driveway, you will see a rock garden behind an orchard on your right, with steps leading up to a golf tee, which provides the highest vantage point for the garden.

A brief stroll downhill brings you to another large pond with even more colorful koi and, most importantly by this time, a sitting area. From there, paths lead through shade gardens, past a swimming pool, to the last of the koi ponds, and back to your starting point.

This garden's estimated size is 7 acres.

PAMELA HARWOOD AND PETER FEDER

  partial 10–4

This all-organic garden, which has evolved over the last 27 years, is designed and entirely tended by its two self-taught owners, one of whom is a board member of the Horticultural Alliance of the Hamptons.

Eager to attract beneficial wildlife, the owners installed numerous birdbaths and flowers that attract pollinators. When deer began decimating the plantings, the owners rethought the design, fenced in the rear of the property, and dedicated the accessible front portion entirely to deer-resistant varieties, like the lengthy hedge of 'Hidcote' lavender that runs along the semicircular gravel driveway.

At the same time, they "took back" the fenced-in rear garden, enjoyed blooms that had been deer-eaten for years, but also redesigned the space, continually adding new varieties. The garden is designed to provide blooms from February through November.

A dedicated herb garden was recently expanded when the owners decided to grow other edibles, such as tomatoes, lettuce, green and yellow zucchini, and cucumber. Some are containerized to protect them from rabbits.

Gourds are trained up the deer fence as ornamentals. Although this is mostly a sunny property, there are two shade gardens: one is a rear garden "room" for afternoon shade and entertaining. The other is a shady woodland garden along the front southeast border that features deer-resistant plants.

NEW Year  No Photography 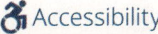 Accessibility  Nibbled Leaf Garden

EAST HAMPTON
ART HOUSE GARDEN OF DELIGHTS
NEW 10–4

Asian fusion, labyrinthine network of foot paths, water features, sculptures, native and decorative plants and trees.

This garden's estimated size is 1 acre.

💬 **TROWEL TALK**

We are creating a space for children and adults where they can delight the senses in a playful way and offer contemplative and meditative places to reflect and rest.
—The Gardener

SAG HARBOR
DONNA'S FARMETTE
NEW 10–4

Including a perennial garden set in place by stone terracing up a hill, a meadow draped under the arms of an ancient mulberry tree, an ornamental kitchen garden, and both a rose and a dahlia garden, there is something in bloom in my garden almost year-round.

Planted primarily with native plants, the garden is a magnet for a wide array of birds, butterflies, insects, and a lot of squirrels. And of course, the outdoor dining area is the perfect spot to take it all in.

This garden's estimated size is ½ acre.

Dutchess County
Sunday, June 23

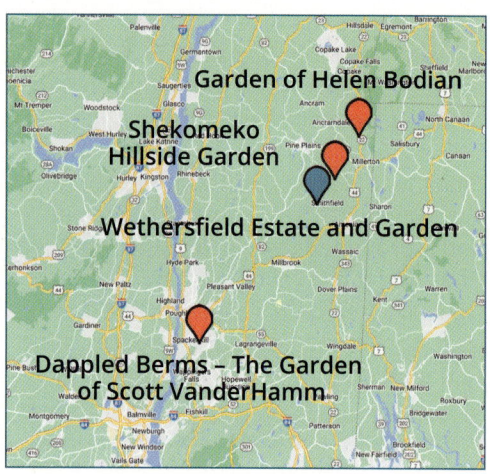

Additional gardens are open nearby:
Litchfield County, CT
  Brush Hill Gardens, Washington, CT
  The Garden of Bunny Williams, Falls Village, CT
  The Garden of Debby and Bart Jones, Cornwall Bridge, CT
  The Garden of Jane Garmey, West Cornwall, CT
  The Garden of Lee Link, Sharon, CT
  Michael's West Cornwall Garden, West Cornwall, CT
  The Shillingford Garden, Salisbury, CT
  The Sumacs, Washington, CT
See page 106.

NEW 5 10 20 '95 Year   No Photography   Accessibility   Nibbled Leaf Garden

MILLERTON

GARDEN OF HELEN BODIAN
  partial 10-4

Over the years, this garden has developed into a landscape for strolling and leisurely observation, having accumulated a series of paths and trails that lead to and around various features, both natural and planted, each arising as a new area developed.

There are four enclosed planted areas, each a distinct garden in itself, and each a consequence of three decades of collecting plants, experimenting with style, and balancing wild with cultivated. Simply listed, they include a square perennial garden, a long rock garden, a walled gravel garden, and a former vegetable garden now turning into something we can't quite name. There are other planted areas that aren't delineated or enclosed, but nevertheless worth notice.

And now in progress, at the edge of a woods and next to a stream, we are making a fernery with a circular seating pattern.

This garden's estimated size is 50 acres (5 acres of gardens).

SHEKOMEKO HILLSIDE GARDEN
NEW    10-4

Situated high in the hills overlooking Dutchess County's Shekomeko Valley, this garden has been lovingly curated by Eileen Naughton for the past 25 years.

The site, a wheat field when the land was purchased in 1997, offers expansive views of the valley and Catskill range to the west, with more intimate garden spaces to the north, east, and south. From the outset, the house was designed to be in sympathy with the land and gardens.

Working with Judy Murphy from Lakeville's Old Farm Nursery, Eileen has expanded and refined the gardens over time.

Stone walls, privet hedges, and boxwood parterres provide structure to the different garden spaces, each variously punctuated with long runs of 'Sargent' crab apples, viburnum, hydrangea, seasonal bulbs, and perennials. June brings a symphony of colors—purple spikes of *Salvia nemorosa*, chartreuse fronds of *Alchemilla mollis*, lipstick-pink weigela, tulips, peonies, bearded iris, brunnera, and more.

This garden's estimated size is 3 acres.

POUGHKEEPSIE

DAPPLED BERMS - THE GARDEN OF SCOTT VANDERHAMM
  partial 10-4

The garden is situated on a 1-acre property within a 1950s (IBM-era) suburban community. As a result of the mature-growth trees which dominate the grounds, a shade perennial garden was created and cultivated over 26 seasons of weekend gardening.

The assembled collection of plants, spread throughout numerous beds and man-made berms, relies heavily on the juxtapositions of color, texture, and form to bring interest and natural beauty to the garden.

One of the highlights of the garden is the collection of more than 427 different hosta cultivars numbering more than 715 specimens, all labeled for ease of identification.

Dappled Berms is one of 25 gardens featured in the book by Linda O'Keeffe, *Inside Outside: A Sourcebook of inspired Garden Rooms.*

This garden's estimated size is 1 acre.

DIGGING DEEPER

The History of Wethersfield Estate & Garden and How Its Responding to Beech Tree Blights
Alaina Mancini, Head of Horticulture and Hillary Henderson
Sunday, June 23, Hours TBD

Wethersfield Estate & Garden
Amenia, NY
$30 Members | $40 General

In 1937 Chauncey Devereaux Stillman purchased two contiguous abandoned farms comprising several hundred acres for use as a summer estate. He built a Georgian-style house designed by Bancel LaFarge at the highest point on the property, overlooking the Taconic Range, the Berkshires, and the Catskills.

Adjacent to the house, he installed a series of garden rooms designed by landscape architect Brian Lynch that include terraces, lawns, mixed borders, a pleached bower, a tea house, a pergola, and a rill.

Between 1947 and 1989, landscape architect Evelyn Poehler expanded the gardens to three acres, creating a strong axial arrangement with various follies and statuary. A 190-foot-long arborvitae allée runs south to north connecting a fountain with motifs from Greek mythology to an oval reflecting pool. A second axis, also originating in the inner garden from the dining room, runs westward moving through a formal garden room with rows of topiary. Overlooking the garden to the north is a balustraded terrace set on a shale wall. Scattered architectural features include a belvedere and a Palladian arch.

Poehler also designed a seven-acre woodland garden, employing a plant palette mostly comprised of native species, in the style of an Italian Renaissance bosco. Sculptures of mythological figures by artists Peter Watts and Josef Stachura are placed along trails and carriage roads.

Maintained by the Wethersfield Foundation since 2017, the house and gardens, along with bordering agricultural fields and forests, comprise the 1,000-acre estate. The agricultural landscape includes windbreak plantings, field diversions, open drains, retention ponds, and wildlife borders-all part of an extensive reforestation effort led by the New York State Conservation Department (now Department of Environmental Conservation) beginning in the 1940s.

We invite you to come, Dig Deeper into the history of Wethersfield Estate & Garden and learn about how Wethersfield is responding to the various beech tree blights impacting historical features in the formal garden.

PRESERVATION PARTNER
PUBLIC GARDEN

WETHERSFIELD ESTATE & GARDEN

257 Pugsley Hill Rd
Amenia, New York 12501

Wethersfield Estate & Garden occupies 1,000 acres in northeast Dutchess County, where it is the highest point in the region with an elevation of 1,200 feet. From that vantage point, it offers majestic views of the Berkshires, the Catskills, and the Taconic Hills.

Comprising a Georgian-style house, classical gardens, a carriage house, and a farm, Wethersfield Estate & Garden is generally considered one of the finest examples of Italian Renaissance gardens in the United States.

Founded by Citigroup heir, philanthropist, and investor Chauncey Stillman in 1938, Wethersfield Estate & Garden is now a nonprofit organization devoted to the proper stewardship of land, habitat protection, conservation, culture, and the arts.

Wethersfield hosts a diversity of formal and native-inspired garden spaces, such as an Arts & Crafts English perennial

Saratoga County
Saturday, June 29

garden, cut flower garden, hedged yew topiaries, and mature tree specimens, and 20 miles of trails for equestrian activities and hiking.

Wethersfield strives to integrate the latest horticultural knowledge to maintain a sustainable and historical garden in a changing world. Wethersfield Estate & Garden is on the National Register of Historic Places and was awarded the 2021 New York State Historic Preservation Award for Excellence in Historic Landscape Preservation.

facebook.com/WethersfieldGarden

instagram.com/wethersfieldgarden

wethersfield.org

SARATOGA SPRINGS
A PLACE TO NEST - MOE'S GARDEN
partial   10–4

Our gardens are on a small city lot. We have utilized the space for small shrubs, perennials, herbs, and vegetables, with very little lawn. We have introduced various plants of our interest: some from grandparents, some from other gardeners, and some from childhood memories of lilacs, violets, and lily of the valley.

I feel that in sharing plants, your garden flourishes. We created raised beds for quite an array of vegetables, and then intermingled tomatoes with perennials. I really enjoy collecting my own seeds and find that the plants do even better the following season, acclimating to their own environment.

It is such a pleasure sitting on the front porch, and walkers will comment on how beautiful the gardens are. I am grateful to be able to share this with them.

This garden's estimated size is 60 × 100 feet.

NEW 5 10 20 95 Year   No Photography   Accessibility   Nibbled Leaf Garden

💬 TROWEL TALK

I make a strong effort to maintain organic gardening, permaculture, and pollinators, and try to utilize the small area to have shrubs, perennials, and vegetables.
My goals are to every year expand my knowledge of plants and our relationship with them.

—*The Gardener*

FOXGLOVE - SARAH PATTERSON'S GARDEN
  10–4

My home is within the city limits of Saratoga Springs, but my hope is that when you are in the garden all thoughts of a city are gone.

You won't find a lawn here, only flowers, trees, and shrubs. I started the garden in 2008 and in 2021 made the biggest structural change. A large sunken area is now filled in. Varieties of trees and shrubs are Stewartia, *Cornus florida*, Magnolia, *Styrax obassia*, Amelanchier, *Ilex* evergreen and verticillata, Viburnum, Hamamelis, and some special evergreens. Digitalis, Geranium, *Alchemilla mollis*, Pulmonaria, Echinacea, Rudbeckia, peony, ferns, and irises are some of the perennials.

This garden's estimated size is ¼ acre.

💬 TROWEL TALK

My first garden was part of the 16 acres I grew up on. It was an old-growth woodland full of native wildflowers and large beech trees. It is where my love of shade gardening started. In 1995 and for a few years after, my garden in Fairfield, CT was part of the first Open Days tours. If any of you went on those tours, we were on Redding Road. I would love to see you again at my home in Saratoga Springs.

—*The Gardener*

SCHUYLERVILLE
SUSIE AND PAUL'S GARDENS
 10–4

These gardens have changed somewhat since I last showed the garden for Open Days, but they still include the formal parterre. I have teamed up with my partner, Paul Schneider, an avid horticulturist and sculptor. With his help we have been able to make more use of the property by opening up beds and growing the more unusual or rare plants that we find.

The rock gardens and containers holding rock garden plants and rocks are multiplying rapidly and are being placed throughout the garden beds along with Paul's sculptures, making for a more interesting overall effect.

This garden's estimated size is ½ acre.

Nearby Counties

- **PUTNAM**
- **WESTCHESTER**

Sunday, June 30

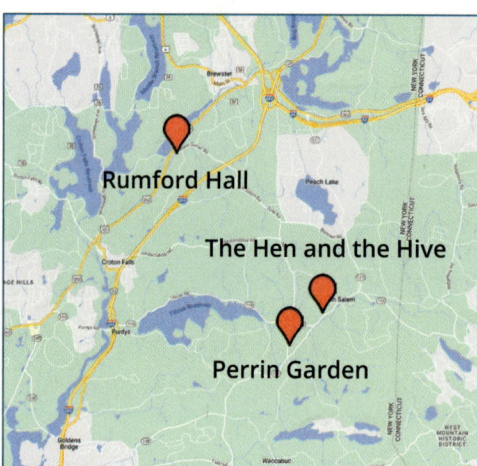

PUTNAM COUNTY
BREWSTER
RUMFORD HALL
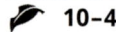 10–4

Rumford Hall is a 15-acre property with mature plantings and monumental boulders in the foothills of the Appalachians. A stone table near the foxgloves is engraved with the date of the house, 1879, and a smokehouse huddles under greenery in a courtyard garden with an old, weathered door.

We have boxwood and roses, a plum allée, weepery, pergolas, orchard, vegetable garden, fernery, and a pool garden with succulents and grasses. Fences are lined with ninebark, honeysuckle, and tapestry hedges. The ruins on the hill are adjacent to a woodland garden enclosed by stone walls. Visitors are encouraged to follow the trails that we have signposted in the hills; the forest has a footbridge and a mountain upholstered in moss.

This garden's estimated size is 15 acres (including woodland trails).

WESTCHESTER COUNTY
NORTH SALEM
PERRIN GARDEN
 10–4

A curved driveway, partially lined with bottlebrush buckeye and fragrant sumac, leads to a rise revealing an English-style country house bordered by an apple orchard to one side, a spring woodland garden on another side, and a grass meadow in the front.

Visitors pass through a series of beech- and yew-lined courtyards to get to the front door. In the rear, formal gardens surrounded by stone walls contain mature perennials and provide lovely views of preserved land in the distance. A small brick and flagstone area surrounded by perennials offers an intimate spot for dining under a sweetgum tree. Below the formal gardens, a transition garden combines native grasses with blueberry bushes and gives way to a wildflower meadow.

The property continues to evolve in its incorporation of more and more native plants to provide a habitat for wildlife and a more sustainable landscape for the future.

This garden's estimated size is 14 acres.

Register online: gardenconservancy.org/opendays   New York   275

THE HEN AND THE HIVE
 10–4

Celebrating 21 years of gardening at the Hen and the Hive, we continue to blend open perennial beds, wildflower meadows, woodlands, and paths, while deer-fencing only vegetables, berries, and a more formal flower garden.

With the majority of our property unfenced, we try to take advantage of interspersing deer-resistant mostly native plantings and an effective spraying regimen. This strategy has been successful and allowed us to cultivate various garden spots throughout the property that incorporate seating areas, stone, and even a bit of water.

Each year has brought new ideas for new areas to enjoy throughout the growing season and beyond. The recent addition of a greenhouse has expanded possibilities and given us a chance to learn new things and extend the growing season in challenging new ways.

A major focus over the past five years or more has been to eliminate as many non-native invasive species as possible and find the treasures that have been struggling to shine for years.

Delaware County
Saturday, July 6

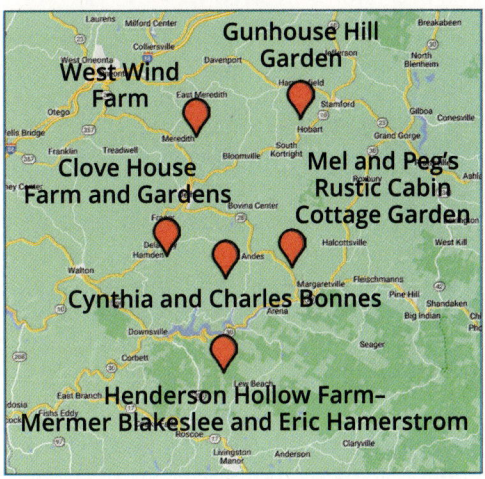

ANDES
CYNTHIA AND CHARLES BONNES
 partial   10–4

Our garden is on a hillside facing the western Catskills, with four ponds descending toward the mountain view. Around the house and large barn, part of a former dairy farm, are several formal garden spaces defined by native stone walls. They include a perennial border, a fountain terrace, and a vegetable garden. An allée of Japanese lilacs ascends the hillside, and informal plantings edge two of the ponds and a connecting stream.

Visitors are welcome to bring a blanket and picnic on the lawn or hike the trails on the property.

NEW 5 10 20 '95 Year

MEL AND PEG'S RUSTIC CABIN COTTAGE GARDEN

  10-4

Perched on the side of a hill deep in the Catskills, our garden takes full advantage of a beautiful, borrowed view that is seamlessly integrated throughout the garden setting.

Wind your way up a long sinewy driveway (don't miss Mel's new rocket on the way up) and you are greeted by the boisterous "garden proper," which was carved out of the steep slope and is held up by a massive boulder retaining wall. Multiple entrances beckon you to enter.

Slip in through a cedar arbor covered in grapes, or take the stone path through the conifer garden, and meander along gravel and mulch paths through a lush array of small trees, shrubs, perennials, and grasses that create a whimsical, enchanted garden experience. Step down the rustic stone staircases, or exit through a mass of hydrangeas, to explore the smaller garden rooms, including a large mixed garden in the shape of a footprint with wide mulch paths, a couple of small shade gardens, a spiral garden, and a small country vegetable garden.

This is a garden that you will find yourself immersed in and one you will experience with all your senses, as you feel an ornamental grass brush your arm, listen to the trickle of the water feature, smell the intoxicating mock orange wafting in the breeze, or relax in an Adirondack chair. The garden is carefully integrated with our living space to create a seamless experience of indoor and outdoor living. A favorite spot to reflect and enjoy is from the wide frontier porch that spans the length of our hand-stripped log cabin. Viewed from this vantage point, the inside and outside come together while you experience a bird's-eye view of the garden and the sweeping mountain vistas.

Despite being a professional landscape designer, our own garden was not designed, but instead is a twenty-year evolution and a labor of love. It is an eclectic collector's garden where we experiment with new plants and techniques. The end result is an exuberant space that is simultaneously wild and orderly.

This garden's estimated size is 1 acre.

💬 TROWEL TALK

If I had only one plant to use for the gardens I create, it would be the *Geranium macrorrhizum*. I don't care which cultivar because I don't care about the flowers. As a matter of fact, I would prefer that they didn't bloom.

The flowers are fine, and most folks love them, but after they are spent, it takes a while for them to fall off and there are too many to deadhead. Flowers or not, this plant makes the most beautiful, fluffy, dense ground cover. The deer don't touch it (fingers crossed), it smells great, it looks good all season (except for the first couple of weeks in the spring when it is growing in ☹), it has great fall color, and it really controls the weeds.

I use it in huge sweeps to create a beautiful architectural line that doesn't need to be edged. I would use it even more if it could take full sun, but it tends to yellow some, even in our fairly cool climate. It is easy to control; we harvest massive amounts of sprigs to clear paths

---

NEW 5 10 20 95 Year  No Photography  Accessibility  Nibbled Leaf Garden

and populate large areas for new clients without ever purchasing a plant. May the force not deliver an invasive species that attacks my beloved big root geranium. We affectionately call them "Macs." I think I would have to shutter my business if that happened.

—Mel Bellar

DELANCEY
CLOVE HOUSE FARM AND GARDENS
NEW 10–4

The Clove House Farm and Garden is shaped by the architectural and environmental features of a mid-nineteenth-century dairy farm.

Wooded land, large period barns, and pastures provide the backdrop for substantial perennial gardens, orchards, and vegetable plots. Two spring-fed ponds and a trout stream combine sumptuous gardens and grounds for an idyllic setting.

This garden's estimated size is 5 acres.

💬 TROWEL TALK

The current owners, James and King, are the third family to live on the property. The remaining 40 acres have shaped the gardeners in equal measure to the work they have accomplished. Maximizing the existing barns and outbuildings and the geography to accentuate rather than to re-create.

Gardening here is a passion and undoubtedly a labor of love.

—James and King

DELHI
WEST WIND FARM
NEW 10–4

Although the property, an old dairy farm, was acquired in 2000—it seemed such a great place to garden—it took many years for the gardens to evolve. A herd of Icelandic horses changed focus early on and landscaping for others took the time away.

Recently, a pergola was added at the end of a cutting garden, as well as more dahlia beds. Lots of annuals interspersed with perennials and shrubs keep everything going in this generally short growing season at 2,000 feet. It is still very much a work in progress!

This garden's estimated size is 1 acre.

HOBART
GUNHOUSE HILL GARDEN
NEW 10–4

We have been restoring and reimagining an 1800 dairy farm for the last twenty years. Our focus has been on the enhancement of the entire 120-acre farm. Gardens and plantings are integrated into the adaptive reuse and interpretation of existing farm structures and sculptures which have a planted component.

Visitors will have the opportunity to walk through the vernacular landscape and see how we have tried to integrate built and natural forms.

This garden's estimated size is 2 acres.

NEW 5 10 20 95 Year    No Photography    Accessibility    Nibbled Leaf Garden

ROSCOE

HENDERSON HOLLOW FARM - MERMER BLAKESLEE AND ERIC HAMERSTROM

  10-4

Our garden began in 1990 on this secluded, defunct farm, taking its form from a dry streambed running down the hillside. The beds are dense, deep, and layered, the plants encouraged to retain some of their wildness, often forming drifts from self-sown seedlings.

Paths extend out of the garden into both woodland and meadow, as the garden reflects and reaches into the surrounding landscape. The stonework is old and ongoing: two planted terraces, a rustic stone bridge, hand-hewn flagstones, rebuilt walls, stone steps snaking through a swampy meadow. There's rusty metal, too. Antique trucks and farm equipment are settled about, and an iron foot bridge crosses the streambed.

The garden was featured in *Garden Design* magazine. The house, barns, and front porch are open to all our visitors.

This garden's estimated size is 2 acres.

💬 TROWEL TALK

Our garden is a collaboration with this place, a secluded hollow with western exposure, rocky soil, hilly land, and hardpan.

From my first days of gardening, I noticed that each bed seemed to know what it wanted, reflecting sometimes the house or barns, sometimes the woods and meadows. And it's still true! The garden constantly pushes back, disappoints, delights, surprises, even startles. It is not a collaboration of equals—the garden always wins.

And as we experience more volatile weather from climate change, I'm increasingly moved by the plants' resilience and fortitude. They are my models.

We lost a huge white pine last winter and now the beds by the front porch are no longer in shade. The tree is gone but the garden remains because it never stops changing. I'm constantly learning (and relearning!) that its beauty is dynamic, always in process, a play, never a still life.

—Mermer B.

Suffolk County
Saturday, July 13

JAMESPORT
WINDS WAY FARM
  partial 10–4

Welcome to Winds Way! Located on the shore of Great Peconic Bay, our North Fork gardens occupy land that was once potato field and pasture. The gardens are designed to complement the historic buildings—an 1836 Greek Revival-style whaling captain's house, an 1872 one-room schoolhouse, an early nineteenth-century barn—that we've moved to our property to create a compelling sense of place.

Included are a small orchard featuring heirloom apples and espaliered fruit trees, a large-scale vegetable garden, a soft-fruit area, and herbaceous and shrub borders teaming with plants that appeal to butterflies and other pollinators.

As avid birders, we've planted many natives to provide food, shelter, and nesting sites for feathered friends.

Plantings vary in style from more formal gardens with historically appropriate plant material to naturalistic settings. They feature shaded and woodland gardens in addition to full-sun areas and a small meadow. All the gardens are connected with meandering paths; garden spaces are defined by hand-cut picket fences, rail fences, and hedges.

We started as weekend gardeners in the mid-1980s and, since retiring in 2001, continue to add new gardens, most recently a gravel garden in front of the schoolhouse. The property also includes farm fields and a woodland protected by conservation easements.

This garden's estimated size is 2 acres of cultivated gardens on a 15-acre property.

💬 TROWEL TALK

We love our gardens—despite the unwitting mistakes made along the way—especially all the creatures who come to visit. While we've been working on our gardens for more than 30 years, we are constantly surprised by a beautifully colored insect, trail of tiny footprints, fly-by visit of a feathered friend, or lovely wildflower volunteer.

Now that we are becoming (or have become) older gardeners, we are learning to let go a little, to let the plants and wildlife have their way. But we will admit that collaboration with mother nature can be challenging at times, and we both love our hoes. So, the journey continues, and we hope to become better stewards as the gardens change along with the gardeners. How wonderful it is to think about the seasons ahead and all they offer.

—Nancy and Richard

MATTITUCK

THE LANDCRAFT GARDEN FOUNDATION

    10-4

In 2020, garden owners Dennis Schrader and Bill Smith formed the Landcraft Garden Foundation, a 501(c)(3) not-for-profit foundation. The Landcraft Garden Foundation is dedicated to inspiring, educating, and promoting gardening, horticulture, and the preservation of our natural environment.

Our mission is to provide a horticulturally diverse garden that offers knowledge of the plant world and acts as a laboratory for experimenting with horticultural techniques, plant diversity, breeding, and design. Ultimately, our goal is to provide the experience of delight that gardens bring to people throughout the world.

Set in the heart of the North Fork's wine region, this 4+ acre public garden surrounds a restored 1840s farmhouse. In 2008, the house went through a major renovation, and the gardens and terraces surrounding it have since been redesigned.

The deck, porches, and stone terraces are filled with hundreds of container plantings. There are many perennial and mixed shrub borders throughout the garden that can be accessed by numerous winding paths. Garden rooms, hedged in by hornbeam and boxwood, feature various themed gardens within.

Additionally, there is a vegetable/herb garden, a formal knot garden, several bog plantings, meadow gardens, and a woodland shade area. The garden also features rustic arbors, trellises, stone walls, and a tiki hut that contains a collection of exotic plants.

The newest meadow garden surrounds the "Ruin"—a subterranean stone grotto partially covered with a sedum green roof. The three roundels located in the eastern part of the garden are made from locust wood harvested from the property. The roundels support climbing roses and seasonal exotic vines and are underplanted with a collection of shade-loving plants.

There are many sitting areas to enjoy the views and a natural clay pond with stream and bridge, and other smaller ponds for water lilies and papyrus. Many of the plantings throughout contain tropicals, subtropicals, tender perennials, and annuals. There are a handful of hardy palms and a large grove of *Musa basjoo*, the hardy banana.

The Mediterranean garden, which has collections of subtropical fruits, also contains the bee yard. The house and gardens are encircled by 10 acres of rehabilitated meadows with mowed paths for viewing native plants and wildlife. The meadow contains grasses, perennials, and shrubs that provide a habitat for deer, foxes, groundhogs, rabbits, box turtles, wild turkeys, and many other birds and insects.

This garden's estimated size is 4 acres (plus 10 acres natural area).

MT. SINAI
TRANQUILITY
 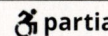 10–4

This garden is open twice this year: May 25 and July 13.

Hundreds of perennials, shrubs, trees, and annuals are combined with water features, lawn art, and recently relocated garden trails that allow the visitor to enter the owner's vision of an Impressionistic garden painting.

Footpaths wind through the extensive garden, allowing visitors to immerse themselves in the sights and sounds of nature and escape the general stress of modern lifestyles.

This garden's estimated size is ¾ acre.

💬 TROWEL TALK

I try to create new gardens each year by moving paths and flower beds. I love explosion of color and use flowers and foliage color to create a visual display.

—The Gardener

Capital Region
Saturday, July 20

CLIFTON PARK
GROWFORME5B
10–4

Eric and Christopher started this garden in 2018 when their new construction home was completed. This is a younger garden featuring a collection of specimen trees, 50+ David Austin roses, 140+ hydrangeas, and a terraced outdoor living space. With a focus on texture, color, and four-season interest, the garden provides a place for relaxing, socializing, and fun.

A traditional suburban lot has been transformed into an ever-evolving sanctuary. For more information, please follow Eric and Christopher on Instagram and YouTube @GrowForMe5b

This garden's estimated size is ½ acre.

GLENVILLE
SONGNI YUAN
NEW 10–12, 12–2, 2–4

Songni Yuan is the garden of David Besozzi, who designed and built this "backyard" Zen garden starting in 2009. The garden consists of both Japanese and Chinese elements.

Although the main garden is referred to as the Zen Garden, over time the garden grew and additional garden areas were added, including a stroll garden, viewing garden, and a border garden known as the "Dragon's Spine." The garden's name, Songni Yuan, is derived from Dave's Chinese name, which he adopted when studying Chinese in the 1980s. The translation is Song (Pine) and Ni (Mud), resulting in the garden name Pine Mud's Garden. The Chinese characters that make up the name are appropriate—the "Mud" (water and earth) gives life to the "Pine" (wood), and all three of these elements exist through a symbiotic relationship.

Dave's own relationship with the garden is very similar. The pine tree is a symbol of longevity, and the garden has done much to improve his mental and physical health over the years—it gives him life, and in turn he helps the garden blossom and grow. They need each other. Throughout the garden there are a variety of grasses, hosta, astilbe, spirea, boxwoods, dwarf maples, ferns, and bamboo. Shade plants dominate the Zen garden area. Japanese styles influence the overall design of the fencing and gate structures, while a series of lanterns populate the garden areas.

The Moon Window in the gazebo area reflects some of the Chinese influences that are also found in the garden, while statues of Buddha and Guanyin (the Goddess of Mercy) look over the garden and ensure a sense of peaceful tranquility. In addition, there is an extensive vegetable garden on the property, just beyond the Sukiya-style Woodland Gate along the edge of the property.

This garden's estimated size is 3,000 sq. ft.

💬 TROWEL TALK

As an educator, I discovered that education is like gardening. Teachers nurture the minds of students with knowledge in the hope of bringing forth new understanding and a joy of learning that will help young people blossom into adulthood.

In the garden, I have to nurture the plants so that they too can grow into blossoms that bring great joy.

—*David Besozzi*

LOUDONVILLE
INSPIRED BY ITALIAN GARDEN DESIGNS
NEW ♿ 10-1, 1-4

Relax and wander through a private retreat for a Mediterranean style home... outdoor living spaces, the sound of water cascading into fountains, a sunken pool terrace surrounded by limestone walls, and gardens showcasing the contrast of all green hardscape and alternating "rooms" that surprise the eye with a rainbow of perennials throughout the summer season.

This garden's estimated size is 1 acre.

💬 TROWEL TALK

Favorite plant? Roses! Plant I've never had any luck with? Roses. First garden? This one, which has been 42 years in the making. No formal training but an obsessive love of plants and landscape design. (I was best described as a "Darwinian" gardener when I started-survival of the fittest and all.)

Design inspirations? The Cranbrook Schools in Bloomfield Hills, MI, and great Italian, French, and British gardens; I love the idea of the landscape directing you through an unexpected turn to have an entirely new vista and experience unfold.

—Susan Fitzgerald

NISKAYUNA
CHERIE GOLD
NEW 🍃 10-4

A suburban oasis, Cherie's gardens reflect a cottage country garden feel. What began as a love of flowers has turned into a passion for collecting and displaying BIG flowering plants and shrubs. The gardens are anchored by specimen trees surrounded by sweeping swaths of flowers.

This garden's estimated size is ½ acre.

💬 TROWEL TALK

Gardening is in my genes, as I recently learned from my 82-year-old cousin. Our grandmother, who came over to America from Austria as a teen, gardened her whole life.

My mom only grew annuals, but we planted tons of them every spring. As a young adult I began to experiment with perennials. My friend Patti Keats, a true artist, initially inspired me to really transform my little gardens into the sweeping swaths of flowers I now have, and she continues to do so with her amazing gardens.

My three adult children all love to garden, and I know that I have passed the love of gardening on to the next generation

—Cherie Gold

NEW 5 10 20 95 Year 🚫 No Photography ♿ Accessibility 🍃 Nibbled Leaf Garden

GARDEN OF GREGORY AND KATHLEEN GREENE

  10–4

Situated on about ⅜ acre, our garden is a mix of formal and informal plantings. As you enter the side garden through a yew hedge, a large bowl made from Vermont marble sits in the middle of a small lawn.

On either side of the lawn there are two borders of perennials and shrubs. Stepping down into the back garden, there is a border to your right that combines shrubs, perennials, and tropicals and a large potted Red Abyssinian banana. The rest of the back garden is divided up by hedges and stone walls along with cut flower gardens, another perennial border, and shade gardens. A small greenhouse and potting shed sit in the back corner of the garden.

Scattered throughout the property are Stewartia, dogwoods, witch hazels, and other small trees along with areas planted for pollinators.

This garden's estimated size is 1/3 acre.

💬 TROWEL TALK

My garden has become a refuge in these challenging times. I find as I enter it the outside world fades away and I become immersed in the garden and nature. Many times, I find myself stopping to observe bumble bees collecting pollen or to listen to bird song. Even the most mundane of tasks gives me pleasure. I feel very fortunate to be surrounded by plants and wildlife.

—*The Gardener*

THE GARDEN OF M. PATRICIA

NEW 10–4

The first garden on our property was started shortly after we bought our home 35 years ago…a bungalow built in 1930 on a very small patch of land. As time went on, we acquired the wooded lots adjacent to our home, we now have more than 2 acres in total and garden on more than an acre.

After we cleared the land of brambles and weeds, the garden was "carved out" among the existing trees, many of which were black walnuts. It took years to realize that the many planting failures we experienced could be attributed to these beautiful, majestic black walnut trees, juglone creating a toxic environment for so many of the plants.

The garden consists of several large "rooms"…the garden off the deck is the earliest, then the garden behind the studio, the garden on the way to the shed (formerly called the "bull pen," holding planting failures…hoping to nurse back to health), the pool garden, and finally, the side garden…the garden with the best view from our home.

The garden beds are curved and not planted in the commonly suggested large groups or drifts of odd numbered plants. There is more layering and repeat planting around the gardens to carry the eye from place to place. Throughout the property the planting style is a mix of shrubs and perennials with lots of clipped boxwood shrubs and hedges to present a somewhat tidy appearance to a garden that has been described as "organized chaos."

This garden's estimated size is 1½ acres.

NEW 5 10 20 '95 Year  No Photography  Accessibility  Nibbled Leaf Garden

💬 TROWEL TALK

As a painter of silk and canvas, the garden has become a living painting, not only changing with the seasons but with the whims and passions of nature and the gardener.

—M. Patricia—the gardener and painter

SCHENECTADY

50 SHADES OF GREEN

NEW 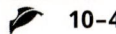 10–4

Sited in New York's first historic district and hidden behind one of the area's oldest homes awaits a reimagined and ever evolving green space designed for pollinators.

What started out as just a basic clean up and weeding gig soon evolved into a growing collection of both native species and rare ornamentals with attracting hummingbirds and other pollinators in mind.

Visitors should be on the lookout for hummingbirds, along with various types of butterflies and bees before being smitten by the secret shade garden only revealed by ducking under an archway smothered by our native "Dutchmans Pipe."

This garden's estimated size is ¼ acre.

💬 TROWEL TALK

Q: What is your favorite plant?
A: So, my favorite plants at the moment include a tropical pitcher plant (*Nepenthes alata*) that I picked up at the Capital District Flower Show, my staghorn fern, Bruce, the generous clumps of *Tillandsia* I found in Florida, and not to forget the always en vogue *Monstera*...So basically, I'm a fan of epiphytes.

Q: Can you describe your first garden?
A: My first garden was at my mom's house in the middle of the city, and the only space available was a 5' × 8' rectangle of the worst soil in between the brick house and the very hot sidewalk, full of all sorts of things you *wouldn't* call pretty. I had no experience at all, but I wanted to do something and always loved flowers. I started in May and by the end of July I had zinnias and sunflowers and stuff just coming into their own, and I just kept adding like a mad man and surprisingly that worked for that situation.

Q: What is a plant you have never had any luck with?
A: Starting poppies from seed, period.

Q: What is your favorite garden tool and why?
A: My hands because there is no replacement.

Q: Who inspired you to garden?
A: Mother Nature herself.

—Christopher K.

NEW 5 10 20 95 Year  No Photography  Accessibility  Nibbled Leaf Garden

Dutchess County
Saturday, July 27

Additional gardens are open nearby:
Litchfield County, CT
   Sculpturedale, Kent, CT
   Juniper Ledge, Lakeville, CT
   Fernwood, Norfolk, CT
   Lagniappe Garden, Washington, CT
See page 117.

Berkshire County, MA
   Garden of Jeffrey A. Steele, Ashley Falls, MA
See page 168.

MILLBROOK
LITHGOW COTTAGE FARM
    10–4

A few years ago, we were able to purchase adjacent property with a pond we'd overlooked for the previous 45 years. Dredging the pond of 100 years of silt was the first improvement we made. Then aquatic plants went in and shrubby willows around the perimeter to attract birds.

Now we're working to develop native grasses in the meadow around the pond. These additions greatly expanded the scope of a garden originally designed around a lily pool and Carpenter Gothic potting shed at the entryway to our house. Here, an informal parterre is planted with ornamental vegetables, annuals, and perennials.

Over the years we've added a mini-rock garden and trough collection at the side of the house and a fountain by a local sculptor near the back porch. A shrubbery on a berm between the road and front lawn also evolved to screen out noise and dust. We continue to tweak and upgrade this wild area leading down to a playhouse and a mowed path around the pond.

This garden's estimated size is 1 acre.

💬 **TROWEL TALK**

I have had no luck with very expensive dwarf conifers that I have been advised need sharp drainage and little water. I have attempted to meet these requirements but not one single success!

—*Bindy Kaye*

MILLERTON
HIGHGROVE COTTAGE
 ♿ partial 10–4

Barbara's garden, atop the beautiful Smithfield Valley in the heart of the Millbrook Hunt Country, is exhibited in vibrant colors in her perennial landscape around her cottage.

Her fashion background shows in the mix of color from an array of roses, crocosmia, Russian sage, Allium 'Globemaster,' lilies, phlox, and many more among stone and cast-iron sculptures and stone walls on different levels. A peach and apple espalier is featured against the charming cottage.

The views show the magnificent landscape of the Smithfield Valley, not a house in sight.

This garden's estimated size is 2 acres.

PRESERVATION PARTNER PUBLIC GARDEN

WETHERSFIELD ESTATE & GARDEN

**257 Pugsley Hill Rd
Amenia, New York 12501**

Wethersfield Estate & Garden occupies 1,000 acres in northeast Dutchess County, where it is the highest point in the region with an elevation of 1,200 feet. From that vantage point, it offers majestic views of the Berkshires, the Catskills, and the Taconic Hills.

Comprising a Georgian-style house, classical gardens, a carriage house, and a farm, Wethersfield Estate & Garden is generally considered one of the finest examples of Italian Renaissance gardens in the United States.

Founded by Citigroup heir, philanthropist, and investor Chauncey Stillman in 1938, Wethersfield Estate & Garden is now a nonprofit organization devoted to the proper stewardship of land, habitat protection, conservation, culture, and the arts.

Wethersfield hosts a diversity of formal and native-inspired garden spaces, such as an Arts & Crafts English perennial garden, cut flower garden, hedged yew

---

NEW 5 10 20 '95 Year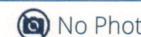

topiaries, and mature tree specimens, and 20 miles of trails for equestrian activities and hiking.

Wethersfield strives to integrate the latest horticultural knowledge to maintain a sustainable and historical garden in a changing world. Wethersfield Estate & Garden is on the National Register of Historic Places and was awarded the 2021 New York State Historic Preservation Award for Excellence in Historic Landscape Preservation.

facebook.com/WethersfieldGarden

instagram.com/wethersfieldgarden

wethersfield.org

Sullivan County
Saturday, July 27

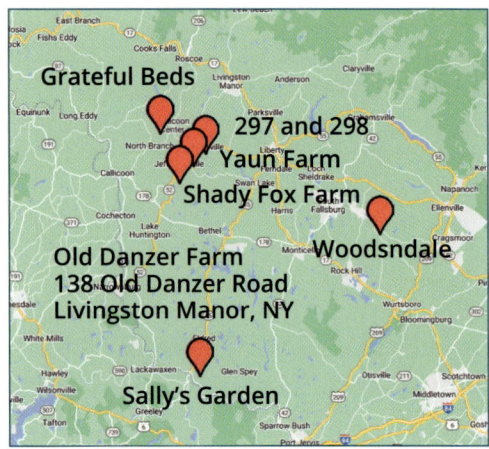

BARRYVILLE
SALLY'S GARDEN
NEW   10–4

Sally's Garden is at the home of Sally Rowe and Anthony Biancoviso. There are two distinct ornamental gardens, one 30 years in the making, the other more recently developed, both designed and created by Sally. They are intimate, lushly planted spaces on less than a quarter of an acre, situated on a historic 12-acre farm property.

The gardens include an impressive collection of trees and flowering shrubs, along with a wide range of herbaceous perennials for shade and sun, all with an emphasis on both native as well as fragrant and pollinator plants. Old stone paths and walls, gentle grass paths, and a small pond round out this delightful, highly personal experience.

Sally's gardening passions, knowledge and adventures are shared in her forthcoming gardening memoir, *Digging Up the Grass: Stories from the Flower Garden*. Pottery studio and gallery of Anthony Biancoviso also on premises.

This garden's estimated size is 1/5 acre.

💬 TROWEL TALK

"I grew this peony from a seed"! This is what I exuberantly tell garden visitors about said plant. I'm unabashedly proud of my accomplishment—that I even took on such a project, especially since I grow so little from seed. An impressive provenance and century-old lineage came with the random seed pack, as they were collected from the heirloom plants grown at Hildene, the Robert Todd Lincoln home in Manchester, Vermont.

For a number of years, not knowing what the flowers would look like, I eagerly awaited the big ta-da—and finally the moment arrived when fifteen baby-pink buds appeared on the plant. When the swollen buds unfurled, I let out an audible wow!

What an enchanting flower, with its slightly wavy, blush-pink single petals, tinged with gentle wisps of a deeper rose-and wide center ring of fluffy yellow stamens. The flowers turned to soft white clouds as they gracefully aged. They had no scent, but I was in love. Hildene calls this peony 'Blush Single'. I adore all my peonies, but I cherish this one above all others. Happily, in early June during the height of peony season, my vases are filled like never before.

—*Sally Rowe*

JEFFERSONVILLE
297 AND 298
♿ partial   10–4

The garden of 298 was designed by a landscape architect from Terremoto Landscape in Los Angeles and installed by The Dirt Diva in Sullivan County. It includes a large number of pollinator species and a wide variety of native and non-native plants appropriate for the area.

The 297 house is Victorian, built as a boarding house in the late 1800s, and the gardens surrounding the house were installed when the house was renovated in 2001. The gardens here are more formal; however, the house now has a field of wildflowers in the backyard that features a different bloom every few weeks throughout the season.

This garden's estimated size is 1 acre.

SHADY FOX FARM
NEW   ♿   10–4

A 100-foot serpentine stone wall is the backdrop for a mixed herbaceous border. The pool garden consists of a collection of summer flowering trees, shrubs, and perennials. The plant selection is deer resistant.

NEW  Year    No Photography    Accessibility    Nibbled Leaf Garden

LIVINGSTON MANOR
OLD DANZER FARM
NEW   10-4

Print maker Madelon Jones and her husband, Kit Jones, a photographer, created the garden over 35 years.

The garden features serpentine fieldstone walls, which frame the view to the pond. Island beds, planted with perennials and shrubs, are punctuated with an ornamental grass collection surrounding the pond.

This garden's estimated size is 45 acres.

MOUNTAIN DALE
WOODSNDALE
  10-4

Working in the film and fashion industry for twenty-plus years, I settled in the Catskills and started a family and a career in environmental science.

No longer working in fabrics, I now paint with flowers, plants, and forms given to me by the natural landscapes of Woodsndale. Woodsndale was conceived to provide a sustainable home for all of us to live in harmony. We have created decorative gardens with more than 80 varieties of plantain lilies, many Asiatic hybrid lilies, varieties of hydrangeas, and much more.

From spring to fall, Woodsndale is a pollinator's paradise and home to wild bees, butterflies, hummingbirds, and, yes, groundhogs, and a herd of deer. Our organic vegetable garden provides for our daily sustenance. The decorative gardens are a gateway to the naturalized woodland gardens that meld into the forest and glacier rocks.

We enjoy having visitors walk through the 2+ acres of gardens and then discover the forest. We encourage you to have a cold drink at the writer's shack, and rest among the rock formations surrounded by the trees. We know you will enjoy listening to the winds and leaves as they create a unique voice for nature's symphony.

This garden's estimated size is 2 acres of garden, plus 4 acres of forest.

💬 **TROWEL TALK**

Gardens are a work in progress. They are constantly changing. Visiting a garden is like walking into an artist's studio and observing a piece of art evolve. I think that if you find a garden that you like, it should be revisited at least every few years. Only then can you fully experience the creator's intentions for choices of plants and their placement and experience the garden in its mature growth.

—Evadne Giannini

NORTH BRANCH
GRATEFUL BEDS
  10-4

Our raised bed garden is 450 square feet, with about twenty complementary varieties of vegetables, herbs, and flowers, including milkweed for the beloved butterflies.

This garden's estimated size is 450 sq. ft.

💬 **TROWEL TALK**

My favorite garden tool is the fabulous

NEW  Year No Photography  Accessibility  Nibbled Leaf Garden

stirrup hoe I got for my birthday. I began gardening as a creative endeavor using flowers in planters around my house. When we decided to put in the raised bed garden, my wife thought it was going to be too big.

However, the joy we have in going to the garden and eating what we harvest is indescribable, as is the joy we have found in sharing our vegetables with friends and neighbors. Throughout this process, we have learned that no garden is too big!

—Isaac Yohanan

YOUNGSVILLE
YAUN FARM
NEW ♿ 🍃 10–4

Yaun Farm was the weekend home of Tony Lepsis and Brian Whitney, owners of North Hill Garden design on Long Island.

The first few years were consumed with the restoration of the farm house and gardens of 20 acres, tree removals and selective pruning, opening up a vista to the pond and the hemlock and laurel woods.

All new plantings revolved around the deer, with mixed borders of spirea boxwood and calycanthus shrubs, planted with epimediums, hellebores, hardy geraniums, and astilbes. Hostas and shade perennials are protected by the house and a six-foot fieldstone wall. The old lilacs created garden rooms for the summer hydrangeas.

The vegetable garden is located on the old barn foundation. The eight-foot stone walls are the backdrop for the raised beds. Trails take you up the hill, past native ferns to the fire pit with views of the mountains.

This garden's estimated size is 20 acres.

Columbia County
Sunday, July 28

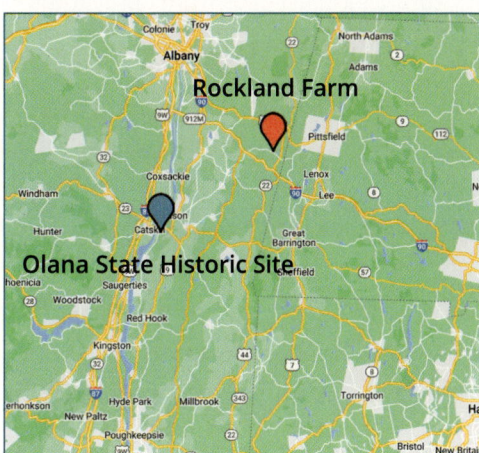

Additional gardens are open nearby:
Berkshire County, MA
 Kingsmont, West Stockbridge, MA
 Walford, West Stockbridge, MA
See page 169.

CANAAN
ROCKLAND FARM
10 ♿ partial 🍃 10–4

Our garden comprises a variety of areas that flow one from another over about 10 acres of our property.

A 450-foot-long rock ledge runs parallel to the front drive and is topped by a dry garden. A raised terrace on the west side of the house features exotic and tropical plants, many in containers.

Behind the house is a sequence of garden rooms: a formal area contained within a raised hornbeam hedge, a perennial garden around our swimming pool, a fishpond with a fountain, a sundial garden, a rock garden, and a fenced vegetable and cutting garden.

A hydrangea allée leads from here either to a lawn, with a seating area nestling within sweeps of perennials, or to steps up to a wooded knoll, with paths offering intermittent views of the garden and the hills beyond and connecting a folly, a pet pergola, a water feature, and a stumpery. A massive pine bench in a pine grove overlooks a 3-acre lake in the middle distance.

Our garden has been featured in magazines and in the books *Great Gardens of the Berkshires*, *Private Edens*, and *Private Gardens of the Hudson Valley*.

This garden's estimated size is 10 acres.

💬 TROWEL TALK

We knew almost nothing about gardening when we bought our house in 1980. There was no garden already here, and we eventually made a start, with the help of friends and the nearby Berkshire Botanical Garden, where we took classes.

The combination of enthusiasm and ignorance led us to create a garden that was too large for us to maintain without help, but we have no regrets and derive great pleasure from it.

—*Madeline and Ian Hooper*

PRESERVATION PARTNER
PUBLIC GARDEN

OLANA STATE HISTORIC SITE

5720 NY-9G
Hudson, New York 12534

The Olana Partnership is a non-profit organization whose mission is to inspire the public by preserving and interpreting Frederic Church's OLANA, a New York State Historic Site and National Historic Landmark within the Hudson River Valley National Heritage Area.

f facebook.com/OlanaFredericChurch/

📷 instagram.com/olanafredericchurch/

🌐 olana.org

Register online: gardenconservancy.org/opendays　　　New York　293

Suffolk County
Saturday, September 7

EAST HAMPTON
POMEROY
♿ 10–2

Hidden on a private lane, our garden has been the object of our affection for 30 years. A row of gingko trees flank the street and driveway. The hemlock hedge on the north side of the front lawn survived woolly adelgid and now thrives.

Proceeding up the driveway and through the white gates, a peony bed frames the porch. The back lawn is divided into an upper terrace and a natural punch bowl below. A serpentine perennial bed divides the two, along with a 'Wintergreen' *Ilex* hedge. A prized cutting garden of zinnias sits atop the stone wall. The tall evergreen border along the back of the property consists of *Cryptomeria* and Leyland cypress. Punctuating it all is a collection of period garden ornaments.

This garden's estimated size is 2/3 acre.

WAINSCOTT
BIERCUK AND LUCKEY GARDEN
  10–2

This garden is open twice this year: May 11 and September 7.

We designed, personally installed, and maintain our four-season garden, which shelters, under a high oak canopy, a collection of rhododendrons, camellias, azaleas, pieris, understory trees, perennials, bulbs, and in season, tropicals.

The maturing garden is adapting to changes in sunlight/brightness due to tree death and deforestation on three sides. The rear right quadrant, the sunniest space, contains a pool designed as a pond with a waterfall and is surrounded with plantings that peak mid-July through October.

Winding paths and stone walls enhance a sense of depth and elevation on a mainly flat acre. There is something in bloom every season.

This garden's estimated size is ½ acre.

💬 TROWEL TALK

Despite being a totally committed sun worshiper (my nickname is Tan Man), my preferred gardening venue is treed shaded space. I've enjoyed the opportunity to create a woodland escape, its coolness a perfect foil to a day of sunbathing. The garden, now a treed peninsula since three adjoining properties have been denuded, is a haven for birds.

—Tan Man

NEW　5　10　20　'95　Year　🚫 No Photography　♿ Accessibility　🍃 Nibbled Leaf Garden

Ulster County
Saturday, September 7

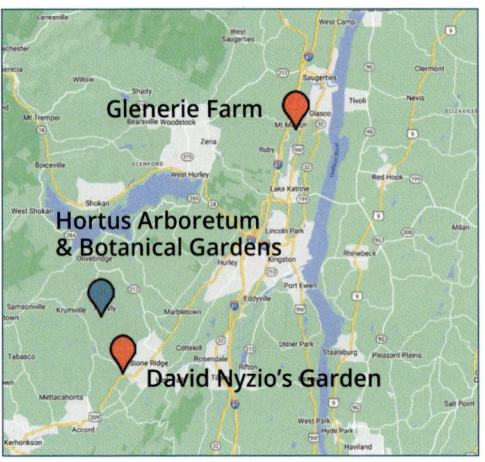

The 2024 Open Days in Ulster County are presented in partnership with Hortus Arboretum and Botanical Gardens

**NONPROFIT PARTNER
2023 GARDENS FOR GOOD RECIPIENT
PUBLIC GARDEN**

HORTUS ARBORETUM & BOTANICAL GARDENS

**76 Mill Road
Stone Ridge, New York 12484**

Our goal is for Hortus to be a "living textbook" of plant life that can be grown in the Hudson Valley.

We began the process of creating a botanical garden/arboretum by planting native trees, shrubs, perennials, and unusual edible plants with a focus on rare and endangered species.

In 2001 we began recording what we planted with detailed plant tags. In 2017 we received Level II Accreditation by the ArbNet Arboretum Accreditation Program and the Morton Arboretum. As a young botanical garden/arboretum, our goal is to grow the largest diversity of plant life in the Hudson Valley accessible to the general public.

This year, Allyson and Scott published *Cold Hardy Fruits and Nuts: 50 Easy-to-Grow Plants for the Organic Home Garden or Landscape* (Chelsea Green Publishing, 2022), an easy-to-use resource for growing healthy, resilient, low maintenance trees, shrubs, vines, and other fruiting plants from around the world.

chelseagreen.com/product/cold-hardy-fruits-and-nuts/

facebook.com/hortusbotanicalgarden

instagram.com/hortusgardens

hortusgardens.org

NEW   Year No Photography Accessibility Nibbled Leaf Garden

DIGGING DEEPER

Dynamic Successional Mosaic Landscape
David Nyzio
Saturday, September 7, 10–12

David Nyzio's Garden
Stone Ridge, NY
$30 Members | $40 General

I am a lifelong naturalist, and my landscaping practices reflect this interest in natural history.

At the turn of the twentieth-century, there were 200,000 houses in NYC. Most of the land in my area, after previously being deforested, was planted with non-native grasses to feed horses. Most of the landscape here is covered in agriculturally adaptive Eurasian plants. It's difficult to imagine what the past plant configurations were.

The principal focus of my landscape project is to reintroduce as many appropriate native plants as possible, as well as remove as many problematic introduced plants as possible.

Tilling the soil is often problematic because it exposes bad memories, that is, the undesirable seed bank present there. It also disrupts the soil and its living community. Plastic covering and solarizing techniques have been effective in preparing soil for plug and seed planting.

Unlike typical gardening practices, my only interest is mowing management. No weeding, watering, mulching, or thinning. Once plants are established, mowing frequency and pattern will be the only management practice.

All plants have different needs and respond to different mowing pressures. My goal is to encourage a diverse plant and animal community that will be more stable as time goes on with less intensive editing of invasives necessary.

It can also be considered a distribution center. The distribution vectors already exist in the form of birds, wind, and water flowing over the bottomland into the creek. The more desirable native plants are here, the more seeds can be spread far and wide.

Photo: David Nyzio

DIGGING DEEPER

Diversity on a Cut Flower Farm
Karin and Dennis Skalla
Saturday, September 7, 2–4

Glenerie Farm
Saugerties, NY
$30 Members | $40 General

Glenerie Farm, started in 2012, has sold specialty cut flowers to their community since 2019.

Learn how owners Karin and Dennis have navigated different enterprises, balancing the promises of permaculture techniques with the realities of a small scale, diversified farm. Discover the processes which best support all aspects of life on the farm–from its flowers, to its livestock, to the native flora and fauna.

Hear from the farmers how they continue to improve the health of the land they steward while growing a wide variety of flowers for wholesale and retail.

💬 TROWEL TALK

Our farming journey together began in 2011. We grow specialty cut flowers for wholesale and retail and offer a cut flower subscription program for our community. We also supply DIY buckets of flowers for brides, or other event planners, interested in doing their own floral arrangements. We grow a wide variety of flowers throughout the season, including more than 150 varieties of dahlias.

We started farming with livestock and still raise goats, ducks, and pigs. We enjoy our horse, dogs, and cats as companions on our journey. One of our guiding farming disciplines is permaculture. We appreciate the thoughtful consideration given to the environment, the land, and the natural floral and fauna existing on the land we are fortunate enough to steward.

In cooperation with our livestock, we produce beautiful compost that allows us to grow beautiful flowers. We feed locally grown, organic, soy-free grains and local hay. Our animals spend their lives outside in the fresh air and are rotated through our 15-acre property to ensure they have access to fresh pasture.

It may surprise some to discover locally grown cut flowers as an alternative to the commonly found, internationally grown blooms. Our farm-grown flowers have a smaller environmental footprint and a relatively longer vase life, and by purchasing local flowers, you're supporting a small business in your own community. We choose to be small scale and diversified to best oversee all aspects of the farm and to continue to improve the health of our land.

— *The Gardeners*

Dutchess County
Saturday, September 21

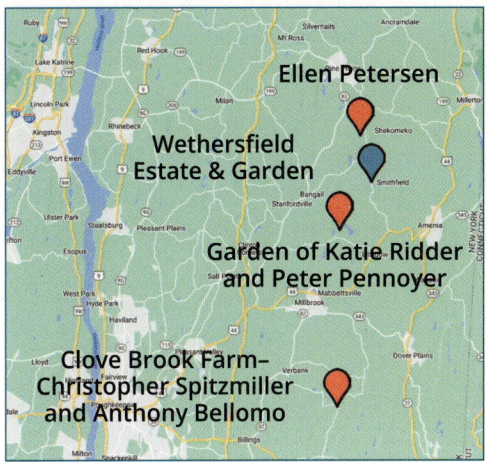

MILLBROOK

CLOVE BROOK FARM - CHRISTOPHER SPITZMILLER AND ANTHONY BELLOMO

 partial 10–4

This garden is open twice this year: June 2 and September 21.

The garden at Clove Brook Farm was started about seven years ago following a restoration of the historic Greek Revival farmhouse. The garden has quickly grown into a series of interconnected spaces, beginning with a horseshoe-shaped garden near the house that is surrounded by a clipped hornbeam hedge and anchored by a dovecote. It's this garden where we have a spectacular show of tulips and sweet peas in spring, followed by towering dahlias in late summer.

A few years ago another large garden "room" was added which centers on an oval swimming pool and Neoclassical style pool house. This garden is also bounded by a hornbeam hedge and includes perimeter beds filled with various herbaceous perennials which evolve throughout the growing season, starting with poppies in early spring, then peonies, roses, lilies, and finally dahlias.

Last year my partner, landscape architect Anthony Bellomo, designed and installed a large kitchen garden which we pack with various vegetables. We are both confirmed garden addicts, and in addition to the more formal garden spaces, continue to add informal and naturalistic plantings throughout the property. We've planted several mixed shrub borders studded with drifts of bulbs, embellished our existing orchard, and collected unique sculptures to establish focal points.

There is nothing more satisfying than tending and fostering a garden, and watching it develop and mature. It's all documented in *A Year at Clove Brook Farm* (Rizzoli, 2021, with foreword by Martha Stewart).

This garden's estimated size is 3 acres.

GARDEN OF KATIE RIDDER AND PETER PENNOYER

 10–4

Our hornbeam-enclosed flower garden with formal bluestone paths frames fourteen flower beds and was inspired by Wave Hill in the Bronx.

The garden is centered on a small terrace with fountain bowl and a wisteria-draped pergola. Our house, designed by my husband, Peter Pennoyer, faces directly onto the garden with a mudroom in the form of a small temple aligning with the central path. The beds feature fastigiate beech, dwarf conifers, grasses, annuals, and ever-developing unusual combinations.

Our landscape architect, Edmund Hollander, designed our property with simple hedgerows and trees, reserving the flower garden and woodland path for me to unleash a less disciplined approach. Our land runs the length of an old farm stone wall. The principal elements align from east to west: meadow, flower garden, greenhouse, woodland path, cutting garden, and, finally, the corn field of the neighboring farm.

to take the path up a little hill. There is a beautiful big Franklinia blooming behind the house.

The garden was included in Jane Garmey's book, *Private Gardens of the Hudson Valley*.

This garden's estimated size is 7 acres.

This garden's estimated size is 6 acres

STANFORDVILLE
ELLEN PETERSEN

   10–4

I have been gardening here for 42 years, but, thanks to the help of Danielle Giulian, I continue to make changes, refining the design, renovating older plantings, and beginning new areas.

One goal is to have interest every month of the year. High summer is the start of the dahlias and phlox and other perennials. Our carefully assembled collection of plants includes more natives every year. I love finding interesting native cultivars like Liquidambar 'Slender Silhouette' but also enjoy the thrill of searching out exotic rarities.

A meadow of *Sporobolus heterolepis* (prairie dropseed) frames "Windblown Couch," a sculpture by Vivian Beer. Robert Murray's "Willow" is next to the pond, and "Portal" by Carla Edwards will entice you

PRESERVATION PARTNER PUBLIC GARDEN
WETHERSFIELD ESTATE & GARDEN

**257 Pugsley Hill Rd
Amenia, New York 12501**

Wethersfield Estate & Garden occupies 1,000 acres in northeast Dutchess County, where it is the highest point in the region with an elevation of 1,200 feet. From that vantage point, it offers majestic views of the Berkshires, the Catskills, and the Taconic Hills.

Comprising a Georgian-style house, classical gardens, a carriage house, and a farm, Wethersfield Estate & Garden is generally considered one of the finest examples of Italian Renaissance gardens in the United States.

Founded by Citigroup heir, philanthropist, and investor Chauncey Stillman in 1938, Wethersfield Estate & Garden is now a nonprofit organization devoted to the proper stewardship of land, habitat protection, conservation, culture, and the arts.

Wethersfield hosts a diversity of formal and native-inspired garden spaces, such as an Arts & Crafts English perennial garden, cut flower garden, hedged yew topiaries, and mature tree specimens, and 20 miles of trails for equestrian activities and hiking.

Wethersfield strives to integrate the latest horticultural knowledge to maintain a sustainable and historical garden in a changing world. Wethersfield Estate & Garden is on the National Register of Historic Places and was awarded the 2021 New York State Historic Preservation Award for Excellence in Historic Landscape Preservation.

facebook.com/WethersfieldGarden

instagram.com/wethersfieldgarden

wethersfield.org

300　New York　　　　　　　　　　Register online: gardenconservancy.org/opendays

Jefferson County
Saturday, October 5

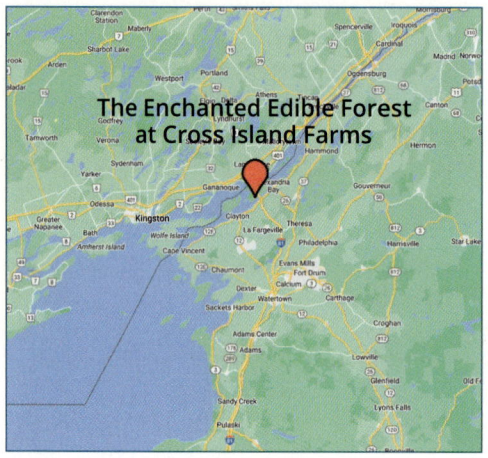

WELLESLEY ISLAND
THE ENCHANTED EDIBLE FOREST AT CROSS ISLAND FARMS

  1–4

This garden is open twice this year: May 18 and October 5.

Over the past eleven years Dani Baker has developed an acre of her certified organic farm as a multi-functional "Enchanted Edible Forest" garden containing more than 300 cultivars of perennial fruits, nuts, berries, flowers, and other edibles.

The garden is elegantly landscaped, including a number of native limestone patios, two small ponds, and a bridge, trellis, and gates fashioned from native white cedar. The word that visitors most often spontaneously use to describe it is "magical."

Based on her experience creating this garden, Dani has written a book, *The Home-Scale Forest Garden: How to Plan, Plant and Tend a Resilient Edible Landscape*, a guide to help others create their own magical edible landscapes.

Learn more at enchantededibleforest.com

This garden's estimated size is 1 acre.

💬 **TROWEL TALK**

I planted several honey locusts to provide usable nitrogen to the surrounding plants. Honey locust trees are either male or female. Earlier this season I spotted some large green pods on one of the trees, and exuberantly exclaimed "It's a girl!"

—Dani Baker

 Year　　　

Ulster County
Saturday, October 19

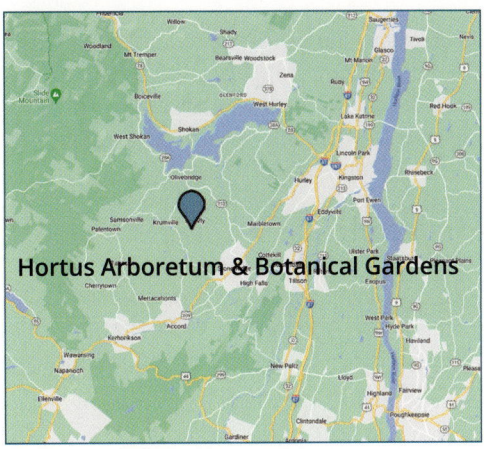
Hortus Arboretum & Botanical Gardens

The 2024 Open Days in Ulster County are presented in partnership with Hortus Arboretum and Botanical Gardens.

**NONPROFIT PARTNER
2023 GARDENS FOR GOOD RECIPIENT
PUBLIC GARDEN**

HORTUS ARBORETUM & BOTANICAL GARDENS

**76 Mill Road
Stone Ridge, New York 12484**

DIGGING DEEPER

Guided Tour of The Enchanted Edible Forest Garden
Dani Baker, Creator: The Enchanted Edible Forest Garden; Author: The Home-Scale Forest Garden
Saturday, October 5, 10–12

The Enchanted Edible Forest at Cross Island Farms
Wellesly Island, NY
$30 Members | $40 General

Take a guided tour of a sustainable edible perennial garden where nature does most of the work.

Use all your senses—see, smell, and taste edible flowers, leaves, herbs, fruits, berries, and perennial vegetables in season. Get inspired—learn how to landscape your own property with aesthetically pleasing, food-producing plants. Become enchanted—experience the ambiance and abundance of a garden modeled after nature.

NEW 5 10 20 '95 Year   No Photography   Accessibility   Nibbled Leaf Garden

Our goal is for Hortus to be a "living textbook" of plant life that can be grown in the Hudson Valley.

We began the process of creating a botanical garden/arboretum by planting native trees, shrubs, perennials, and unusual edible plants with a focus on rare and endangered species.

In 2001 we began recording what we planted with detailed plant tags. In 2017 we received Level II Accreditation by the ArbNet Arboretum Accreditation Program and the Morton Arboretum. As a young botanical garden/arboretum, our goal is to grow the largest diversity of plant life in the Hudson Valley accessible to the general public.

This year, Allyson and Scott published *Cold Hardy Fruits and Nuts: 50 Easy-to-Grow Plants for the Organic Home Garden or Landscape* (Chelsea Green Publishing, 2022), an easy-to-use resource for growing healthy, resilient, low maintenance trees, shrubs, vines, and other fruiting plants from around the world.

chelseagreen.com/product/cold-hardy-fruits-and-nuts/

facebook.com/hortusbotanicalgarden

instagram.com/hortusgardens

hortusgardens.org

DIGGING DEEPER

Fruiting Plants From Around the World for your Garden
Scott Serrano and Allyson Levy
Saturday, October 19, 11–1

Hortus Arboretum & Botanical Gardens
Stone Ridge, NY
$30 Members | $40 General

Prepare to get inspired (and hungry) while learning to surround your home and grace your table with rare and beautiful fruits, and nuts.

Allyson Levy and Scott Serrano are both botanical artists who moved to the Catskill Mountains twenty-four years ago. Their interests have expanded well beyond paper and canvas, and they now garden all year long at Hortus, a nonprofit, accredited botanical garden and arboretum.

Trying plants from around the globe, their goal is to create a "living textbook" of plant life, particularly edibles, that can be grown in New York's Hudson Valley.

These range from hardy citrus to ancient medlars, new types of quince that can be eaten raw, and a host of unusual berries and nuts.

Allyson and Scott are passionate about sharing their expertise and this walking tour will be filled with practical tips to ensure you can enjoy such bounty, too.

Refreshments featuring some of these choice edibles will be served.

Asterisk Farms - Sullivan, OH
Photo: Dana Depew

305

Ohio

Open Days dates and times by County, Town, and Garden

LORAIN

Sullivan
Asterisk Farms
 Saturday, September 28, 10–4

SUMMIT

Akron
Becky's Wild and Wonderful Garden
 Saturday, August 10, 10–2

OHIO

Summit County
Saturday, August 10

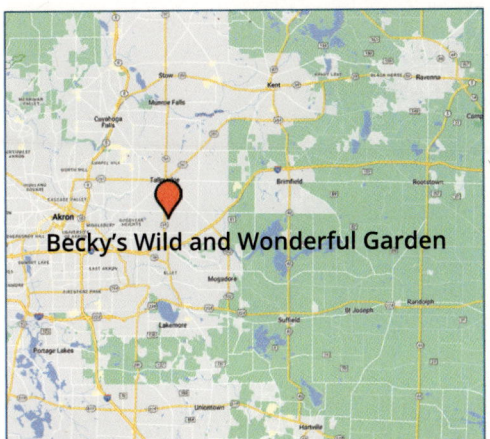

AKRON
BECKY'S WILD AND WONDERFUL GARDEN
NEW 🍂 10–2

Tucked away in an urban neighborhood, I have been developing my small lot into a wildlife and pollinator friendly garden. The garden is twenty years in the making, with a maple tree shade garden in the front of my home and full sun to more shade in the backyard.

The garden beds are meadows of many different perennials, with splashes of colorful tropical and annual plants. I grow several different kinds of berries and have a small vegetable room, where I grow my vegetables. There are two huge river birches in the back of the property that can get pretty wet in spring and fall, so there are winterberries, buttonbushes, and an array of different perennials and annuals.

The property has a natural hedgerow, giving me privacy from my neighbors. I grow most of my plants myself from seed, so there will be plants you won't see at the local greenhouse.

This garden's estimated size is 5,000 sq. ft.

💬 **TROWEL TALK**

My garden inspiration started with my mom, who was a gardener up into her 80s. She loved flowers and I think I inherited her love of them. She also had a pretty large vegetable garden back in the 70s. She gave my sister and me a little plot behind the garage, to grow our own little garden.

From then on, wherever life took me, I started growing my own plants and creating small gardens.

—Becky Ramskogler

NEW 5 10 20 95 Year   📷 No Photography   ♿ Accessibility   🍂 Nibbled Leaf Garden

DIGGING DEEPER

Urban Pollinator Gardening
Becky Ramskogler
Saturday, August 10, 2–4

Becky's Wild and Wonderful Garden
Akron, OH
$30 Members | $40 General

Take a tour of an established pollinator garden, boasting natives, tropicals, and vegetable plants. I also grow berries. I'd like to show the diversity of growing many plants in a small space and how these plants provide food and shelter for the many insects that visit.

Learn how easy it is to create a similar garden at your home!

Lorain County
Saturday, September 28

SULLIVAN
ASTERISK FARMS
NEW   10–4

Asterisk Farms was started in 2018 when artist Dana Depew acquired a vacant and abandoned 13-acre farmed-out property and has been renovating the space with found objects into a communal agricultural space that has pick-your-own dahlia gardens and farm-to-table dinners.

This garden's estimated size is 3 acres.

💬 TROWEL TALK

I like to grow dahlias. I do not like groundhogs, I cannot grow strawberries for some reason. I really have a disdain for groundhogs.

—Dana Depew

Garden by the Pond, Brookline, NH
Photo: Brian Jones

Become a Garden Host or a Regional Ambassador

See page 374 or contact us at **opendays@gardenconservancy.org** to learn more.

Nature's Flow - Chadds Ford, PA
 Photo: the Garden Host

Pennsylvania

Pennsylvania

Open Days dates and times by County, Town, and Garden

BUCKS

New Hope
Paxson Hill Farm
  Saturday, June 22, 10–4

CHESTER

Phoenixville
Donald Pell Gardens
  Saturday, June 15, 10–4

DELAWARE

Chadds Ford
Nature's Flow
  Saturday, June 15, 10–4
WynEden
  Saturday, May 11, 10–4
Swarthmore
Belvidere
  Sunday, June 23, 10–4
Hedgleigh Spring
  Sunday, June 23, 10–4

MONTGOMERY

Flourtown
Vicki's Garden
  Saturday, June 15, 10–4
Wyndmoor
Lenbury West
  Saturday, June 15, 10–4

PHILADELPHIA

Philadelphia
Surprise Oasis on the Edge of Philadelphia
  Saturday, June 15, 10–4
Home Place Garden
  Saturday, June 15, 10–4

Register online: gardenconservancy.org/opendays   Pennsylvania   313

Delaware County

Saturday, May 11

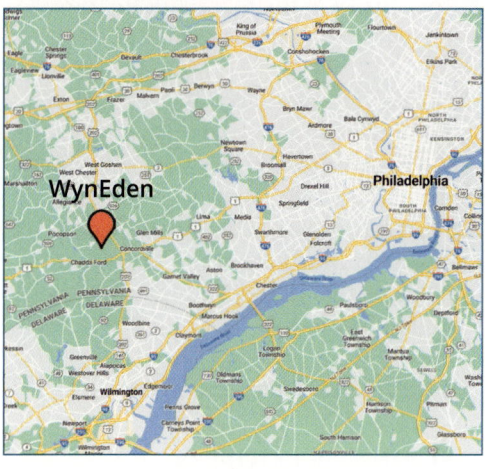

An additional garden is open nearby:
New Castle County, DE
   Thistle, Wilmington, DE
See page 131.

CHADDS FORD
WYNEDEN
  10–4

WynEden is a bucolic, 10-acre reverie set between two hills covered with mature trees. The southern hillside, where the house sits, is covered with more than 10,000 hostas cascading down in wide bands of three different colors.

The middle of the property has a 1-acre pond containing hundreds of water lilies and lotus. This pond is fed by a smaller, two-tiered feeder pond with an Asian-style garden. Here koi swim in the shade of a large thicket of bamboo. A small waterfall tumbles down from the upper tier to the main tier of this pond, which features a zigzag Asian footbridge.

Behind the bamboo, a large bog garden featuring a granite Japanese lantern is surrounded by an extensive planting of rhododendron.

This garden's estimated size is 10 acres.

NEW 5 10 20 '95 Year   No Photography   Accessibility

Nearby Counties

- **CHESTER**
- **DELAWARE**
- **MONTGOMERY**
- **PHILADELPHIA**

Saturday, June 15

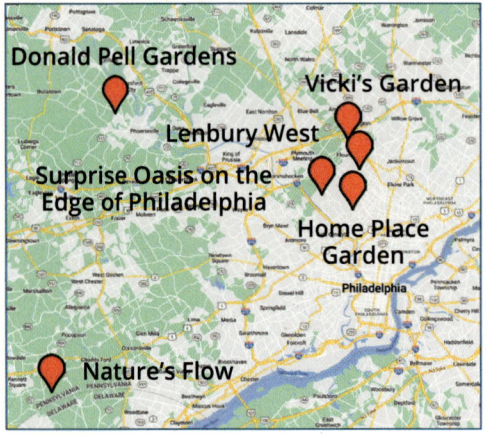

An additional garden is open nearby:
New Castle County, DE
  Old Oaks on Owl's Nest Rd, Wilmington, DE
See page 132.

CHESTER COUNTY
PHOENIXVILLE
DONALD PELL GARDENS
🖋 10–4

Tour the private studio gardens of award-winning garden designer Donald Pell. Since 2008, Pell has been converting this 14-acre farm into a lush landscape of naturalistic gardens in the New American style.

The farmhouse, Oval, and woodland gardens focus on exploring the beauty of plants in defined spaces that create an experience of place. Gravel pathways surrounding a historic stone farmhouse lead visitors through tall blocks of grasses and forbs, providing an intimate reaction to unique plants and novel combinations as they arrive at the rear natural-stone patio with sweeping views south.

Here, viewers overlook the Oval, where large-scale perennial plantings are laid out in block and intermingled compositions to mimic natural habitats while showcasing form, texture, and color. Monolithic slab steps lead toward the grand American pecan tree that is the centerpiece of the woodland garden.

This garden's estimated size is 4 acres.

DELAWARE COUNTY
CHADDS FORD
NATURE'S FLOW
🖋 10–4

When we moved here in December 2010, our realtor described the property as an empty palette for a gardener.

Throughout that first winter, my design evolved to emphasize indigenous plants in a naturalistic flow throughout the garden. We planted more than 200 trees and shrubs in the first year, and in November of 2011, we seeded a native plant meadow in the front area.

Two smaller meadows were planted in succeeding years, one in the far back to emphasize native grasses, and another one close to the back of the house in order to enjoy all the life a meadow provides.

A seasonally wet area has a thick planting of moisture-loving native plants. My passion also includes many conifers. In 2019, a small bog garden was installed.

This garden's estimated size is 4 acres.

💬 TROWEL TALK

I love to think of this garden as being in harmony with nature. There's an emphasis on native plants, since they are so important in the complex relationships that make a healthy ecology. Walking in the garden with the community of life that exists and the beauty of the plants is always a source of great joy in my life.

—Nora S

DIGGING DEEPER

Meadow Installation and Maintenance
Nora Sadler
Saturday, June 15, 4–6

Nature's Flow
Chadds Ford, PA
$30 Members | $40 General

Three native plant meadows were installed on the property in 2011, 2014, and 2017. The largest meadow is a little under an acre, and the other two are much smaller.

Site preparation, installation, and maintenance will be discussed. Knowing the wildlife value for bees, butterflies, and insects plus other ecological benefits makes this gardening journey so rewarding.

Photo: the Garden Host

MONTGOMERY COUNTY
FLOURTOWN
VICKI'S GARDEN
NEW 10–4

The centerpiece of this 1869 farmhouse and garden is an old barn foundation that has been beautifully repointed with found bits of pottery and glass from the yard. Key goals in the planting of the garden were cohesiveness, a focus on the view from the house, and a nod to the historical context of the setting.

The garden is composed of many "rooms" that flow from one to another with sinewy lines, massed plantings, and crisp edges. "Art," mostly in the form of rusty metal pieces, is sprinkled throughout the garden to introduce a bit of whimsy and to provide a nod to the history of the site.

Mature plantings from 30 years of gardening are being gradually replaced with grasses, meadow plants, and more deer resistant species.

This garden's estimated size is 2/3 acre.

WYNDMOOR
LENBURY WEST
 10–4

Laura and Matt have developed their half-acre parcel for the last 30 years. Their home is a modified Mid-century Modern precast concrete prototype—a product of an optimistic building boom in the 1940s. That's when the enormous White Marsh Hall built by financier Edward T. Stotesbury began to be dismantled after his death.

The Axels' land cascades downhill over 30 feet and so the development of exceptional gardens required thoughtful and finessed terracing and pathways. Laura has gathered her botanical exotica from her personal connections that have charmed the region's horticultural educators, curators, writers, and designers.

The gardens are dynamic with surprises quietly tucked behind the robust specimens on display.

This garden's estimated size is ½ acre.

PHILADELPHIA COUNTY
PHILADELPHIA
SURPRISE OASIS ON THE EDGE OF PHILADELPHIA
♿ partial   10–4

In 2002, I moved to this property and pretty much removed all the gardens and started over. I built a greenhouse which is fully irrigated and houses all the hanging baskets and perennials we will use throughout the growing season.

I designed the gardens around the pool to be "show gardens" so that I could show my clients the diversity of beautiful plant material we can grow in our area. There are dozens of varieties of trees, shrubs, and perennials with many different plant habits, tendencies, and colors. Hydrangeas and conifers of many types provide the backbone to this garden.

We are surrounded by 400 acres of the Schuylkill Nature Center, so the vastness of trees in the background make it hard to believe that this is located in the city of Philadelphia.

HOME PLACE GARDEN
10–4

Located on a corner in the middle of West Mt. Airy Village, our 25-year-old garden is densely planted with perennials, shrubs, and vines, all under a canopy of mature maples. This woodland garden combines plants with distinct foliage shapes, colors, and textures.

When not gardening, I am a full-time artist, which allows me to combine my love of gardens with my art. The garden contains many of my handmade objects discreetly positioned among the plants. Featured are a rooftop garden, a doorway to nowhere, and a ceramic tree.

This garden's estimated size is 3,000 sq. ft.

💬 TROWEL TALK

My mother, Ernestine, and my grandmother, Indiana Hutson, were both master gardeners. I can remember going on plant hunting trips with Mommy and watching her decorate her garden with colorful annuals and lush ground covers.

I have since gone on to create my own well-documented garden and even more satisfying, making art based on my love of gardens with many of those works finding homes in museums and private collections.

—Syd C.

Bucks County
Saturday, June 22

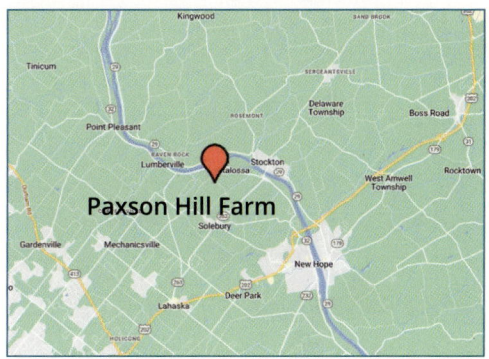

An additional garden is open nearby:
Somerset County, NJ:
  The Gardens at Federal Twist, Stockton, NJ
See page 216.

NEW HOPE
PAXSON HILL FARM
 10–4

Nestled in scenic New Hope, Paxson Hill Farm encompasses 30 acres of imaginative landscapes sure to bring delight to avid gardeners and nature lovers alike. Winding, naturalistic paths lead you through a variety of ever-evolving gardens inspired by world travels and a keen eye for design.

You will find elaborate ponds, a large hedge maze to get lost in, a conifer garden, formal and "not so formal" gardens, and even a Hobbit House. A true hidden gem and a perfect stop on a tour of Bucks County!

This garden's estimated size is 19 acres.

Delaware County
Sunday, June 23

An additional garden is open nearby:
New Castle County, DE
   Peggy Anne and Dan's Home Garden, Wilmington, DE.
   See page 133.

SWARTHMORE
BELVIDERE
10–4

Belvidere is the home garden of Andrew Bunting, Vice President of Horticulture at the Pennsylvania Horticultural Society and formerly the Scott Arboretum and Chicago Botanic Garden.

Andrew purchased the 1/3rd acre property in Swarthmore in 1999. At the front of the house is a gravel garden which uses water-wise plantings. Around the foundation are planted unusual shrubs and vines.

In the backyard, a large bluestone patio runs the lengths of the back of the house and is a showcase for many ornamental containers.

The detached stone garage was converted into a summer house in 2006. The front entrance to the summer house opens into a Mediterranean-like garden while the entrance has more of a tropical feel. To the back right is a large tropical garden planted with red Abyssinian bananas, bromeliads, and cannas during the summer. At the back of the property is a densely planted woodland garden with a pond; a utilitarian area with compost bins and a potager that alternates yearly between vegetables and cut flowers.

In 2012, a joint project with his neighbors was completed which is the addition of the Vassar Farm, a 40' x 100' suburban farm created at maintained by Andrew on his neighbor's property.

This garden's estimated size is 1/3 acre.

HEDGLEIGH SPRING
10–4

Hedgleigh Spring spans four generations of the Cresson family, beginning with the purchase of a "gentleman's farm" by Ezra T. Cresson in 1883.

The central feature of the current garden, designed and built by his son William, is an early twentieth-century flower garden. The flower garden is surrounded by a series of garden rooms including shade gardens, a small naturalistic pond, a stream and waterfall, and a vegetable garden. An old springhouse sits beneath towering old oak and black gum trees among large plantings of azaleas and camellias.

The utilization of the varied microclimates of this garden has lead to a large and varied plant collection. Charles Cresson, the current owner, is author of three books on gardening, a lecturer and consultant.

This garden's estimated size is 2 acres.

NONPROFIT ORGANIZATION

SWARTHMORE HORTICULTURAL SOCIETY

The Swarthmore Horticultural Society is a non-profit that operates in the Borough of Swarthmore.

The Society designs and maintains 13 public gardens and we are dedicated to enhancing Swarthmore's public spaces and promoting the value of horticulture and nature to the community. These gardens are all on public spaces and can be easily accessed by the public.

Many of the gardens showcase seasonal plantings including bulbs in the spring and provocative summer displays.

facebook.com/Swarthmore-Horticultural-Society

instagram.com/swarthmorehort

swarthmorehorticulturalsociety.org/

The Garden at Power Street - Providence, RI
Photo: the Garden Host

Rhode Island

Open Days dates and times by County, Town, and Garden

NEWPORT

Little Compton
Sakonnet
Sunday, July 21, 9–5:30

PROVIDENCE

Providence
College Hill Urban Oasis
Saturday, September 14, 10–12, 12–2, 2–4
Sycamore Farm Community Garden
Saturday, September 14, 10–4
The Garden at Power Street
Saturday, September 14, 10–4

WASHINGTON

Westerly
Thompson's Corner
Saturday, July 13, 10–1, 1–4

Washington County
Saturday, July 13

WESTERLY
THOMPSON'S CORNER

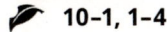 10–1, 1–4

This garden has evolved over the last twenty years. It contains more than 25 species of trees, including a London Plain tree which was planted to commemorate Westerly's Tercentenary in 1969. There is a grove of paw paw trees started from seed and a ginkgo tree which is a descendent of a tree in Westerly's Wilcox Park, an arboretum.

Although less than three-quarters of an acre in a village setting, there are two water features, a summer kitchen, a small boat barn, and an outhouse which is now the world's smallest "she shed" on the grounds of this antique farmhouse. The emphasis has been on using natives to create a naturalistic settling.

This garden's estimated size is ¾ acre.

Newport County
Sunday, July 21

LITTLE COMPTON
SAKONNET

 9–5:30

Sakonnet Garden is a hidden exotic garden embedded within a native coastal fields landscape, a long-term project of John Gwynne and Mikel Folcarelli.

This ongoing experiment in design, scale, and plantings began as an acre-sized spring woodland garden and is subdivided into spaces separated by high windbreak hedges and stone walls that enable growing of many Zone 7 plants.

Each space has its own mood and horticultural objective. These woodland areas are very different in summer— mostly shady and green, but with the "subtropical quadrant" at peak of exuberance.

A new "pollinator plus" summer garden is a colorful walk-through perennial border conceived as a biodiversity maze. Thousands of flowers produce nectar for

---

NEW 5 10 20 '95 Year   No Photography   Accessibility    Nibbled Leaf Garden

butterflies, bees, especially native bees, and other insects important for pollination. Clipped topiary ilex begins to mimic the Nupé house posts from Ghana.

Please note that Sakonnet Garden manages registration for this event. Tickets must be purchased through Sakonnet's website. Open Days credits are not accepted.

For more information, please visit gardenconservancy.org/opendays

This garden's estimated size is 1+ acre.

Providence County
Saturday, September 14

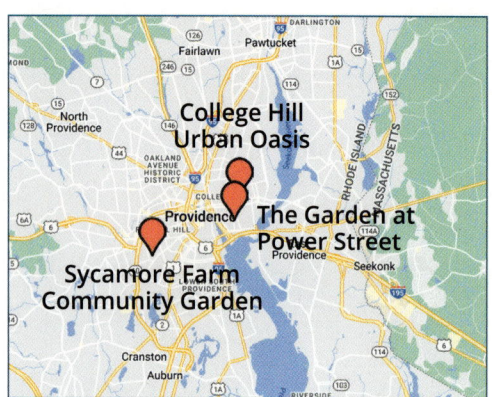

An additional garden is open nearby :
Bristol County, MA
 Landscape Designer Andrew Grossman's Display Gardens, Seekonk, MA
See page 173.

PROVIDENCE
COLLEGE HILL URBAN OASIS
 partial   10–12, 12–2, 2–4

Designed by Andrew Grossman, this urban garden in the heart of College Hill near Brown University is a miniature paradise. Located at the intersection of two quiet streets in the Stimson Avenue historic district, it is enclosed by a tall board fence with lattice insets.

The garden features a boisterous arrangement of hydrangea bushes and hydrangea trees accented by a contemporary fountain amid pots of tall grasses and flowers.

This garden's estimated size is 1,200 sq. ft.

NEW 5 10 20 95 Year    No Photography    Accessibility    Nibbled Leaf Garden

SYCAMORE FARM COMMUNITY GARDEN

  partial 10–4

Sycamore Farm is an urban agriculture oasis in Providence's historic West End neighborhood. Visitors will delight in touring a whimsical mix of organically grown vegetables, berries, herbs, and flowers in raised beds tended by nine neighboring families and the garden owner who lives on the property in a newly constructed home.

A beehive dwells under the boughs of an old beech tree that takes up a full third of the farm. The perimeter fence and deck are made of tamarack that was hewn and milled in Rhode Island. A water feature wends through the garden, from downspouts to a little pond. This rock river solves two problems: drainage from the new house's roof and what to do with the piles of newly excavated foundation stones and pebbles—the remains of two buildings that were buried decades ago on this double lot.

Decades ago, a community garden grew up on the then vacant lot. The present owner, an urban agriculture advocate, purchased the lot when it fell into neglect. Still a work in progress, Sycamore Farm is once again happily flourishing and providing joy to all who garden within or who walk and drive by it.

This garden's estimated size is a double city lot.

TROWEL TALK

I got hooked on community gardens as early as 1995 when my neighbors and I in Omaha, NE revitalized a vacant lot where a young man had been murdered in a drive-by shooting. Since then, it's been a privilege to work alongside urban agriculture heroes across the country and around the world. Most recently it's been a delight to share my own garden in Providence, RI with neighbors and passersby who are amazed by the variety and vigor of all manner of crops, berries, and fruit trees.

—*Katherine Brown*

THE GARDEN AT POWER STREET

 10–4

This is a new garden: the borders were built in 2017 and planting began in the fall of 2018. A city lot 70 × 70 feet, the garden is mostly filled with flowering perennials and features a summer house folly.

Previously there was no garden, just a worn-out lawn. Laura Willson designed the structure, and Kevin Bacon built the stone wall. The design pays homage to Colonial Revival gardens of 100 years ago.

This garden's estimated size is ⅛ acre.

A Behind the Garden Gate garden - Kiawah Island, SC
Photo: the Nonprofit Partner

South Carolina

South Carolina

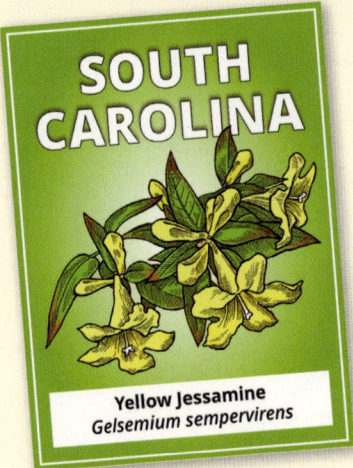

SOUTH CAROLINA

Behind the Garden Gate: Charleston-Area Open Days

Saturday, May 25 and Saturday, June 1

Hours: 9–2

COMING SOON

Enjoy an extraordinary opportunity to visit the Low Country's finest private gardens at the height of the spring season.

This season, our first weekend features gardens on Kiawah Island, then gardens in historic Charleston for the following weekend. Six different gardens are on tour each Saturday, and details will be announced soon.

Event registration, garden descriptions, photographs, and more information can be found at gardenconservancy.org/open-days/charleston-2024

NONPROFIT PARTNER

CHARLESTON HORTICULTURAL SOCIETY

The Charleston Horticultural Society provides quality educational programming that supports efforts, both big and small, to create beautiful, sustainable green spaces, fosters community partnerships; and preserves our legacy of horticulture in the South Carolina Lowcountry.

The Charleston Horticultural Society is in its 23rd year serving our community as the leader in horticulture educational outreach and programming in the SC Lowcountry. We offer a wide array of formal and informal educational activities such as workshops, classes, lectures, and other programming that furthers the art and practice of gardening, design and environmental sustainability.

facebook.com/ChasHortSoc

instagram.com/ ChasHortSoc

chashortsoc.org

Garden of Bill Noble - Norwich, VT
Photo: the Garden Host

Vermont

Vermont

Open Days dates and times by County, Town, and Garden

WINDHAM
Westminster West
Gordon and Mary Hayward's Garden
   Sunday, June 30, 10–4

WINDSOR
Norwich
Garden of Bill Noble
   Sunday, June 30, 10–4
Springfield
Woodland Farms
   Sunday, August 11, 10–4

Register online: gardenconservancy.org/opendays   Vermont   333

Nearby Counties

- **WINDHAM**
- **WINDSOR**

Sunday, June 30

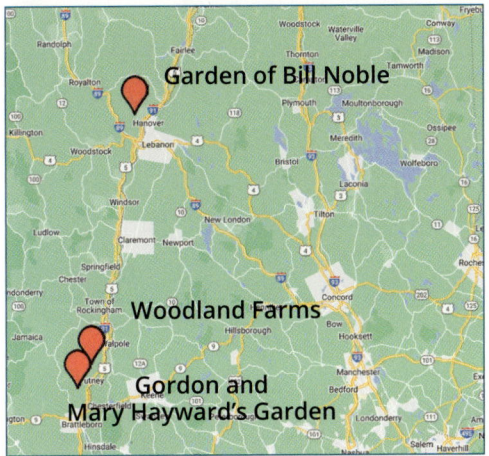

Additional gardens are open nearby:
Cheshire County, NH
   Boggy Meadow Farm, Walpole, NH
   Gardens of Bruce and Ellen Clement, Westmoreland, NH
   Shooting Star Farm, Spofford, NH
See page 194.

WINDHAM COUNTY
WESTMINSTER WEST
GORDON AND MARY HAYWARD'S GARDEN
   10–4

Gordon and Mary Hayward's 1½-acre garden surrounds their 220-year-old farmhouse in southeastern Vermont.

Over the past 38 years, they have developed a hybrid of Old England and New England gardens to reflect Gordon's growing up on an orchard in northwestern Connecticut, and Mary's growing up on a farm outside Chipping Campden in the North Cotswold Hills of England.

The garden, the subject of their book *The Intimate Garden* (WW Norton, 2005), comprises fourteen garden rooms. One area includes a pair of 90-foot perennial borders that terminate in a post-and-beam gazebo framing views of 20 acres of meadows.

More than 40 planted terra-cotta pots and many garden ornaments, several from England, figure into the mood of this garden.

This garden's estimated size is 1½ acres.

WINDSOR COUNTY
NORWICH
GARDEN OF BILL NOBLE
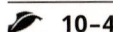 10–4

Originally a hillside farm with a rambling house, barns, stone walls, and fields, enhanced with views of neighboring farms and distant mountains, the garden has grown to include perennial and shrub borders, rock gardens, a vegetable garden, and orchard.

The main flower garden began as an old-fashioned mixed border, inspired by the gardens of the nearby Cornish Artists' Colony. Remnants of barn foundations offer settings for alpine and rock garden plants, ferns, and other specialty plants grown primarily for foliage value.

Plantings have recently expanded with new shrub borders and meadow plantings. The garden is chronicled in Noble's book,

NEW Year   No Photography  Accessibility  Nibbled Leaf Garden

Spirit of Place: The Making of a New England Garden.

This garden's estimated size is 2 acres.

NEARBY NURSERY
THE BUNKER FARM

**857 Bunker Road
Putney, VT 05346**

The Bunker Farm is a family-run farm that produces naturally pasture-raised meats, specialty annual and perennial flowers, and award-winning maple syrup.

facebook.com/thebunkerfarm

instagram.com/thebunkerfarm

thebunkerfarm.com

Windsor County
Sunday, August 11

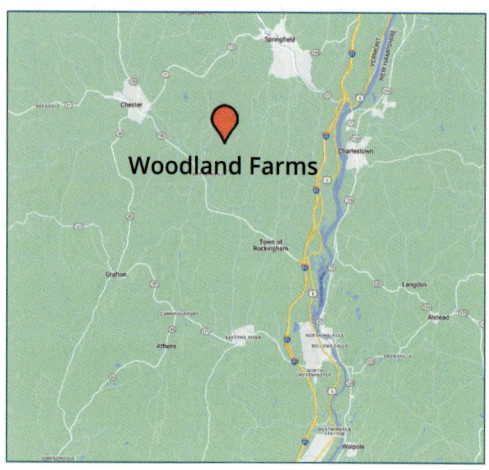

Additional gardens are open nearby:

Cheshire County, NH
  Distant Hills - Garden of Michael and Kathy Nerrie, Walpole, NH
  Hollows End, Gilsum, NH
See page 196.

SPRINGFIELD
WOODLAND FARMS
 10–4

The gardens at Woodland Farms have been evolving for twenty years around an oak-and-stone dwelling built to suggest a medieval Anglo-Norman house mysteriously come to rest on 300 acres in Vermont.

The "ruins" of ancient Celtic structures (created by dry stonewaller Dan Snow) and substantial terraces, steps, and pathways (built by Scott Bolotin) provide the bones for a hands-on, owner-designed, richly varied landscape.

Distinct garden areas include shrubs, perennials and grasses, dwarf conifers, meadows, and uncommon trees. Featured are perennials that last spring through fall, attracting pollinators and birds.

Chickens are kept, and there is an extensive drystone-walled organic vegetable garden. Stone-and-timber outbuildings, large expanses of grassland, hayfields, berry bushes, a northern-kiwi arbor, and a mixed-fruit orchard complete the design of this small manor farm.

Woodland Farms has been featured in *Gardens Illustrated* and *Martha Stewart Living* magazines.

This garden's estimated size is 20 acres.

Clay Hill Garden - Boyce, VA
Photo: RL Johnson

Virginia

Virginia

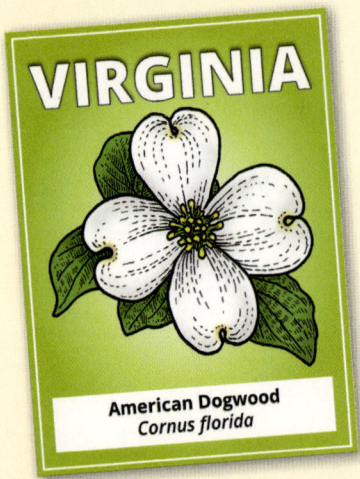

Open Days dates and times by County, Town, and Garden

CLARKE

Boyce
Clay Hill Garden
Sunday, October 6, 10–4

FAIRFAX

Great Falls
Domaine St. Charles
Saturday, June 8, 10–4
Gardens of Ellen and Allie Ash
Saturday, June 8, 10–4
Sandra's Secret Garden
Saturday, June 8, 10–1, 1–4

FAUQUIER

Marshall
Poke Gardens
Sunday, October 6, 10–12, 12–2, 2–4

Fairfax County
Saturday, June 8

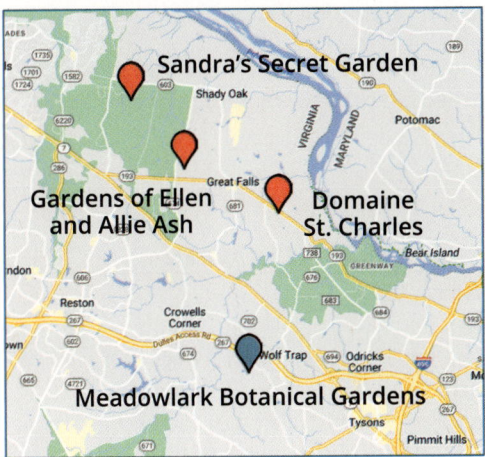

GREAT FALLS
DOMAINE ST. CHARLES

 10–4

This is a French country manor home set on two and one half acres of property. It features French style gardens with four water features, a pool, spa, and cabana. The property features extensive garden paths and terraces, pea gravel driveway and paver garage court. Entry gates lead through an allée featuring a Provençal wall fountain at the driveway terminus.

Cross axial alignment creates distant focal points and maximizes the breadth of the grounds. The garden features a wide variety of flowering trees and shrubs, featuring a "fragrant collection" of plants and over 10,000 perennials.

This garden's estimated size is 2½ acres.

💬 TROWEL TALK

My father introduced me to gardening and the art of "dry walling". Our family is Welsh by background and the dry stack wall techniques have been passed down 8 generations.

My father and I spent time visiting the National Arboretum and other public botanical gardens. I started my landscape design company in high school and trained under several garden designers and landscape architects in Washington DC. My design style is reflective of study, travel, and application.

It is difficult to identify one plant that could be considered "my favorite" given the varied applications, climatic zones, and sun exposures. I've become more interested in native species and their application in urban gardens.

My favorite garden tool is the Italian grape hoe.

—Charles O.

GARDENS OF ELLEN AND ALLIE ASH
10–4

Surrounded on all sides by giant American holly trees, the Ashes built their contemporary house in 1981 and the gardens have slowly grown to encompass most of their five-acre property.

After entering the gate, you are greeted by a perennial bed that includes flowering shrubs as well as perennials and annuals. The centerpiece of the backyard is a pool with a large covered eating pavilion. Also sharing the backyard are many small specialty gardens for roses, sedums, vegetables, show-quality dahlias, and a

---

NEW 5 10 20 95 Year  No Photography ♿ Accessibility  Nibbled Leaf Garden

goldfish inhabited lily pond.

But the highlight is the almost two-acre woodland garden. Its meandering moss trails are lined with a combination of shade and sun plants plus numerous sculptures and whimsical garden accessories.

Already growing on the property were hundreds of hollies, oaks, hickories, and dogwoods to which have been added azaleas, rhododendrons, laurels, pieris, daphne, viburnums, camellias, and hydrangeas.

Filling out the smaller spaces are more than thirty types of hostas, and countless varieties of hellebores, tiarella, pulmonaria, tricyrtis, primula, aquilegia, ferns, clematis, native groundcovers, heaths, trillium and numerous large and small bulbs.

The garden had been lovingly planted and tended by the owners, Ellen and Allie Ash.

💬 TROWEL TALK

I love dahlias and grow them to show. I usually get a few on the Court of Honor plus lots of blue ribbons.

I grew up in Manhattan in a two bedroom apartment with a tall plant and a short plant. At my first house, I had two tomato plants and a rose bush. In the next 50 years, I've expanded a lot and now have well over a thousand plants.

I love hybrid lilies and always over order with the rationale that I can always find room for a few more. When my husband and I travel, we love to buy whimsical outdoor sculpture. Sometimes we buy something just because the title makes us laugh.

I love to share my garden and inspire others to become involved in gardening.

Peonies don't like me! People always offer me rooted cuttings and I warn them that I will probably kill them.

I love using a big screwdriver to get out weeds in my sedum garden. It cost me all of $1.

—Ellen Ash

SANDRA'S SECRET GARDEN
NEW   10–4, 1–4

The garden covers a little over half an acre, with hardscape features including a flagstone path through the garden. Because of the number of trees, the garden does not include many plants that require a lot of direct sun.

The majority of the flowers are impatiens, caladiums, hostas, and begonias. There is a (recirculating) stream running through the garden which empties into a 13,000-gallon koi pond.

This garden's estimated size is ½ acre.

NEW 5 10 20 '95 Year  No Photography  Accessibility  Nibbled Leaf Garden

PUBLIC GARDEN
NOVA PARKS - MEADOWLARK BOTANICAL GARDENS

9750 Meadowlark Garden Ct
Vienna, Virginia 22182

Meadowlark Botanical Gardens is a 95-acre public garden with notable features such as a Korean Bell Garden, a Mediterranean Greenhouse Collection, Potomac Valley Collection. We are also the host of a wedding venue (The Atrium) as well as a winter light show (Winter Walk of Lights).

Meadowlark Botanical Gardens is a part of NOVA Parks - the best of Northern Virginia through nature, history, and great family experiences

facebook.com/MeadowlarkGardens

instagram.com/meadowlarkbotanicalgardens

novaparks.com/parks/meadowlark-botanical-gardens

Nearby Counties

- **CLARKE**
- **FAUQUIER**

Sunday, October 6

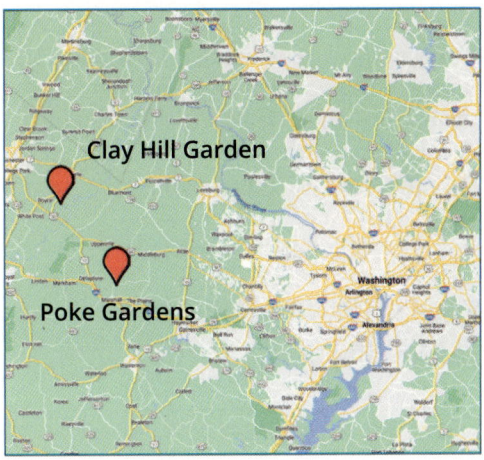

CLARKE COUNTY
BOYCE
CLAY HILL GARDEN
NEW   10–4

My husband and I have lived at Clay Hill for more than forty years and the gardens have grown and changed along with the property and ourselves.

We have created a series of terraces with a Gothic-inspired greenhouse at the center where I grow orchids, palms, and cycads.

My principal gardening passion is growing dahlias. We currently grow nearly a hundred in special beds that cater to their requirements. In September and October, they are at their peak of beauty.

We also have a large vegetable and cut flower kitchen garden, in addition to our wonderful, very old boxwood bushes of which we are especially proud.

This garden's estimated size is 3 acres.

💬 TROWEL TALK

I am very passionate about dahlias and through the years I have learned to grow them quite well. They don't require a lot of work but the more you fuss over them the more they will reward you!

—Elizabeth

FAUQUIER COUNTY
MARSHALL
POKE GARDENS
NEW 10-12, 12-2, 2-4

Poke Gardens is situated on 9 acres just outside Marshall, Virginia. The gardens began almost 30 years ago with a small vegetable garden at the bottom of a hill below a shady house in the woods.

The sloping site seemed to suggest a series of terraces falling to the east and south and the gardens evolved in through the years with that idea in mind. The kitchen garden is just above the main property gates and supplies the house all summer.

The garden gates at a tool shed just across the drive from the vegetable garden lead to the main garden which is a series of "rooms" loosely defined by color. First is a hydrangea hill with over 40 varieties then a double shady border leaning toward blues silvers and yellows. There are steps up to a pavilion with a garden of deep shade plants. The end of the "Blue Garden" is now dominated by a mature contorted Mulberry 'Unryu'- "Dragon in the Clouds". at the end of the gravel path is another pavilion overlooking the valley toward the Bull Run Mountains or looking across the lower garden toward the pool terrace and house.

The winding path is broken by grass lawns steps and bridges crossing a water feature that spills from the pump house into a tank then into a winding stream. The first area is built of hedges of old peony varieties (some from my grandmother's garden) on one side and mixed pink leaning perennials on the other. The next terrace with a squire lawn is mostly planted primarily for the high summer garden. The course through the gardens over bridges and boardwalks and through woods finally reaches a pond garden.

The path continues back up the hill passing the Sylvan Theatre, up rustic steps to a circular fern garden with an obelisk folly in its center. The existing woods of hickory, chestnut, oak, and tulip poplar are planted deeply with azaleas in drifts of white and pink with deeper more jewel like colors at the far end of the woods.

It is a garden to wander and explore, to find places to sit in the shade and discover the interior views and those borrowed from the beautiful Piedmont of Virginia.

This garden's estimated size is 5 acres.

NEW 5 10 20 '95 Year    No Photography    Accessibility   Nibbled Leaf Garden

💬 TROWEL TALK

The gardening books of Gertrude Jekyll were my first inspiration when I finally got organized enough to "plot" garden layouts. The idea of rooms, of course, comes from the Arts & Crafts gardening movement in England.

I like using hardscape to shape the land and then plant to obscure that definition. I've always pushed out Zone 7 limits. Rarely successfully. I had a magnificent "Lady Banks" rose trained onto a 12' tower for several years. It was ultimately killed to the ground by an early heatwave followed by a deep freeze.

—*Dana Westring*

Shades of Green - Sammamish, WA
Photo: the Garden Host

Washington

346 Washington

Open Days dates and times by County, Town, and Garden

KING

Redmond
Novelty Creek
   Saturday, June 1, 10–4
Rutherford Creek Gardens
   Saturday, June 1, 10–12, 12–2, 2–4
Sammamish
Shades of Green
   Saturday, June 1, 10–4
Vashon Island
Austin Donnelly
   Sunday, June 9, 10–4
Carhart Garden
   Sunday, June 9, 10–4
Froggsong Gardens
   Sunday, June 9, 10–4
The Garden at the Corner of Dock and Dock
   Sunday, June 9 2024, 10–4
The Halstead Garden
   Sunday, June 9, 2024, 10–4
Victorian Stumpery Garden
   Sunday, June 9, 10–4

KITSAP

Bainbridge Island
Dragon's Lair - The Demianew Gardens
   Saturday, June 22, 10–4
The Piraino Garden
   Saturday, June 22, 10–4
The Skyler Garden
   Saturday, June 22, 10–4

King County
Saturday, June 1

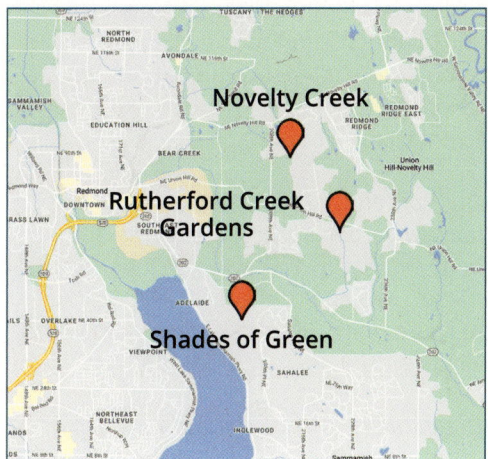

REDMOND
NOVELTY CREEK
NEW   10–4

Novelty Creek was designed around three large ponds connected by cascading waterfalls, and fed by a year-round, 60-gallons-per-minute artesian spring. The ponds were dug in 1979 when the house was built, but the garden didn't truly begin in earnest until twelve years later.

Gardening around the unlined, natural blue clay ponds is a challenge. To survive, plants must thrive in either a bog or hard-packed clay. At the entry, a massive arbor blends with the post and rail fencing, as well as the pergola nearer the pasture. The free-standing stone moon gate near the front door is in keeping with the "circles" throughout the property.

This garden's estimated size is 1 acre.

TROWEL TALK

Favorite plant: *Primula bulleyana* (candelabra primrose). I started with a handful of plants, and they have self-seeded through the years so that now they are, really and truly, a ground cover, choking out other plants in their way (too bad for those wimpy plants). The primulas not only provide color in late spring and early summer, but they have grown as a ground cover; they suppress all weeds and are slug-proof, a must here in the Pacific Northwest.

Favorite gardening tool: hori-hori knife. A must for a hands-on gardener.

—*The Gardener*

RUTHERFORD CREEK GARDENS
NEW   10–12, 12–2, 2–4

Our little bit of England, a 2-acre English Country Garden made and maintained by an English country couple.

In the main gardens, the mixed borders are planted with 'must-have' sustainable perennials, mixed in with flowering shrubs and specimen trees against a borrowed backdrop of tall native evergreens.

The garden rooms and pathways are connected by rose-covered archways and wisteria-supporting pergolas, taking you through the shady grove of sequoia and cedar trees and emerging in the meadow in front of the Chicken Cottage.

The "No Mow Meadow" is planted with spring and summer bulbs and then gets its first mow in July, supplying hay for the chickens! Close by is the Pavilion, designed and built by the owners. This is a shady or sheltering spot to sit and view the more formal Parterre Garden with its four clematis-supporting Tuteurs.

Pick a path and wander along the ferny creek edge or take the long east border to the beech pleached hedge. West of the house is the greenhouse and a gravel garden, with a few indulgent tropical plants.

Woodchip paths take you around the deck to the Daisy Steps and then to the top of the Gabion Garden, a terrace of planted gabion walls and connecting steps. From here steps and sloping paths take you to the natural area of "Soggy Bottom," next to the creek and a natural wildlife pond, and then you can follow the creek, emerging back in the gravel garden. The paths are edged by more gabion walls and in places topped with Fern Tables.

This garden's estimated size is 2 acres.

💬 TROWEL TALK

Always on my right hip are my trusty Felco secateurs. I have lost a few pairs in the garden over the years and even sent a pair through the shredder once!

It is with what I imagine will be the delight of an archaeologist that I will then find a pair thought lost in a garden or the compost bins, and I will lovingly clean, sharpen, and return them to the holster to prune another day.

—*Alison the Gardener*

SAMMAMISH
SHADES OF GREEN
NEW   10–4

Welcome to Shades of Green, a shade garden based on foliage colors, textures, and shapes. Our garden design goals were to find perfect plant combinations, create serene outdoor spaces, and make a garden to enjoy year-round.

Our garden design challenges were long, narrow garden spaces, and gardening beneath mature trees. We feel we've met these goals and challenges, and we love to share our gardening experiences with visitors.

This garden's estimated size is 8,500 sq. ft.

Register online: gardenconservancy.org/opendays   Washington 349

King County
Sunday, June 9

VASHON ISLAND

AUSTIN DONNELLY
NEW   10–4

Hidden in plain sight on Morgan Hill, Mary Liz Austin's garden is a portal to a verdant knoll of bewitching beauty; thoughtful planting combinations include a variety of sun-loving perennials, a mix of grasses, and whimsical garden art.

A visit to her garden reveals a window into the heart of a true artist, a creative soul who transforms ordinary into the exceptional through the alchemy of hard work, imagination, and the love of nature.

This garden's estimated size is 1 acre.

💬 TROWEL TALK
I am a landscape/nature photographer as my profession, and I try to create my garden beds so they have an interesting foreground as well as background features. I like to photograph the natural world with a wide-angle lens, and I have this same tendency with my garden, using sight lines, color, and texture to help with seeing the big picture so to speak. My other want is that visitors feel a sense of intimacy despite being adjacent to a busy road.

—Mary Liz

CARHART GARDEN
10–4

Our 2½-acre Northwest-style four-season garden with mixed shade and sun has evolved over twenty years.

The diverse collection of plants includes a mixture of unusual and rare woodland plants and ferns among Japanese maples, species rhododendrons, and unusual conifers. Many paths afford an opportunity to pause and reflect among the naturalistic plantings of cedars and firs, as well as stewartias, hydrangeas, and shade-tolerant perennials. Hillside paths lead down to a waterfall and pond.

An antique Indonesian garden shed offers an Asian touch to our garden. Washington State artists as well as international sculptors enhance our garden with art.

This garden's estimated size is 2½ acres.

FROGGSONG GARDENS
 10–4

Froggsong Gardens, a 6-acre estate garden, is a blend of formal and informal design. A roundel garden, parterre garden, stone ruin, rose garden, and a knot garden support a variety of cottage garden perennials.

NEW 5 10 20 '95 Year

The "Queen's Garden" with arches of repeating hornbeams and a new Sunken Garden are the latest additions. The garden has been featured in *Sunset*, *Fine Gardening*, *Better Homes and Gardens*, and recently a book *Private Gardens of the Pacific Northwest* by Brian Coleman.

This garden's estimated size is a 6-acre garden on 17 acres.

💬 **TROWEL TALK**

Our garden was scotch broom and brambles when we moved here 40 years ago.

—*Lucinda Stockett*

THE GARDEN AT THE CORNER OF DOCK AND DOCK

NEW  10–4

One hundred years ago, this lot was under the vast industrial wharf of a large shipyard. For the past few years, Sylvie and Todd have created a multifaceted waterfront oasis framed by towering redwood, sycamore, and palm. (Yes, palm trees in the Pacific NW!)

The beach-facing lower yard and fire pit are encircled by saltwater friendlies and Northwest natives. Large beds of azalea, rhododendron, maple, and dwarf pine and more weave to the upper garden. The hops-covered bench and green-canopied gazebo (the "Belvedere") provide comfortable vantage points for resting, conversation, and meals.

The semicircle, short-cropped lawn for games tops the colorful landscape that's bejeweled with sculptures, carvings, and mosaics.

Beyond the main house, past the lilacs and lavender, is the orchard with apple, pear, plum, and persimmon.

This garden's estimated size is 1 acre.

💬 **TROWEL TALK**

From the get-go, as a little girl, Sylvie thrived when gardening with her parents in Belgium and the south of France.

A particular passion was stacking rocks to build walls and terraces so common in Provence. So, it's no surprise to find dry-stacked walls in her newest garden as it rises over Quartermaster Harbor. Sylvie always maintains a "kitchen garden" for herbs, greens, and "tisanes" (verbena is a favorite), and her gardens surprise with delightful colors and textures in every season.

Todd and Sylvie designed the garden to protect the shoreline by reducing rapid run-off over the sunbaked, hardened turf of a barren lawn. Ideally, the roots and mulching increase the permeability of the heavy clay soil. For the past six years, the garden has claimed first prize in the neighborhood sunflower competition (measuring height and width of flower), another testament to Sylvie's green thumb!

To encourage pollinators, Todd has built a couple "top bar" beehives and tries to keep ahead of swarms!

—*Todd and Sylvie*

NEW Year

THE HALSTEAD GARDEN

  partial   10–4

This half-acre 22-year-old garden complements the 1908 Craftsman styled home in Dockton on Maury Island, which is connected to Vashon Island by a land bridge.

When the owners moved here in 2000, there was no garden on the property. Today, the garden is interactive, authentic, and personal. Topiary shrubs, familiar perennials, garden art, winding paths, a labyrinth, dry creek bed, areas for meditation and inspiration, and a spectacular view of Quartermaster Harbor greet the visitors.

This garden's estimated size is ½ acre.

VICTORIAN STUMPERY GARDEN

NEW   10–4

My former wife, Pat Riehl, created this garden in 2010 with the help of British fern expert Martin Rickard.

The idea of using stumps as a major garden element was first used in mid-nineteenth-century England. Stumps are removed from the ground, arranged either on their side or upside down. Areas around them are planted with ferns or other shade-loving plants. There are 250 stumps arranged in a 10,000 sq. foot area. There is a stump tunnel and a stump grotto. You will walk down a set of stairs and go through the tunnel.

Douglas fir tower overhead, and thirteen tree ferns on either side of the pathway. There are two fern tables, a fern chair, and fern bench to engage your eye. It is a magical place.

This garden's estimated size is 1/3 acre.

💬 TROWEL TALK

Pat's first garden was small, in Seattle, with poor soil and no sun. She became aware of ferns after meeting Sue Olson, fern expert and writer. Ferns became her passion.

She found a garden space on Vashon Island and transformed it with the stumpery, seven garden beds, and a conifer garden with 100 dwarf and miniature conifers. There was not a plant she did not like, especially snowdrops. Jim Fox, a garden writer and nursery buyer, was a big mentor who once said, "Pat is the only person I know who could make stumps grow."

—*The Apprentice Gardener*

Kitsap County
Saturday, June 22

BAINBRIDGE ISLAND
DRAGON'S LAIR - THE DEMIANEW GARDENS

partial   10–4

We are situated on a hill overlooking beautiful Puget Sound. Our property includes both shady woodland and full sun areas, so we are able to grow a diverse selection of plants.

We have several goals for ourselves as caretakers of our property. One is to have something in bloom from early spring through fall. The other is to use water and our labor resources efficiently. In addition, we love fragrance and color. So we have used many different types of plants throughout our gardens to achieve these goals. We also have many garden accents made of glass that give the garden a playful feeling.

In spring we have a profusion of bulbs and early blooming perennials such as epimediums and terrestrial orchids. As spring gives way to summer, we have blue Himalayan poppies, more orchids, peonies, delphiniums, and finally roses. Midsummer is full of Oriental lilies, roses, and many other perennials.

Late summer gives us perennial lobelia, sedum, and many fuchsias. A collection of arisaemas blooms throughout the season in the various beds. We have fruits, vegetables, and herbs in sunny beds, so we enjoy our own organic produce throughout the season. Grasses add texture as well as low water requirements.

We have two mature ponds that give us many hours of pleasure. Waterlilies give us color and habitat for many goldfish and frogs that hatch out and mature each year.

This garden's estimated size is ¾ acre cultivated, ¾ acre forest.

💬 TROWEL TALK

We are lucky to have been the caretakers of this property for the last 30 years! Our first years were spent creating the beds and continuing to expand our collection of plants. We have had many iterations over the years and have continued to create the hardscaping.

We still love terrestrial orchids and continue to collect them. In the last year we have been completely redoing our irrigation system. We had continued to add on and change the previous one over the years and it had started to leak in many areas. And of course, there have been additional products that work better than the original system.

And, as we are aging, we have begun to take out some of the more fussy, demanding plants and replace them with things that require less maintenance. We are using rare conifers that will grow very slowly and require less work, but still be interesting.

And for pops of color, more glass decorations! Our gardens really are living and will continue to evolve!

—Paul

THE PIRAINO GARDEN

 10–4

Our 29-year-old garden is secluded within a green frame of bamboo, Mexican evergreen climbing hydrangea, fir, and cedar trees. It is a blend of Asian and Northwestern garden styles, designed for leisurely discovery and contemplation.

Planted and organically maintained solely by the two of us, the garden features variations of leaf size, shape, texture, and hue, combined with brighter color accents that change through the seasons. Look for five varieties of clumping bamboo, several varieties of Japanese maple, collected stones, artwork, and small bits of whimsy.

The garden now borders on the newly established Rockaway Bluff Nature Preserve. We have been busy replanting sections of the garden due to our increasingly dry climate and increased shade from our tree friends. Some of the garden art pieces were designed by us, and the large rock sculpture is by a local island artist.

We look forward to sharing our peaceful corner of Bainbridge Island with you.

This garden's estimated size is 1/4 acre.

TROWEL TALK

We love plants that play well with others—beautiful in their own right but not taking anything away from others. Our garden is a home to wildlife, including our miniature schnauzer.

We do not care to be perfect; we strive to be interesting.

—*The Mindful Duo*

THE SKYLER GARDEN

 10   partial   10–4

Surrounded by waves of cedar pickets and an iron gate made by the owner, this private 1/3-acre site sits at the end of a quiet cul-de-sac. Nestled among tall firs, vine maples, rhododendrons, azaleas, viburnum, and magnolias, these gardens have been a work in progress for more than 30 years.

Stroll the pathways, each leading to a different garden room, and you will discover seemingly endless groupings of hosta, helleborus, hebe, barberries, spiraea, farfugium, euphorbia, and more than 100 varieties of ferns—the gardener's passion. These gardens have interest throughout the year with hardscape and water features. Enjoy the serenity of these gardens.

THE GARDEN CONSERVANCY NORTHWEST NETWORK

The Garden Conservancy Northwest Network (GCNN) is a member-supported association of gardens, parks, and horticultural organizations.

It is dedicated to connecting people and gardens, creating engaging educational programming, fostering an appreciation of plants, and preserving gardens as vital cultural resources.

Our members include:

Western Washington
Albers Vista Marcovina Gardens - Bremerton
Far Reaches Botanical Conservancy - Port Townsend
Heronswood Garden - Kingston*
Meerkerk Gardens - Green bank

Metro Seattle
Bellevue Botanical Garden - Bellevue
Bloedel Reserve - Bainbridge Island
Dunn Gardens - Seattle
Elisabeth C. Miller Botanical Garden - Seattle
Highline SeaTac Botanical Garden - SeaTac
Historic Seattle - Seattle
Kruckeberg Botanic Garden - Shoreline
Mukai Farm & Garden - Vashon
PlantAmnesty - Seattle
Streissguth Gardens - Seattle
UW Botanic Gardens, Washington Park Arboretum and Seattle Japanese Garden - Seattle

South Sound
Lake Wilderness Arboretum - Maple Valley
Lakewold Gardens - Lakewood
PowellsWood Gardens - Federal Way
Soos Creek Botanical Garden & Heritage Center - Auburn

Eastern Washington
Yakima Area Arboretum - Yakima

Western Oregon
Delbert Hunter Arboretum and Botanic Garden - Dallas

Metro Portland
Peninsula Park Rose Garden - Portland
Rogerson Clematis Garden - West Lynn

*2023 Gardens for Good Grant Recipient

Register online: gardenconservancy.org/opendays   Washington 355

GCNN MEMBER PUBLIC GARDEN
LAKEWOLD GARDENS

**12317 Gravelly Lake Drive SW
Lakewood, Washington 98496**

A nature and garden lover's paradise, Lakewold Gardens is a national and Washington State historic landmark that features landscape architecture surrounded by rare and native plants-far from ordinary, but only one mile from Interstate 5!

Whether you visit in the dead of winter or the peak of summer, this horticultural haven offers 10 acres of beautiful blooms and hidden discoveries for every season.

 facebook.com/LakewoldGardens

 instagram.com/lakewoldgardens

 lakewoldgardens.org

GCNN MEMBER PUBLIC GARDEN
YAKIMA AREA ARBORETUM

**1401 Arboretum Dr
Yakima, Washington 98901-8513**

The Yakima Area Arboretum is a horticultural paradise. Established in 1967, this 46-acre treasure trove in central Washington is a living tribute to the wonders of nature.

It's not just a garden; it's a vibrant tapestry of over 1000 tree, forb, grass, and shrub species carefully curated to thrive in the Inland Northwest by utilizing our 200+ days of sunshine in the fertile Yakima Valley.

At the Arboretum, we're not just about beauty; we're about fostering a deep connection with the natural world. Our mission is clear: "To inspire people of all ages to discover and connect with nature through a diverse collection of trees and shrubs hardy to the Inland Northwest." Here, you'll find inspiration for your own garden. It's not just a place to visit; it's a place to learn.

We champion sound arboricultural practices, sustainable gardening, and

NEW 5 10 20 '95 Year   No Photography   Accessibility   Nibbled Leaf Garden

public participation, offering a wealth of knowledge and resources for gardeners like you.

Come, explore our living museum, and let the Yakima Area Arboretum ignite your passion for gardening. Discover the richness of the curated flora, exchange ideas with fellow enthusiasts, and enjoy part of a community gem that shares your green-thumbed passion.

facebook.com/YakimaAreaArboretum

instagram.com/yakimaareaarboretum

ahtrees.org

GCNN MEMBER PUBLIC GARDEN

BELLEVUE BOTANICAL GARDEN

**12001 Main St
Bellevue, Washington 98005**

The Bellevue Botanical Garden welcomes over 400,000 visitors each year to learn about gardening and explore nature. We curate a vast collection of 3,000 unique varieties of plants spread throughout 53-acres in 12 thematic garden spaces.

The Garden hosts a wealth of educational classes for children and adults, along with many community events benefiting Bellevue and the horticulture community at large.

Our two hallmark events, Arts in the Garden and Garden d'Lights are thriving along with the Trillium Store gift shop and Copper Kettle Coffee Bar.

Today, Bellevue Botanical Garden serves as a beautiful and safe space of respite. The success of the Garden is the outcome of a vibrant and diverse community, a collaboration between the City of Bellevue, the Bellevue Botanical Garden Society, and nine other partner groups.

NEW 5 10 20 '95 Year   No Photography   Accessibility   Nibbled Leaf Garden

Register online: gardenconservancy.org/opendays   Washington   357

In just the past year we had more than 400 individual volunteers contribute over 16,000 hours of work to the Garden.

facebook.com/BellevueBotanical/

instagram.com/bellevuebotanical

bellevuebotanical.org

GCNN MEMBER
PUBLIC GARDEN

THE E.B. DUNN HISTORICAL GARDEN TRUST

**13533 Northshire Rd NW
Seattle, Washington 98177**

The historic 7.5-acre gardens were founded in 1915 as part of the estate of the Dunn family as their summer home. The Olmsted Brothers firm was commissioned to emphasize the natural features of the land, taking advantage of the gradual slope of the property to emphasize the sweeping views of the Puget Sound and the Olympic Mountains.

Today, the original landscape remains complete with curving paths, the Great Lawn, and the Woodland Garden. Our mission is to " preserve and enhance Dunn Gardens as a public resource, celebrating the original 1915 Olmsted design and showcasing the evolution of garden design in the Pacific Northwest."

facebook.com/TheDunnGardens/

instagram.com/dunn.gardens

dunngardens.org

NEW 5 10 20 95 Year   No Photography   Accessibility   Nibbled Leaf Garden

358 Washington

Register online: gardenconservancy.org/opendays

GCNN MEMBER PUBLIC GARDEN

KRUCKEBERG BOTANIC GARDEN FOUNDATION

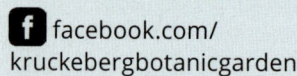 facebook.com/kruckebergbotanicgarden

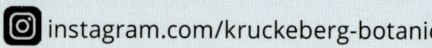 instagram.com/kruckeberg-botanic

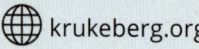 krukeberg.org

**20312 15th Ave NW
Shoreline, Washington 98177**

The mission of the Kruckeberg Botanic Garden Foundation is to maintain and develop a living collection of native and rare plants that serves as a gathering place for the community to learn, be inspired, and feel connected to the natural world.

The Kruckeberg Botanic Garden was founded in 1958 when Dr. Art Kruckeberg and his wife Mareen moved to a 4-acre farmhouse in Shoreline.

Over the ensuing decades they created the Garden, growing nearly every plant from seed or cutting.

Art and Mareen took an informal, naturalistic approach to design, combining Northwest native plants with unusual and rarely cultivated species collected from the West coast and around the world. The result is a unique Puget Sound woodland garden.

NEW 5 10 20 '95 Year    No Photography   Accessibility    Nibbled Leaf Garden

Register online: gardenconservancy.org/opendays   Washington   359

GCNN MEMBER PUBLIC GARDEN

PUGET SOUND PUBLIC GARDENS

The Pacific Northwest is richly endowed with public gardens of all sorts. If you're looking for native plants or exotics, a natural landscape or a full-to-bursting perennial border, a botanical garden or a sculpture garden, you can find your place here.

The Puget Sound Public Gardens website was created to bring together in one place a listing of public gardens in the Puget Sound region as a gateway resource for garden visitors. Peruse the Gardens page to sort destinations by location and plan your tour. Visit our guest photography galleries on our popup page—featuring garden photos by local artists, photographers, and enthusiasts—to see how others capture these diverse gardens. And, don't miss the P.O.V. page—our Garden Directors' Point of View, revealing their special perspective and insight into the gardens under their care.

instagram.com/pugetsoundpublicgardens

pugetsoundgardens.org

GCNN MEMBER PRESERVATION PARTNER

SOOS CREEK BOTANICAL GARDEN FOUNDATION AND HERITAGE CENTER

29308 132nd Ave SE
Auburn, Washington 98092-2141

Today's 23-acre Garden is located on a portion of land purchased in the late nineteenth century by Maurice Skagen's Norwegian ancestors.

In 1891 Ole Evensen Oie purchased 160 acres from the Northern Pacific Railroad, later increasing the holding to 200 acres. Oie and his family farmed the land for many decades. In 1968 Maurice acquired the first 5-acre parcel, which became the nucleus of the Garden, and began to plant.

At that time it was pasture land, overgrown with blackberries and Alder saplings. It also had, and still does have, native plants such as Douglas Fir, Western Red Cedar, Vine Maples, Big Leaf Maple, Trillium and Skunk Cabbage.

Over the years, friends Maurice Skagen and James Daly have expanded what was to become a legacy for the community. Today, in addition to the native plants,

NEW 5 10 20 95 Year   No Photography   Accessibility   Nibbled Leaf Garden

there are thousands of hybridized specimens, nearly all planted by Maurice. In the 1980's Maurice toured gardens in England and Japan, coming away inspired to create "stroll gardens." He purchased many unusual plants during these trips such as tree peonies from Kyoto and Sorbus cultivars from England.

Since then, specialty nurseries around the Pacific Northwest have provided innumerable additions to our collections.

Soos Creek Botanical Garden provides a diversity of gardens for the public to enjoy, including inspirational gardens based upon international, regional, and historical gardens, while providing education and conservation of horticulture, the environment, and history.

Come celebrate the seasons with us in the heart of south King County.

facebook.com/SoosCreekBG

GCNN MEMBER PRESERVATION PARTNER

RHODODENDRON SPECIES FOUNDATION & BOTANICAL GARDEN

**2525 S 336th St
Federal Way, Washington 98003**

The Rhododendron Species Botanical Garden, located between Seattle and Tacoma, is a 22-acre woodland garden that is home to the largest collection of Rhododendron species in the world.

Visitors will experience a diverse botanical collection in a forest of Douglas fir, western red cedar, hemlock, and other native plants. The garden is also home to beautiful companion plants, including the famous Himalayan Blue Poppies, Camellias, Magnolias, Japanese maples, and many rare plants.

The Rhododendron Species Foundation is a non-profit organization dedicated to the conservation, research, acquisition, evaluation, cultivation, public display, and distribution of Rhododendron species.

The Foundation provides education relating to the genus and serves as a unique resource for scientific, horticultural, and general gardening communities worldwide.

facebook.com/RhodyGarden

instagram.com/RhodyGarden

RhodyGarden.org

Glasshouse in the Prairie - Fredonia, WI
Photo: the Garden Host

Wisconsin

Wisconsin

Open Days dates and times by County, Town, and Garden

OZAUKEE

Fredonia
Glasshouse in the Prairie
　Saturday, August 10, 10–4
　Saturday, August 11, 10–4

Mequon
Bonniwell Garden
　Saturday, August 10, 10–4
　Sunday, August 11, 10–4

Saukville
The Farm on Hilly Lane
　Saturday, August 10, 10–4
　Sunday, August 11, 10–4

WISCONSIN

The 2024 Open Days in the Milwaukee area are presented in partnership with The Garden Club of Greater Milwaukee.

NONPROFIT PARTNER

GARDEN CLUB OF GREATER MILWAUKEE

The Garden Club of Greater Milwaukee (GCGM) has over 200 members and is the largest garden club in Wisconsin. Our mission is to educate members and the community about the art and science of gardening, floral design, landscape design and horticulture. We embrace best practices that promote sustainability, protect the environment, and conserve our natural resources.

We volunteer in our community to share our passion for the natural world, including our partnership with the Garden Conservancy in hosting Open Days, Digging Deeper and Garden Master events in Milwaukee and surrounding counties throughout the summer.

facebook.com/gcgmke

instagram.com/gcgmke

gardenclubgreatermilwaukee.org

Milwaukee Area
Sunday, May 5

The Shapson Garden

DIGGING DEEPER

Cultivating Edible Mushrooms: A Mushroom Inoculation Workshop
Steve Shapson and M. J. Jansen
Sunday, May 5
Three sessions: 9:30, 12:30, 3:30

The Shapson Garden
Mequon, WI

NEW   Year No Photography Accessibility Nibbled Leaf Garden

This Digging Deeper event with wild mushroom foragers, Steve Shapson and M. J. Jansen, introduces you to the world of cultivating mushrooms.

Besides learning about mushrooms, you will be participating in a workshop where you will inoculate specially harvested logs with shiitake, oyster, and chestnut mushrooms spawn as part of an assembly-line process.

The price of the workshop includes one of each type of log with the option to purchase additional logs. Your logs can be placed in a shady spot on your property or integrated into a shade border. Complete written instructions for taking care of your logs, along with other information about cultivated and wild mushrooms, will be provided as part of the workshop.

This Digging Deeper is not appropriate for children under the age of 15. Please wear clothing that you won't mind getting dirty.

Milwaukee Area
Saturday, August 10
Sunday, August 11

FREDONIA
GLASSHOUSE IN THE PRAIRIE
NEW 🍃 10–4

Nestled in the tranquil embrace of nature, Dawn and Steve's gardens and prairie are a testament to their love of nature and Dawn's passion for gardening.

What was once an empty farm field more than a quarter century ago has blossomed into a captivating haven. Today it boasts 7½ acres of prairie cultivated by Dawn and Steve. Their hard work alone has molded the 12-acre landscape into a symphony of hardscape, gardens, and prairie. In the heart of this natural space, you'll find their home, a quaint garden shed, and a recently added glasshouse.

This 20 × 14 ft multipurpose glasshouse extends their growing season into the realms of spring and fall. It's not only for plants; it's where they host dinner parties under the stars and intimate gatherings in the evening glow of the glasshouse's beautiful chandelier. Their glasshouse, surrounded by their gardens and prairie, is a testament to their love of nature and the joy it brings them.

This garden's estimated size is 12 acres.

💬 TROWEL TALK

We knew nothing about establishing a prairie almost 30 years ago when we purchased our property. We seeded about 7 acres by hand, several years before we started building the house, and built a drag and pulled that thing back and forth...just the two of us.

We came back every so often to see if it was doing anything. Years 1 and 2 were disappointing. Year 3, I recall driving up and seeing these cars stopped along the road...they were taking pictures of all the blooming lupine in our prairie. We were so excited!

—Dawn and Steve

MEQUON
BONNIWELL GARDEN
NEW 10–4

The Bonniwell house, featuring wood, glass, and stone with a metal roof, was built in 2004 and overlooks a large, landscaped pond that we stock with fish. The gardens at the immediate rear of the home and the swimming pool are rectangular and are bordered by hedges, stone, flagstones, or wood.

The manicured landscape is less structured as it reaches the existing woods that consist of maple, birch, hickory, and oak.

Over the years the following were added to this 6-acre property: the vegetable garden, the woodland paths, the perennial collections, and, in 2022, the pickleball court. My favorite part about the court is the beech hedge in lieu of a fence.

I have tried to create many different "rooms" for a wide variety of different experiences in each. All the plants selected in each "room" were chosen for a timed bloom throughout the year.

This garden's estimated size is 6½ acres.

💬 TROWEL TALK

I love to garden to create beautiful spaces for people to enjoy.

My go to tool is the Felco #2 Pruner ☺

My favorite plant is the red bud, but I have never had success with Lupine.

—Peter K

SAUKVILLE
THE FARM ON HILLY LANE
NEW 🌿 10–4

As stewards of the Hemlock Family Farmstead, established in 1846, we are deeply committed to preserving its rich history while creating a peaceful oasis.

Our eleven-year restoration journey is a testament to our dedication. We have cultivated colorful cottage-style gardens interspersed with charming spaces that evoke feelings of a bygone era. The picturesque views are enhanced by woodland meadows, wetlands, and tranquil ponds.

We are passionate about organic and

biodynamic practices. We have been beekeepers for seven years and proudly serve as a designated Monarch Waystation. Our methods both depend upon and help to protect a variety of vital pollinators.

We maintain the historic elements of the property while enjoying the use of the original outbuildings as they stand today. We have breathed new life into the farmstead through thoughtful renovation of the farmhouse and preservation of the barn and summer kitchen.

New projects include creating a vegetable garden, establishing a chicken coop, and enhancing the pond banks with new plants. Our greatest joy comes from sharing the gardens and the property with others! We are captivated by the variety of bees and butterflies that add life to the thousands of flowers in the gardens and meadows. We enjoy watching for new bird species that visit or nest in the gardens, woodlands, and ponds.

The tranquility and pastoral beauty of the property is often captured through our photography and the paintings of plein air artists who visit this special place.

This garden's estimated size is 3 acres.

Edna Mae Garden, Los Angeles, CA
Photo: Matt Harbicht

Become a Garden Host or a Regional Ambassador

See page 374 or contact us at **opendays@gardenconservancy.org** to learn more.

Get Involved 371

LIKE WHAT YOU'VE SEEN?

GET INVOLVED

Open Days are only made possible by YOU!

Become a volunteer, Garden Host, or Regional Ambassador.

Celebrating and sharing America's gardens since 1995

Get Involved

OPEN DAYS CALIFORNIA • Los Angeles • 2023

Adams Family Garden
Casa Nancia
The Edna Mae Garden
Urban Wildlife Habitat

Photos: Matt Harbicht

GET INVOLVED

gardenconservancy.org/opendays

Get Involved 373

GET INVOLVED

328 North
The Barn
Ilona's Garden
Wit McKay

Photos: Brian Jones

OPEN DAYS MASSACHUSETTS • Berkshire County • 2023

Celebrating and sharing America's gardens since 1995

GET INVOLVED

Become a Garden Host

Visiting Open Days is just one of the ways that you can support the Garden Conservancy's mission. We're keen to expand the program and Open Days is best spread by those who know and love the program. Why not consider becoming a Garden Host or Regional Ambassador?

We are always on the lookout for gardens throughout the US that highlight exceptional design and smart ways to garden. Gardens take many forms—from beautiful estates, to small farms combining form and function, to tiny backyard jewel-box gardens—all are welcome.

We celebrate the diversity of America's gardens and gardening traditions through the Open Days program and invite you to share your garden as a Garden Host.

Opening your garden through Open Days is a rewarding experience unlike any other. If you are proud of the work you've done in your garden and are ready to share with others, you may be a perfect candidate to serve as a Garden Host.

Contact our office at opendays@gardenconservancy.org to begin your journey as a Garden Host.

Become a Regional Ambassador

Are you passionate about the wonders of great gardens, and engaged in your regional gardening community? Are you looking to become involved in a fun, rewarding, and worthy project? You might be a perfect fit to be a Regional Ambassador!

Ambassadors help make the program run—they identify great gardens, arrange Open Days logistics, help to organize volunteers, and raise awareness of the Garden Conservancy through regional channels.

Be on the lookout for virtual informational sessions for prospective Regional Ambassadors throughout the winter months to learn more about this role. If you are ready to commit to this rewarding experience, contact our office to learn more.

Call
845.424.6500, M–F, 9–5 ET

Email
opendays@gardenconservancy.org

Visit
Gardenconservancy.org/opendays

High Elevation Garden - Steamboat Springs, CO
Photo: Phillip Carruthers

gardenconservancy.org/opendays

Get Involved 375

Wit McKay Garden, Berkshire County, MA
Photo: Brian Jones

Celebrating and sharing America's gardens since 1995

The Frank and Anne Cabot Society for Planned Giving

In 2021, the Garden Conservancy created the **Frank and Anne Cabot Society** for planned giving, established to recognize and thank our friends, members, and Fellows who have generously included the Conservancy in their estate plans. The Cabots founded the Garden Conservancy in 1989 with the goal of guiding the transition of significant private gardens into vibrant public resources, a mission that continues to be central to all that we do.

With the creation of the Cabot Society, we celebrate those whose generosity supports the future of the Garden Conservancy, ensuring that the legacy of extraordinary gardens is available for generations to come.

There is no minimum dollar amount to become a member of the Frank and Anne Cabot Society. Benefits include complimentary admission to virtual programs and Open Days, recognition in the Conservancy's Annual Report, and a token of our appreciation created in partnership with Janet Mavec, celebrated jeweler and longtime friend of the Garden Conservancy.

For more information, or to join, please contact Director of Development Bridget Connors at bconnors@gardenconservancy.org or 845.424.6500 ext. 228.

Anne and Frank Cabot photo courtesy of Caroline Burgess / Stonecrop Gardens

gardenconservancy.org/opendays

Membership Matters

Just like you, we believe gardens play an essential role in our history, culture, and quality of life.

The Garden Conservancy's members are not only our most committed supporters, they also play a vital role in helping us provide access to outstanding gardens through Open Days, help fund our educational programs, and advance our preservation work.

Are you passionate about gardens?
Join a growing national community that shares your interests while helping us *preserve, share, and celebrate America's gardens and diverse gardening traditions for the education and inspiration of the public.*

We offer vast opportunities for our members to learn and exchange information and ideas about gardening, sustainability, design, and preservation through our educational programming and publications. Our virtual talks offer a way to join the conversation regardless of location or season!

Membership opportunities start at just $50 and include a full year of exclusive benefits including:

- Free copy of our *Open Days Directory*
- Complimentary member credits redeemable for Open Days garden admissions or virtual talk registrations
- Additional Open Days garden admissions available at a 50% discount
- Special member-pricing for all our educational programs
- Subscription to the Garden Conservancy's print and electronic newsletter, containing articles about Conservancy projects, garden restoration, events, and tours
- Invitations to special members-only events
- Digital subscription to *Better Homes & Gardens*

Ilona's Garden, Williamstown, MA
Photo: Brian Jones

Celebrating and sharing America's gardens since 1995

the art and science of east coast gardening

DIG IT!
MAGAZINE

www.dig-itmag.com

for people who love gardens

articles and interviews
garden profiles
exclusive garden bus trips

Stunning home and garden features in every issue + 3 additional pages of garden inspiration.

HOMES

Receive an entire year of *SLHL* for only

$12
NINE FABULOUS ISSUES

To take advantage of this offer, send your check along with name and addresses to:
St. Louis Homes + Lifestyles
255 Lamp & Lantern Village
Town and Country, MO 63017

Subscribe Online:
stlouishomesmag.com/content/subscribe

Gardens by Date

MARCH

SATURDAY, MARCH 2
California (Riverside County)
Palm Springs
Casa de las Ardillas, 10–4
Casa Madrina - Godmothers Cottage, 10–4
Casa Mazamitla, 10–4
Dry Falls Garden, 10–4
Monte Vista Garden, 10–4

APRIL

SATURDAY, APRIL 13
New Jersey (Essex County)
Nutley
The Mountsier Garden, 10–4

SUNDAY, APRIL 21
California (Los Angeles County)
Altadena
The Abascal Family Garden, 10–4
Pasadena
Bennett-De Beixedon Garden, 10–4
The Schumacher Garden Retreat, 10–4

SUNDAY, APRIL 28
California (Los Angeles County)
Sherman Oaks
Longridge, 10–4
Studio City
Sustainable Storybook Garden, 10–4
Wrightwood Estates Hillside Garden, 10–4

SUNDAY, APRIL 28
New York (Westchester County)
Bedford
The Great Hill Schoolhouse, 10–4
Lewisboro
The White Garden, 10–4

gardenconservancy.org/opendays

MAY

SATURDAY, MAY 4
Alabama (Jefferson County)
Birmingham
Louise Wrinkle's Southern Woodland Garden, 10–4
Rooms with Views, 10–4
The Butrus Garden, 10–4
The Dancer, 10–4

SATURDAY, MAY 4
California (Marin County)
Bolinas
Visions of Paradise - Sally Robertson Garden and Studio, 10–4
Ross
Old Oak Hill, 10–4
Stinson Beach
The Panoramic Garden, 10–4

SATURDAY, MAY 4
Massachusetts (Berkshire County)
Richmond
Black Barn Farm, 10–4

SATURDAY, MAY 4
New Jersey (Essex County)
Nutley
The Mountsier Garden, 10–4

SATURDAY, MAY 4
New Jersey (Somerset County)
Far Hills
The Hay, Honey Farm, 10–4

SATURDAY, MAY 4
New York (Columbia County)
Hillsdale
Wombat Crossing, 10–4

SATURDAY, MAY 11
California (Alameda County)
Albany
Keeyla Meadows Gardens and Art, 10–4
Berkeley
Aging Gracefully, 10–4
Berkeley
Catalina Sculptural Pollinator Paradise, 10–4
Oakland
Ann Nichols' Garden, 10–4
Piedmont
A Garden for Birds, 10–4
Piedmont Oasis, 10–4

SATURDAY, MAY 11
Delaware (New Castle County)
Wilmington
Thistle, 10–4

SATURDAY, MAY 11
Massachusetts (Hampshire County)
Amherst
Kinsey-Pope Garden, 10–1, 1–5

SUNDAY, MAY 11
Massachusetts (Middlesex County)
Groton
Garden of Pepe and John Maynard, 10–4

Celebrating and sharing America's gardens since 1995

SATURDAY, MAY 11
Massachusetts (Worcester County)
Boylston
Berry Garden, 10–4
Petersham
Swift River Farm, 10–4
Worcester
Garden of Matt Mattus and Joe Philip, 10–4

SATURDAY, MAY 11
New York (Suffolk County)
East Hampton
Glade Garden–Abby Jane Brody, 10–3
The Garden of Dianne B., 10–3
Sag Harbor
The Hunting-Cooper Garden, 10–3
Wainscott
Biercuk and Luckey Garden, 10–3

SATURDAY, MAY 11
New York (Westchester County)
Bedford Hills
Bedford Cross Farm, 10–4
Chappaqua
The Little Garden That Could, 10–4
Mount Kisco
Rocky Hills, 10–4
Ossining
A Garden for Birds and Pollinators, 10–12, 12–2, 2–4

SATURDAY, MAY 11
Pennsylvania (Delaware County)
Chadds Ford
WynEden, 10–4

SATURDAY, MAY 18
California (San Francisco County)
San Francisco
Geary Street Gardens, 10–4
The Cottage Garden, 10–12, 12–2, 2–4
Twin Palms, 10–4

SATURDAY, MAY 18
California (San Mateo County)
Pacifica
Pacifica Collector's Garden, 10–4

SATURDAY, MAY 18
Massachusetts (Essex County)
Manchester
Highgarden/High Contente, 10–4

SATURDAY, MAY 18
Massachusetts (Middlesex County)
Stow
Glenluce Garden, 10–4
Weston
Spencer-Scott Garden, 10–4

SATURDAY, MAY 18
New Jersey (Bergen County)
Demarest
Hawks Off the Palisades, 10–3
Mahwah
Magic Mountain Sanctuary, 10–3
Wyckoff
Janet Schulz, 10–3

SATURDAY, MAY 18
New York (Dutchess County)
Amenia
Broccoli Hall–Maxine Paetro, 10–4
Wassaic
Neverest, 10–2

gardenconservancy.org/opendays

SATURDAY, MAY 18
New York (Jefferson County)
Wellesley Island
The Enchanted Edible Forest at Cross Island Farms, 10–12, 12–2, 2–4

SATURDAY, MAY 25
Connecticut (New London County)
Stonington
Kentford Farm, 10–4

SATURDAY, MAY 25
New York (Suffolk County)
Mt. Sinai
Tranquility, 10–4
Old Field
Two Grey Achers, 12–4
Wading River
Woodland Garden - Bill and Veronica Schiavo, 10–4

JUNE

SATURDAY, JUNE 1
Colorado (Denver Metro Area)
Centennial
Pine Gardens, 10–4
Denver
Jim and Dorothy's Garden, 10–4
Panayoti Kelaidis Quince Garden, 10–4
Prairie Paradise, 10–4
Virginia Vale Garden, 10–4

SATURDAY, JUNE 1
Maryland (St Mary's County)
Hollywood
Butterfly Alley, 10–12, 12–2, 2–4
Leonardtown
Dragonfly, 10–12, 12–2, 2–4
Lexington Park
Allen's Heirloom Homestead, 10–12, 12–2, 2–4

SATURDAY, JUNE 1
Massachusetts (Franklin County)
Greenfield
Phoenix House Gardens, 10–4
Sunderland
Maples of Silver Lane, 10–4
Swampfield, 10–4

SATURDAY, JUNE 1
Massachusetts (Hampden County)
Springfield
Our Color-Filled Retreat, 10–4

SATURDAY, JUNE 1
Massachusetts (Hampshire County)
Amherst
Flying Pig Farm, 10–4
Florence
Culver's Garden, 10–4

Celebrating and sharing America's gardens since 1995

SATURDAY, JUNE 1
New Jersey (Essex County)
Montclair
Anna's Pollinator Haven, 10–4
Cynthia Corhan-Aitken, 10–4
Nutley
The Mountsier Garden, 10–4

SATURDAY, JUNE 1
Washington (King County)
Redmond
Novelty Creek, 10–4
Rutherford Creek Gardens, 10–12, 12–2, 2–4
Sammamish
Shades of Green, 10–4

SUNDAY, JUNE 2
Connecticut (Litchfield County)
Falls Village
Church House-The Garden of Page Dickey and Bosco Schell, 10–4
Roxbury
Japanese Gardens at Cedar Hill, 10–4
Washington
Isabel and Winston Fowlkes, 10–2
West Cornwall
Roxana Robinson - Treetop, 10–4

SUNDAY, JUNE 2
New York (Dutchess County)
Amenia
Broccoli Hall–Maxine Paetro, 10–4
Millbrook
Clove Brook Farm - Christopher Spitzmiller and Anthony Bellomo, 10–4
Millbrook
Squirrel Hall, 10–4

SATURDAY, JUNE 8
California (San Joaquin County)
Tracy
Hutton, 10–4

SATURDAY, JUNE 8
Colorado (Pueblo County)
Pueblo
Conrad Family Garden, 10–4
Midway Xeric Garden, 10–4
Pollinator Garden, 10–4

SATURDAY, JUNE 8
Connecticut (Fairfield County)
Fairfield
Inwood Cottage Garden, 10–4
Greenwich
Chelmsford, 10–4
Garden of Allison Bourke, 10–4
New Canaan
Ann and Haig's Garden, 10–4
Southport
The Gould Garden, 10–12, 12–2, 2–4
Westport
Greens Farms Botanical Gardens, 10–4
Prospect Gardens Westport, 10–4
Rosebrook Gardens, 10–4

SATURDAY, JUNE 8
Virginia (Fairfax County)
Great Falls
Domaine St. Charles, 10–4
Gardens of Ellen and Allie Ash, 10–4
Sandra's Secret Garden, 10–1, 1–4

SUNDAY, JUNE 9
California (San Francisco County)
San Francisco
English Tudor Residential Garden, 10–4
New England in San Francisco, 10–4
The Gaddam Residence, 10–4
San Francisco Native Garden, 10–4

gardenconservancy.org/opendays

SUNDAY, JUNE 9
New York (Ulster County)
New Paltz
Ying and Yang in Tillson, 10–4
Saugerties
Ann Krupp Bryan, 10–4
Riverhill - Joe and Tamara DiMattio, 10–4
West Shokan
Secret Garden, 10–4

SUNDAY, JUNE 9
Washington (King County)
Vashon Island
Austin Donnelly, 10–4
Carhart Garden, 10–4
Froggsong Gardens, 10–4
The Garden at the Corner of Dock and Dock, 10–4
The Halstead Garden, 10–4
Victorian Stumpery Garden, 10–4

SATURDAY, JUNE 15
Connecticut (Hartford County)
Farmington
Oldgate, 10–4
Glastonbury
The Murray Gardens, 10–4
The Stubenrauch Gardens, 10–4

SATURDAY, JUNE 15
Delaware (New Castle County)
Wilmington
Old Oaks on Owl's Nest Rd., 10–4

SATURDAY, JUNE 15
Massachusetts (Middlesex County)
Pepperell
The Stone Sphere, 10–4

SATURDAY, JUNE 15
New Hampshire (Hillsborough County)
Hollis
Hollis Village Edible Garden, 10–4
Lakeside Retreat, 10–4
Manchester
New Shire Gardens, 10–4
Nashua
The Garden On Briarwood, 10–4

SATURDAY, JUNE 15
New York (Columbia County)
Claverack
Ketay Garden, 10–4
Peter Bevacqua and Stephen King, 10–4
Hudson
Flying Pig Acres, 10–4
Versailles on Hudson, 10–4
West Taghkanic
Arcadia - Ronald Wagner and Timothy Van Dam, 10–4

SATURDAY, JUNE 15
New York (Nassau County)
Glen Cove
Kippen Hill, 10–4
Locust Valley
Garden of Carol and Jim Large, 10–4
Port Washington
The Gardens at Sands Light, 10–4
Roslyn Harbor
Shade Haven - Susan and Steve King, 10–4

Celebrating and sharing America's gardens since 1995

SATURDAY, JUNE 15

New York (Westchester County)
Bedford
Brae Willows, 10–4
Rabbit Hill, 10–4
Croton on Hudson
Rivermere on the Hudson, 10–4
Mount Kisco
The Greneker Retreat, 10–4
Pound Ridge
James and Ellen Best's Sara Stein Garden, 10–4

SATURDAY, JUNE 15

Pennsylvania (Chester County)
Phoenixville
Donald Pell Gardens, 10–4

SATURDAY, JUNE 15

Pennsylvania (Delaware County)
Chadds Ford
Nature's Flow, 10–4

SATURDAY, JUNE 15

Pennsylvania (Montgomery County)
Flourtown
Vicki's Garden, 10–4
Wyndmoor
Lenbury West, 10–4

SATURDAY, JUNE 15

Pennsylvania (Philadelphia County)
Philadelphia
Surprise Oasis on the Edge of Philadelphia, 10–4
Home Place Garden, 10–4

SUNDAY, JUNE 16

New Jersey (Hunterdon County)
Califon
Treetop, 10–12, 12–2, 2–4
Pottersville
Bird Haven Farm, 10–4
Jardin de Buis, 10–4

SUNDAY, JUNE 16

New Jersey (Morris County)
Chester
Windance, 10–4

SUNDAY, JUNE 16

New Jersey (Somerset County)
Bernardsville
Mountain Top, 10–4

SATURDAY, JUNE 22

Connecticut (Fairfield County)
Fairfield
Garden of Kathryn Herman, 10–4
Greenwich
Sleepy Cat Farm, 10–12, 12–2, 2–4

SATURDAY, JUNE 22

New Jersey (Hunterdon County)
Stockton
The Garden at Federal Twist, 10–4

SATURDAY, JUNE 22

New York (Suffolk County)
Bridgehampton
Entwood Garden, 10–4
Pamela Harwood and Peter Feder, 10–4
East Hampton
Art House Garden of Delights, 10–4
Sag Harbor
Donna's Farmette, 10–4

SATURDAY, JUNE 22

Pennsylvania (Bucks County)
New Hope
Paxson Hill Farm, 10–4

SATURDAY, JUNE 22

Washington (Kitsap County)
Bainbridge Island
Dragon's Lair - The Demianew Gardens, 10–4
The Piraino Garden, 10–4
The Skyler Garden, 10–4

gardenconservancy.org/opendays

SUNDAY, JUNE 23
Connecticut (Litchfield County)
Cornwall Bridge
Garden of Debby and Bart Jones, 10–4
Falls Village
Garden of Bunny Williams, 10–1, 1–4
Salisbury
The Shillingford Garden, 10–1, 1–4
Sharon
Garden of Lee Link, 10–4
Washington
Brush Hill, 10–4
The Sumacs, 10–4
West Cornwall
Garden of Jane Garmey, 10–4
Michael's West Cornwall Garden, 10–4

SUNDAY, JUNE 23
Delaware (New Castle County)
Wilmington
Peggy Anne and Dan's Home Garden Sunday, June 23, 10–4

SUNDAY, JUNE 23
New York (Dutchess County)
Millerton
Garden of Helen Bodian, 10–4
Shekomeko Hillside Garden, 10–4
Poughkeepsie
Dappled Berms - The Garden of Scott VanderHamm, 10–4

SUNDAY, JUNE 23
Pennsylvania (Delaware County)
Swarthmore
Belvidere, 10–4
Hedgleigh Spring, 10–4

SATURDAY, JUNE 29
Massachusetts (Franklin County)
Greenfield
Mary Chicoine's Garden, 10–4
Leverett
Earthworks Garden, 10–4

SATURDAY, JUNE 29
Massachusetts (Hampden County)
West Springfield
Suburban Garden in Transition, 10–4

SATURDAY, JUNE 29
Massachusetts (Hampshire County)
Amherst
Kinsey-Pope Garden, 10–1, 1–5

SATURDAY, JUNE 29
New York (Saratoga County)
Saratoga Springs
A Place to Nest - Moe's Garden, 10–4
Foxglove - Sarah Patterson's Garden, 10–4
Schuylerville
Susie and Paul's Gardens, 10–4

SUNDAY, JUNE 30
New Hampshire (Cheshire County)
Walpole
Boggy Meadow Farm, 10–4
Spofford
Shooting Star Farm, 10–4
Westmoreland
Gardens of Ellen and Bruce Clement, 12–4

SUNDAY, JUNE 30
New York (Putnam County)
Brewster
Rumford Hall, 10–4

SUNDAY, JUNE 30
New York (Westchester County)
North Salem
Perrin Garden, 10–4
The Hen and the Hive, 10–4

Celebrating and sharing America's gardens since 1995

SUNDAY, JUNE 30

Vermont (Windham County)
Westminster West
Gordon and Mary Hayward's Garden, 10–4

SUNDAY, JUNE 30

Vermont (Windsor County)
Norwich
The Garden of Bill Noble, 10–4

JULY

SATURDAY, JULY 6

New York (Delaware County)
Andes
Cynthia and Charles Bonnes, 10–4
Mel and Peg's Rustic Cabin Cottage Garden, 10–4
Delancey
Clove House Farm and Gardens, 10–4
Delhi
West Wind Farm, 10–4
Hobart
Gunhouse Hill Garden, 10–4
Roscoe
Henderson Hollow Farm - Mermer Blakeslee and Eric Hamerstrom, 10–4

SATURDAY, JULY 13

Colorado (Denver Metropolitan Area)
Denver
SummerHome Garden, 10–4
The Bosler House Gardens, 10–12, 12–2, 2–4
Lakewood
Grummons Desert Garden, 10–4

SATURDAY, JULY 13

Connecticut (Windham County)
Ashford
My Gardens of Serenity, 10–4
Tranquil Refuge, 10–4

SATURDAY, JULY 13

New Jersey (Bergen County)
Franklin Lakes
Blue Meadow Farms, 10–3
Lakeside Garden, 10–3
Ho-Ho-Kus
Lourdes and Alfredo's Garden, 10–3
Mahwah
Sisko Gardens and Sculpture Site, 10–3
Wyckoff
Janet Schulz, 10–3

gardenconservancy.org/opendays

SATURDAY, JULY 13
New York (Suffolk County)
Jamesport
Winds Way Farm, 10–4
Mattituck
The Landcraft Garden Foundation, 10–4
Mt. Sinai
Tranquility, 10–4

SATURDAY, JULY 13
Rhode Island (Washington County)
Westerly
Thompson's Corner, 10–1, 1–4

SATURDAY, JULY 20
Connecticut (New Haven County)
Cheshire
Goin' to the Dogs, 10–12, 12–2, 2–4
Hamden
Woodland Ridge, 10–4
Oxford
Garden of Susan and Richard Kaminski, 10–4

SATURDAY, JULY 20
Massachusetts (Essex County)
Marblehead
Ticehurst, 10–4
Salem
Renaissance Italy Comes to River Street, Salem, 10–4

SATURDAY, JULY 20
New York (Capital Region)
Clifton Park
GrowForMe5b, 10–4
Glenville
Songni Yuan, 10–12, 12–2, 2–4
Loudonville
Inspired by Italian Garden Designs, 10–1, 1–4
Niskayuna
Cherie Gold, 10–4
Garden of Gregory and Kathleen Greene, 10–4
The Garden of M. Patricia, 10–4
Schenectady
50 Shades of Green, 10–4

SUNDAY, JULY 21
Connecticut (Hartford County)
Burlington
Garden of Robin Lensi, 10–4
The Salsedo Family Garden, 10–4
Canton
Sudden Delight, 10–4
The Marsted's Garden of Whimsy, 10–4
Glastonbury
The Murray Gardens, 10–4

SUNDAY, JULY 21
Rhode Island (Newport County)
Little Compton
Sakonnet, 9–5:30

Celebrating and sharing America's gardens since 1995

SATURDAY, JULY 27
Connecticut (Fairfield County)
Sherman
Cooke-Gribble Garden, 10–4

SATURDAY, JULY 27
Connecticut (Litchfield County)
Kent
Sculpturedale, 10–4
Lakeville
Juniper Ledge, 10–4
Norfolk
Fernwood, 10–4
Roxbury
Lagniappe Garden, 10–4

SATURDAY, JULY 27
Illinois (Chicago Area)
Highland Park
Highland Park Residence, 10–4
Lake Forest
The Cottage, 10–4
The Gardens at 900, 10–4
Mettawa
Mettawa Manor and Kurtis Conservation Foundation, 10–4

SATURDAY, JULY 27
Massachusetts (Berkshire County)
Ashley Falls
Garden of Jeffrey A Steele, 10–4

SATURDAY, JULY 27
New York (Dutchess County)
Millbrook
Lithgow Cottage Farm, 10–4
Millerton
Highgrove Cottage, 10–4

SATURDAY, JULY 27
New York (Sullivan County)
Barryville
Sally's Garden, 10–4
Jeffersonville
297 and 298, 10–4
Shady Fox Farm, 10–4
Livingston Manor
Old Danzer Farm, 10–4
Mountain Dale
Woodsndale, 10–4
North Branch
Grateful Beds, 10–4
Youngsville
Yaun Farm, 10–4

SUNDAY, JULY 28
Massachusetts (Berkshire County)
West Stockbridge
Kingsmont, 10–4
Walford, 10–4

SUNDAY, JULY 28
New York (Columbia County)
Canaan
Rockland Farm, 10–4

AUGUST

SATURDAY, AUGUST 3
Illinois (Dupage County)
West Chicago
The Gardens at Ball, 10–12, 12–2, 2–4

SATURDAY, AUGUST 3
Massachusetts (Hampden County)
Holyoke
Rock Valley Paradise, 10–4
Springfield
A Country Garden in the City, 10–4
Our Color-Filled Retreat, 10–4

SATURDAY, AUGUST 10
Ohio (Summit County)
Akron
Becky's Wild and Wonderful Garden, 10–2

SATURDAY, AUGUST 10
Wisconsin (Milwaukee Area)
Fredonia
Glasshouse in the Prairie, 10–4
Mequon
Bonniwell Garden, 10–4
Saukville
The Farm on Hilly Lane, 10–4

SUNDAY, AUGUST 11
New Hampshire (Cheshire County)
Gilsum
Hollows End, 10–4
Walpole
Distant Hill Gardens - Garden of Michael and Kathy Nerrie, 10–4

SUNDAY, AUGUST 11
Vermont (Windsor County)
Springfield
Woodland Farms, 10–4

SATURDAY, AUGUST 11
Wisconsin (Milwaukee Area)
Fredonia
Glasshouse in the Prairie, 10–4
Mequon
Bonniwell Garden, 10–4
Saukville
The Farm on Hilly Lane, 10–4

SATURDAY, AUGUST 24
Connecticut (Fairfield County)
New Canaan
New Canaan Meadow, 10–4
Redding
InSitu, 10–4

SATURDAY, AUGUST 24
New Hampshire (Monadnock Region)
Hancock
Skatutakee Farm, 10–5
Jaffrey
The Garden of Nan Quick, 10–4
Peterborough
Fry Garden, 10–4
Michael and Betsy Gordon, 10–4

SATURDAY, AUGUST 24
New Jersey (Hunterdon County)
Stockton
Bellsflower Garden, 10–4
Pretty Bird Farm, 10–4

Celebrating and sharing America's gardens since 1995

SEPTEMBER

SATURDAY, SEPTEMBER 7
New Jersey (Essex County)
Montclair
Anna's Pollinator Haven, 10–4
Nutley
The Mountsier Garden, 10–4

SATURDAY, SEPTEMBER 7
New York (Suffolk County)
East Hampton
Pomeroy, 10–2
Wainscott
Biercuk and Luckey Garden, 10–2

SATURDAY, SEPTEMBER 14
Connecticut (Fairfield County)
Weston
Frances Palmer's Garden, 10–4
Wells Hill Farm, 10–4
Westport
Prospect Gardens Westport, 10–4

SATURDAY, SEPTEMBER 14
Massachusetts (Bristol County)
Seekonk
Andrew Grossman's Garden, 10–4

SATURDAY, SEPTEMBER 14
Massachusetts (Middlesex County)
Carlisle
Gardens at Clock Barn - Home of Maureen and Mike Ruettgers, 10–4

SATURDAY, SEPTEMBER 14
New Jersey (Bergen County)
Mahwah
Sisko Gardens and Sculpture Site, 10–3

SATURDAY, SEPTEMBER 14
Rhode Island (Providence County)
Providence
College Hill Urban Oasis, 10–12, 12–2, 2–4
Sycamore Farm Community Garden, 10–4
The Garden at Power Street, 10–4

SATURDAY, SEPTEMBER 21
New Jersey (Somerset County)
Far Hills
The Hay, Honey Farm, 10–4

SATURDAY, SEPTEMBER 21
New York (Dutchess County)
Millbrook
Clove Brook Farm - Christopher Spitzmiller and Anthony Bellomo, 10–4
Garden of Katie Ridder and Peter Pennoyer, 10–4
Stanfordville
Ellen Petersen, 10–4

SATURDAY, SEPTEMBER 28
Massachusetts (Franklin County)
Leverett
Earthworks Garden, 10–4

SATURDAY, SEPTEMBER 28
Ohio (Lorain County)
Sullivan
Asterisk Farms, 10–4

gardenconservancy.org/opendays

OCTOBER

SATURDAY, OCTOBER 5
Connecticut (Fairfield County)
Greenwich
Sleepy Cat Farm, 10–12, 12–2, 2–4
Southport
The Gould Garden, 10–12, 12–2, 2–4

SATURDAY, OCTOBER 5
New York (Jefferson County)
Wellesley Island
The Enchanted Edible Forest at Cross Island Farms, 1–4

SUNDAY, OCTOBER 6
Virginia (Clarke County)
Boyce
Clay Hill Garden, 10–4

SUNDAY, OCTOBER 6
Virginia (Fauquier County)
Marshall
Poke Gardens, 10–12, 12–2, 2–4

SATURDAY, OCTOBER 12
Connecticut (New London County)
Stonington
Kentford Farm, 10–4

SATURDAY, SUNDAY 19
California (East Bay Area)
Berkeley
Berkeley Pollinator Playground, 10–12, 12–2, 2–4
Berkeley Urban Oasis, 10–12, 12–2, 2–4
Marcia's Garden, 10–4
Oakland
Oakland Cramscape, 10–4
Meadow's Edge, 10–1, 1–4
Zumba Gardens, 10–4

SATURDAY, OCTOBER 19
Massachusetts (Franklin County)
Sunderland
Swampfield, 10–4

SATURDAY, OCTOBER 19
Massachusetts (Hampden County)
Holyoke
Rock Valley Paradise, 10–4

SATURDAY, OCTOBER 19
Massachusetts (Hampshire County)
Amhearst
Kinsey-Pope Garden, 10–1, 1–5

Celebrating and sharing America's gardens since 1995

Notes

Notes

Celebrating and sharing America's gardens since 1995

Notes